PRAISE FOR
ROCKET *dreams*

"Marina Benjamin asked an ingeniously simple question: Whatever happened to the Technicolor dreams of the Space Age? Her search for answers led to a vast subcontinent of popular culture that I, for one, never knew existed—a place where technology merges with our persistent longing for transcendence. The result is a deeply insightful combination of reportage and meditation, and it just may contain the code for where the species is headed. I was entertained, educated, fascinated."

—James Tobin, author of *Ernie Pyle's War* and *To Conquer the Air: The Wright Brothers and the Great Race for Flight*

"*Rocket Dreams* is her quicksilver tour, teasing out the threads of imagination that once streamed into space, around a world that has shrunk but has grown complicated. Agile insights and melodic phrasing make the trip a lot of fun."

—*The Evening Standard* (London)

"What is clever about Benjamin's book, and sets it apart from the usual threnody to the men with the 'right stuff,' is that it identifies the crossover points between cyberspace and outer space. . . . This book is an eloquent response to a historical failure."

—*The Independent* (London)

MARINA BENJAMIN

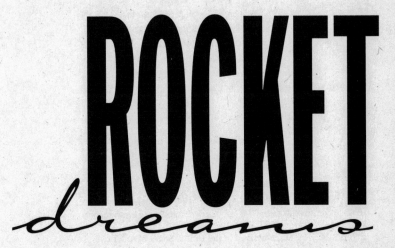

ROCKET
dreams

How the Space Age Shaped Our Vision of a World Beyond

FREE PRESS

NEW YORK LONDON TORONTO SYDNEY

Not A.R

gift 2022

*f*P

FREE PRESS
A Division of Simon & Schuster Inc.
1230 Avenue of the Americas
New York, NY 10020

First Free Press trade paperback edition 2004

FREE PRESS and colophon are
trademarks of Simon & Schuster, Inc.

For information about special discounts for bulk purchases,
please contact Simon & Schuster Special Sales at
1-800-456-6798 or business@simonandschuster.com

Manufactured in the United States of America

1   3   5   7   9   10   8   6   4   2

Library of Congress Cataloging-in-Publication Data
Benjamin, Marina.
Rocket dreams : How the space age shaped our vision of a world
beyond /Marina
Benjamin
p.   cm.
Includes bibliographical references and index.
1. Astronautics—United States—History. 2. Astronautics—Social aspects. I. Title.
TL796.5.U5B37 2003
303.48'3—dc21   2002045590
ISBN 0-7432-3343-3
ISBN 0-7432-5534-8 (Pbk)

TO GREG KLERKX

acknowledgments

It would not have been possible for me to write this book without the generous help of friends and colleagues who offered discussion, opinions, and advice, made introductions on my behalf, wrote references for me, or simply let me bend their ears with space talk. I would therefore like to offer my heartfelt thanks to Anne Goldgar, David Sexton, Simon Schaffer, Edward Marriott, Alison Roberts, Eden Ross Lipson, Barry Bone, Barbara Steinmetz, and Francis Spufford, all of whom supported the project in different ways. Special thanks are due to Tim Jordan, who was my internet consultant for the duration and who—in addition to passing on the latest insider info on net culture—managed to wangle me a much-prized invitation to the cyber-community Brainstorms. My agent, Henry Dunow, offered valuable insights throughout the writing process and was a thoughtful and sensitive first reader: thanks, Henry. I also owe a large debt to my editor, Bill Rosen, whose enthusiasm for space and the Space Age matched my own, and whose careful and intelligent editing helped me write a better book. Not least, I am grateful to the Society of Authors for awarding me a travel grant that allowed me to zip all over the United States in the cause of research and to the Rockefeller Foundation for offering me a writing fellowship in Bellagio, Italy, to work amid the tranquil gardens of the Villa Serbelloni. Above all, I owe my greatest debt to Greg Klerkx, my most stringent critic and most ardent fan, my partner both in life and in space mania.

contents

introduction

Sitting between the subtropical party towns of Daytona Beach and Vero Beach on Florida's eastern coast, Brevard County is a strip of humid backwater, mosquito infested and stiflingly hot. Everywhere you go the air is soupy, but it hangs more heavily in the northern and eastern districts, where the exotic-sounding Indian and Banana Rivers have sliced the land into spindly fingers and created steamy lagoons full of squawking wildlife and lazing alligators. Rising out of this prehistoric landscape is Merritt Island, a fat belt of white middle-class suburbia shaped like a clothespin and shored up by coastal dunes and brackish marshland. It is a place of little apparent distinction. With its rickety beach houses, green-blue swimming pools, and dowdy strip malls, Merritt Island looks like a poor cousin to the Florida Keys and life there follows the same idling rhythms of fishing and sunbathing. The island is an unlikely destination, yet each year it pulls to its swampy shores thousands of people from around the world. Driving east from Orlando, north from Palm Beach, and south from Jacksonville, the tourists pour in to visit what has become known as the Space Coast. In particular, they come to Cape

Canaveral, the unassuming nub of shore land from where mankind took its greatest leap toward the stars.

A few years back, I followed the crowds to Merritt Island, genuinely curious to discover what was so spacey about the Space Coast. I wanted to take in whatever the tourist industry had to offer, cruise along coastal roads where Mercury astronauts once raced Corvettes, and size up the Saturn V moon rocket, now reposing in a huge storage hangar like a dozing giant. Beyond that I was open. I would see where fancy led me. Although I decided to trek out to the cape on a whim (I was in Florida for work, and visiting the Space Coast is one of the things you do when you're in Florida), I knew from the outset that I would end up taking the trip to heart, because, for me, revisiting the Space Age entailed revisiting a part of myself I had left behind long ago: the child whose space-related hopes were boundless. Growing up in central London, idolizing the astronauts from afar, I had tracked the moon landings with a diligence that bordered on obsession. If a flag had been planted, a buggy deployed, a crater explored, or moon rocks scooped into specimen boxes, I knew about it. Too young to witness Yuri Gagarin's famed feats or John Glenn's heroics, my head was filled instead with Apollo trivia. Crew members? No problem. Mission objectives? I was on it. What's more, I'd made a point of acquainting myself with the geography of the solar system, fully expecting that Jupiter and Saturn, Ganymede, Eos, and Callisto would in no time become as familiar as the outlying stops on the London Tube.

What I did not know when I set out for the cape nearly thirty years later was that this pilgrimage would produce only questions; it was as if the space fanatic in me had suddenly reawakened, demanding to know why the future had not unfolded as promised.

Some of the questions that nagged me were germane to the ongoing American space program, a schizophrenic enterprise that seems to lack any kind of continuity with the past. After the glory years of the space race and moon landings, NASA (the National Aeronautics and Space Administration) shrank from the challenges of exploration in order to putter around in Earth orbit, belying its homespun tales of enterprise and daring. Why was the Moon abandoned? Why hadn't we struck out for Mars? And if space was a "new ocean" waiting to be explored, as John F. Kennedy once proclaimed, why hadn't commercial backers stepped in to establish the equivalent of trade routes? Other questions were more reflexive in nature, as they threaded back into my childhood dreams and threatened to expose them as delusions, or else reminded me why so many of us once invested so much in NASA's dream peddling. Was I naïve to believe we'd simply hop from the Moon to the planets and thence to the stars? Or did the prospect of leaping off the planet really speak to some deep-seated urge in the human soul? When it came to the hard-sell mythology of the space race, was I dupe or co-conspirator?

What happened after Apollo is a familiar story; funds were cut, jobs were lost, programs scrapped, and space ambitions curtailed, while telecommunications satellites burgeoned into a profitable business. But the history of the post-1969 space program sheds little light on the fate of the utopian, escapist, and conquistadorial hopes that originally enlivened the effort to put humans in space and meant so much to a generation of Space Age dreamers like me. What it highlights instead is how rapidly those hopes were frustrated by what we were—or in this case weren't—ultimately willing and able to do. In the early days of space exploration, even those extraterrestrial aspirations that today strike us as outlandish—building moon bases, constructing floating space colonies, terraforming distant worlds—went hand in hand with the development of space technology. Indeed, the two were so tightly coupled it was often difficult to tell which was driving which. But then the exigencies of politics and the limits of engineering wrenched them apart and they have gone their separate ways ever since. Technology looked to the market, to science, and to business for inspiration: the aspirations, as well, went elsewhere. This is the story I wish to tell.

What follows concerns the imaginative legacy of Apollo and the subsequent career of a handful of interrelated dreams once fueled by the moon landings, but then deprived of further such nourishment. What happened to those dreams? Did they dry up "like a raisin in the sun," to paraphrase the poet Langston Hughes, or did they find an alternative means of survival? I found that the dreams often ran to ground in subtle ways, altering our understanding of what it meant to reach the Moon, for example, or encouraging existing beliefs about the fundamentally enchanted character of space. More important, I learnt that while the dreams, hopes, aspirations—call them what you will—associated with leaping into space are admittedly harder to map than developments in technology, their course seems at least as logical and has evolved faster than that of the technology.

My journey to trace an alternative history of the Space Age took me across a broad landscape of ideas and into some unlikely corners of philosophy and culture; from the "gospel of flight" (a virtual religion that produced its own pilgrims and prophets) through Gaia and environmentalism, Noetics and the New Physics, to SETI@home (a collective hunt for alien radio signals) and thence to the outer frontiers of cyberspace. I began to see how much we internalized our outward-bound aspirations, even before it became clear that human life would not be expanding across the solar system any day soon. The impact of seeing the Earth from space focused our energies on the home planet in unprecedented ways, dramatically affecting our relationship to the natural world and our appreciation of the greater community of mankind, and prompting a revolution in our understanding of the Earth as a living system. It is no accident, I think, that the first Earth Day on April 20, 1970, coincided with Apollo's return to Earth; or that a new school of spiritualism based on charting the deep space of the human psyche has been developed by one of the astronauts. Nor is it hard to understand why, in the wake of an exploration curtailed, people should be drawn to an innovative model for the domestic economy sprung free from the American space program by NASA administrator James Webb.

The urge to reach out and somehow get beyond the limits of the known world did not disappear altogether, however; and that is why a tour of the post–Space Age environment would be incomplete without a visit to Roswell, New Mexico—a place that is in so many ways a distorting mirror of our extraterrestrial ambitions. Roswell first came to public attention in 1947 because of claims that a flying saucer crashed in its midst and it has since become the "magnetic north" of UFO belief—a belief that began its most dramatic growth not in 1947, or 1957, or 1967, but at precisely the time the space program began its descent. For many people, the enduring mystery surrounding the place is a hedge against having to relinquish a fundamental yearning for contact.

In taking time out to revisit Roswell, I do not wish to give the impression that in the aftermath of Apollo and the moon landings, no fresh ideas made their way onto NASA's drawing boards, dooming us to endlessly playing out our fantasies of evolution, expansion and contact in increasingly convoluted ways. There were new ideas—and one of the most daring and popular was the scheme to create sealed-off colonies in space, where thousands of people might live in a Nirvana of neopastoral self-sufficiency. Extremely influential in the 1970s, this dream has also mutated over time, and while few people today believe we will literally migrate into space, vast numbers of people are doing just that elsewhere and building experimental colonies in cyberspace.

These are just some of the stopping points in the book—enough to suggest that the post-1969 narrative of the Space Age dramatically illustrates the never fully resolved tension between the human urge to explore and the urge to commune, or create communities. Explorers, in their purest form, have always been those who want to leave existing communities, often, to be sure, in search of the utopian ideal of a better one, but also in the belief that to pursue the dream of being truly free, it is necessary to quit their known society. In contrast to this distinctively human pressure to move outward, the desire to dwell together in communities falls in line with our perpetual attempts to bring the outside in: to tame the wild unknown, to colonize new lands, to find a common identity, and to erode the difference between here and elsewhere. Like the force of gravity, this impulse to commune always brings us back to ourselves.

Cast in these terms, the task of characterizing the post-Apollo climate finds a ready analogy in the solving of a problem in introductory physics: the ballistic trajectory, an equation that describes the path of an unpowered projectile that has exhausted its initial momentum and is forced to descend to Earth. Where it lands, and how quickly, is affected only by gravity and atmospheric friction. In basic physics, the challenge may be simplified for the purposes of convenience; we assume away an atmosphere and arrive at a single, elegant solution. In the real world, however, you have lots of friction and thus lots of solutions: your projectile, in other words, could land anywhere.

CHAPTER 1

THE SKY'S THE LIMIT

The drive east from Orlando to Cape Canaveral offers few distractions; no bustling towns, no enclaves of industry, no arresting examples of modern architecture. In fact, there's very little evidence of human habitation. Instead, the most memorable markers along this topographically challenged stretch of flat scrubby grassland, used mainly for cattle grazing, are jumbo-size billboards advertising out-of-town multiplexes and surf 'n' turf combo specials. On my trip to Merritt Island, it struck me that even the freeway seemed out of place here, for as I took in the boundary where asphalt met earth I kept noticing the intrusion of big yellowing clumps of grass. You felt that given the merest chance the swamp would rise up and swallow the highway, reclaiming it so completely that future visitors would never know it had been there.

This is not how it was supposed to be. In the early sixties, the economic boom created by the space race promised that the featureless scrub would be replaced by a sprawl of construction. Just as Florida's coastal swamps had made way for control towers and gantries, so the inland area between Orlando and Port St. John would become the nerve center of a latter-day high-tech economy. As William Atwill remarks in his book *Fire and Power*, in the dreams of the developers, business managers and engineers would file out of their shiny new tract houses and take to the roads in two neat lines, one driving west to the aerospace contractors in Orlando, the other heading east to the launch complex at the cape. Something similar, after all, had happened in the birch and pine woodlands northeast of Moscow where Zvyozdny Gorodok was located. Better known as Star City, this was the cosmonaut training center where Yuri Gagarin spent a year in intensive preparation for his 1961 Vostok mission. Then, it consisted of a simple hostel, some standard-issue barracks, and a number of low buildings housing training facilities. In time it would grow into a small town, with its own community of scientists, its own bars, hotels, sports clubs, and administration centers, and with a large Air Force base catering to the cosmonauts' every need situated just to the south at Chkalovsky.

Perhaps the Soviet example was what inspired one Floridian visionary to purchase a large tract of land halfway to the cape and proceed to subdivide it into lots, pave the streets, put down curbing, and build a half dozen homes on speculation. With a flourish of Space Age enthusiasm, he named the seedling development Rocket City. Given that the $700 million extension of the Atlantic Missile Range at Cape Canaveral, carried out between 1961 and 1966, had created 20,000 jobs directly and a further 30,000 indirectly, it was not unreasonable to expect side benefits. But Rocket City never grew into a satellite settlement servicing the needs of the new economy. It didn't even acquire another half dozen homes. Instead, like the developer's dream that inspired it, it crashed almost as soon as it was floated, the unnoticed, second-order victim of NASA cutbacks in personnel and contracts, which began in 1966 with the completion of Project Gemini and which, with the exception of a few temporary blips, have continued ever since. Star City has fared no better. Its speedily erected infrastructure is today coming apart at the seams, even though to all intents and purposes the city continues to serve the Russian space industry.

Without the benefit of a crystal ball, the construction magnates can hardly be blamed for thinking they'd arrived in developer's heaven. All the usual economic indicators promised gold. Between 1950 and 1968 the population of Brevard County climbed from 23,000 to 239,000, as engineers, scientists, and aerospace workers arrived from all over America, first to work on an expanding rocket development program and then to work for NASA. They brought with them their wives, children, and family pets, and their influx created a surge in school enrollment and health-care needs, not to mention a burgeoning consumer base. Next came a demand for teachers, nurses, police, and other municipal and retail workers, and all the while government money poured into the region. For a time, at least, it looked as if nothing could stem the growth that would turn Brevard into the ultimate company town.

In her autobiography *Space: A Memoir*, published in 1998, novelist Jesse Lee Kercheval has written movingly about what it was like growing up on the Space Coast amid the constant development and the perpetual talk of technology that made her and her classmates feel as if they were already citizens of tomorrow. When Kercheval was ten, her schoolteacher father accepted a job in Florida and moved the whole family to Cocoa. The year was 1966 and the space-related building frenzy was at its peak. As a bedroom community to the rocket launchers, Cocoa was a town rising out of the swamp, a veritable city of the future being built out of concrete and hope. Its pastel-colored houses had air-conditioning and mosquito control (the twin pillars of civilization in subtropical climes), and many of them boasted swimming pools—ever the mark of upward mobility. Only the backyards, heaped with sand, refused to bow to the cultivating influence of futurism. Kercheval lived in a brand-new development called Lunar Heights. It was shaped like a miniature solar system, with concentric rings of low-slung concrete blockhouses orbiting a cluster of four Identikit homes that sat on a central island. Behind the development, she played a game called Space in which she'd roll down the sand hills pretending to be a "gravity wave," while from the street in front of her house she watched Gemini 10 shoot into the skies overhead. From that point on, she was certain that by time she was finished with high school we'd all be vacationing on Mars.

Kercheval captures perfectly the unexpected ordinariness of Florida's honeymoon with space by reminding us that in a place where every space "shot" shook household windows, where every hotel, motel, and bar was named after a planet or rocket ship, where you could feast on a "Gus Grissom" sandwich, listen to WRKT Rocket Radio, and dine at the Moon Hut, such thinking was par for the course. Here in Brevard, space was daily fare, the bread and butter of the local economy and the backbone of the community. True, it was also the talk of the town. But all the breathless expectation it inspired would have meant very little were it not for the concrete sense in which space had become fused with the idea of expanding real estate.

Now, as I headed toward the cape on a near empty freeway, surrounded by scrub, what surprised me most was how so much history could have been so quickly erased. It was as if the Space Age had never happened.

Strangely, the last obvious vestiges of Kercheval's hoped-for future are the region's roads, and there's an interesting history behind their construction. In 1961, a young Titusville lawyer called Max Brewer was instrumental in setting up the Joint Community Impact Committee—essentially a board of local bigwigs whose job was to assess NASA's impact on the local economy and advise the space agency on the community's needs. Brewer, who appears to have been quite the operator, also had a seat on the Florida State Road Board, and thanks to his machinations more than half of the $150 million that NASA extracted out of federal government to support "essential services and facilities" in Brevard ended up being plowed into roads, bridges, harbors, and airport expansion—in other words, transportation to and from the Space Center. Today, this elaborate transport network seems simply to link one failed dream to another.

Roads aside, the bottom fell out of the new economy relatively early. Already in 1969, the very year in which Neil Armstrong and Buzz Aldrin touched down on the surface of the Moon, unemployment in Brevard was up and the county was littered with vacant stores, motels, and, in the new developments in the north, houses. That same year, Disney decided to postpone indefinitely plans to build a futuristic Space Age city where the employees of Disney World (which was under construction at the time) would live. The result was that Disney World was built while EPCOT, which stood for Experimental Prototype Community of Tomorrow, was, at least in its original conception, shelved. Instead of a utopian village, the Space Coast got a theme park.

Jesse Lee Kercheval felt the forces of change a little later, in 1972, when the fathers of so many of her friends were being laid off work. She writes: "We knew that this was the beginning of the end. Soon whole companies would be shutting down." And indeed, whole companies did shut down. Then, as the jobs disappeared, families who'd only recently moved to the cape moved out again. Schools and hospitals closed, committees disbanded, and, as it was attempting to do along the highway, the swamp began quietly reasserting itself.

Today there's little nourishment for space pilgrims in Brevard County, even at the cape itself. Back in the 1960s, the desolate plain that stretched out to meet the sea was lined with a row of launch towers, from each of which a single Mercury astronaut was sent into the skies. First there was Alan Shepard's tower, nearest the sea, then Gus Grissom's, John Glenn's, Scott Carpenter's, Wally Schirra's, and

Gordon Cooper's. Surveying the towers from the ground, the Italian journalist Oriana Fallaci admired their lofty skeletal symmetry; the towers, she said, were "the cathedrals of an age that . . . has substituted technology for liturgy." The launch towers, of course, are long gone, and other than winning a seat in the gallery to watch a shuttle launch, the Space Age tourist of today is pretty much confined to the Kennedy Space Center (KSC)—a stark modernist construction whose aspect inspires nothing that approaches religious sentiment. Instead, what the center's pale concrete uniformity instantly calls to mind is a barely settled colony. From a distance, its low-level buildings, starkly functional walkways, and surrounding expanses of featureless paving appear to have been pressed from a single giant mold. Farther back, from the causeway, the place looks deserted, as though marooned on some distant, half-drowned planet whose inhabitants long ago departed in search of more hospitable lands.

NASA's denizens alighted here in the first place only because the Air Force's missile testing range happened to be based at the cape. It still is—and it's busy as ever launching both satellites and unmanned missions (for example, the Cassini probe, scheduled to reach Saturn in 2004). But at the KSC Visitor Complex, the Rocket Garden marking this association contains a clutch of upended missiles—an Atlas, Titan, Gemini, and Redstone—that look so lackluster, so tired, they speak only of yesterday. And yesterday is where the Space Center and its surrounding attractions are for the most part stuck, caught up in a loop of reminiscence for Apollo that begins at the Astronaut Hall of Fame, where first-generation memorabilia takes center stage, and comes full circle at the back-to-basics education center. If you are looking to see a Saturn V rocket, touch a moon rock, groan under a simulation of multiple G forces, or look over the shoulders of the technicians at Mission Control, you've come to the right place, for almost everything at the cape is geared to reproducing the initial wonder of space exploration and not the routinization that followed.

The day I went around the visitor complex, it looked flat and dull under a cloudy sky, like a moon colony in the Earth's shadow. I parked amid acres of empty lot, then walked to the main compound, where a handful of people milled about, apparently unable to decide whether to visit the education center or the cinema. I opted for the bunkerlike cinema, where two short films on the history of Mir and the dream of floating space colonies neatly summed up the Space Age's eternal shortfall: the distance between aspiration and achievement. The cinema, though, was where NASA permitted itself the indulgence of a little free-form thinking. It was where the agency played its fantasy card.

Settling into my red velvet seat, I watched *Quest for Life*, an animated feature that borrowed much of its imaginative scope from NASA's Origins Program, a brand-new (at the time) initiative focusing on astrobiology, or the study of life in the solar system. The film began sensibly enough with the 1997 Pathfinder mission to Mars, following with NASA's plans to send further remote probes and automated rovers to the red planet. But then the story swerved unexpectedly into reckless fantasy—reckless because it was presented as a kind of future de facto. Suddenly, animated astronauts were heading for Mars in the year 2014. After executing a perfect soft landing, they bounced about on the Martian surface, evidently delighted by its low gravity, and collected a few rocks. Then a probe resembling a giant dentist's drill was shown being dispatched to Europa, one of Jupiter's moons. With an evil-sounding whir, it penetrated the satellite's ice-capped ocean, plunging beneath into a liquid world filled with thousands of swirling microbes.

It goes without saying that NASA scientists would like nothing better than to discover life elsewhere in the solar system; that is the whole point of the Origins Program. And if they cannot unearth living organisms, a genuine fossil will suffice, since any evidence at all would strongly support the argument that life is a universal occurrence not confined solely to Earth. But *Quest for Life* was pure wish fulfillment. It deliberately fudged the line between promotion and propaganda and actively spread misinformation. Scientists studying the "ocean" on Europa, for example, cannot yet confirm the existence there of liquid water. Recent data collected by Galileo, a super-smart surveyor probe sent to study the outer planets of the solar system, seems to suggest that there's an electrically charged layer of some mysterious substance stirring roughly five miles below the moon's ice crust. But even if this were liquid, it may not be water, and the only plan on the table involves sending an orbiter carrying a radar sounder designed to bounce radio waves off the ice. Even then, the "hydrobots" in *Quest for Life* would have been a long time coming, but one of Sean O'Keefe's first acts as new NASA administrator, in the spring of 2002, was to cancel the Europa orbiter. As for a manned mission to Mars, umpteen proposals for such missions lie gathering dust on the shelves of the Johnson Space Center, but if you scrutinize the space agency's website, the word about manned missions to Mars is, well, nonexistent.

Between *Quest for Life* and the Astronaut Hall of Fame, the impression I took away from the KSC was of an agency caught between a vanished past and a possibly never-to-be-realized future. It's not an ideal image for an agency eager to prove to its critics that it has not lost its way, but it conveniently diverts attention from the fact that beneath the public relations boasts, NASA's chief business these days, other than maintaining its big-ticket programs (the Space Shuttle, the International Space Station), is public education.

Before leaving Cape Canaveral, I took an illicit drive down a road signposted "No Access." For a few hundred yards there was nothing but scrub, and before long I caught sight of a sentry box housing the security guard who would soon turn me back. Even so, the impromptu escapade was not entirely in vain because in the far distance, perched on a horizon that dropped away to goodness knows where, stood the vast outline of the legendary Vehicle Assembly Building, known simply as the VAB. Built on a scale so lavish it almost defies comprehension, the immense gray and black structure is tall enough to house the Statue of Liberty almost twice over and capacious enough to swallow the Pentagon whole. Its innards, meanwhile, are endlessly rearrangeable, like a giant construction toy. When the VAB first opened for business, assembly workers reported that confused eagles and vultures would circle the building, mistaking it for an island. Even more bizarrely, clouds had a habit of forming inside it and sometimes it would rain.

Despite the day's being overcast, the sun showed its face for a brief moment, turning this colossal monument to rocket science into a gleaming Lego cube. For an instant, I was thrown back in time and could clearly picture the scenes of barely controlled prelaunch excitement that Norman Mailer described so vividly in *Of a Fire on the Moon.* The whole theater of humanity would be present, impatient for spectacle; royalty, politicians, military heroes, gaggles of reporters and photographers, and behind them, fanning out along the beaches, the "families of poor Okies." Then, slowly, ceremoniously, the Saturn V moon rocket would be rolled out of the VAB to take its place on the launch pad. With its flanks steaming in symbolic anticipation of the sheer effort of lift to come, it would be greeted by cheering and laughing and talking and crying, as irrepressible bubbles of expectation fizzed inside rational heads, turning adults into giddy schoolchildren.

As I left the cape, I found myself thinking about the difference between the actual past and the public memory of the past. I had come here looking for the former, expecting to see the fingerprints of history stamped all over the landscape, and instead I found myself surrounded by the latter. In many ways, of course, the two are polar opposites: history is evanescent, public memory, ever present. The past dies to be replaced in perpetuity by reconstructions and imitations. In the case of the Space Age, I discovered, the artifacts, simulations, re-creations, and monuments that combine to create public memory loom so much larger than remembered history that one may easily be tricked into feeling that the glory days never ended.

Back at my desk, far away from the scene where Apollo made history, I can see my pilgrimage for the nostalgic journey it was. No one these days would claim that we lived in the Space Age. Ask people to characterize our current times and they'll say that we live in the Information Age or the Age of Globalization. At a pinch, and with a quick shake of the crystals, they might say that the New Age had finally dawned. But the Space Age, with its air-whipped promises of interstellar travel and cosmic conquest, seems to have slipped definitively into the past from where nothing can retrieve it—no Shuttle launch or Mars probe, no multilimbed deep-space telescope or shiny new orbiting space station. Nothing can re-create those scenes Norman Mailer described, nor bring back the feelings behind them. Today when we think of the Space Age, we think of the Cold War and the birth-control pill, Elvis and flower power, of a time-warped era forever sealed off from the present.

Yet, for all that, I don't want to shrug off my nostalgia so casually, because what I had been attempting to recapture at the cape was something more than the sum of the Space Age's parts—something more than a montage of rockets and gantries, architecture and landscape. I was after inspiration. I wanted to recapture the sense of hope with which all things related to space filled me as a child, as it filled the adults around me: I wanted to remember the taste of dreaming about our Space Age future.

Visiting Cape Canaveral showed me that this dream went beyond run-of-the-mill space fantasies—fantasies that saw Pan Am, for example, the commercial airline NASA designated its official civilian space carrier, taking bookings in 1968 for its *Clipper* flights to the Moon, scheduled to depart in the year 2000. Or that had Space Age pundits predicting a high-tech tomorrow in which, as one of them put it, "we should gradually accept the space vehicle just as our ancestors finally got round to accepting the wheel or the boat." I wanted to reacquaint myself with some of the more nebulous underpinnings of the Space Age dream: a desire to know where we stood in the cosmic order, a yearning for contact and communion, a quest for new horizons and frontiers, for human expansion, and even for salvation. These are the desires we have always projected onto space and always will, irrespective of whether or not we have the transport infrastructure in place to get us there en masse or the technology that would allow us to stay there for good.

Ever since humans began forging covenants with powerful deities in the sky, we have sought to connect our earthly existence to a higher realm. For if we could somehow relate what happened down here to what happened up there, then we might fit our small lives into the bigger picture. But that's only part of the story. More often than not, the ways in which we've conjoined terrestrial and celestial affairs have conferred on humanity, or on some portion of humanity, a form of elevation. Think of the enhancement of status that comes, say, with being a "chosen people" or the privileged perspective of prophets and astronauts. Add to this the fact that in our thirst for ascension, we have co-opted angelic intermediaries, ecstatic transports, astral planes, and other analogues of Jacob's ladder, and you might say that as a species we have indulged in a kind of perpetual Space Age dreaming, where traveling upward and traveling toward enlighten-ment are one and the same. Almost universally, the pull of space has been understood to elicit in us a kind of spiritual phototropism, or flowering, a desire to believe that it is the better part of ourselves that responds to the call of the heavens. And so, when we dream of space travel, we dream of freedom and beauty, perfection and tran-scendence: we dream of what we might become.

In the twentieth century, technology was pressed into the service of these dreams, peaking with the styling of space colonies and moon bases as hothouses of social experimentation. Numerous Space Age prophets, from Russian visionary Konstantin Tsiolkovsky at the end of the nineteenth century and the British physicist J. D. Bernal, writing just in the pre-rocket era, to Dandridge Cole, Krafft Ehricke, and Gerard O'Neill in the 1970s, believed that beneath the glassy domes of such colonies existing social problems might be ironed out and new theories of community tested; in the best-case scenarios, they imagined mankind reborn. Earlier in the twentieth century, similar hopes of self-betterment had been pinned to the fuselage of the Ford Tri-Motor and its kin, to the extent that the airplane was widely seen as a millennial harbinger that would herald a great new day in human affairs. Historian Joseph Corn, who understood the move for what it was—a leap of faith—has called the new engine of idealism a "winged gospel." The message it preached was that once mankind perfected the art of bearing itself aloft, the soul too would fly; we would end war, poverty, and inequality and would finally come to see that the similarities that exist among diverse peoples vastly outclass the differences. As one early aviator cited by Corn put it, for the flier, "the small, petty differences of life become lost in insignificance, as the great eternal truths become more and more evident."

At the center of the winged gospel was the idea that flying was somehow divine—an idea that hooked directly back into Christian theology with its longing for ascension and rapture and its worship of God in heaven. And so you had aviators experiencing all manner of epiphanies as they sailed through the skies, just like Saint-Exupéry. They had visions of world peace, the oneness of all humanity, or the essential lightness of being, and they fancied themselves messengers of these grandiose insights. Ultimately, says Corn, some of them dreamed that "mere mortals, mounted on self-made mechanical wings, might fly free of all earthly constraints and become angelic."

One such fantasist was Alfred Lawson, an aviation engineer and the editor of *Aircraft* magazine. In 1916 Lawson predicted that the Aviation Age would eventually see the birth of "a superior type of man . . . Alti-man—a superhuman who will live in the upper stratas of the atmosphere and never come down to earth at all." Lawson supposed that this ethereal being would not emerge until the year 3000, but that once he had appeared he would quickly master the skies and begin performing various miraculous feats for the benefit of his earthbound ancestors (beings whom Lawson bluntly dubbed "Ground-man"). Controlling the weather was chief among Altiman's future wonders.

Not content with simply prophesying, Lawson worked his aerial insights into a semireligion called Lawsonomy, which he defined as "the knowledge of life and everything pertaining thereto." Lawsonomy covered the usual bases of a totalizing social fantasy; economics, philosophy, physics, chemistry, mechanics, law, and the sciences of man. But, in addition, it promised those who embraced it quasimagical powers, enabling them to "move onward and upward to a much higher plane of intelligence."

In manifestations more modest than Lawson's, the winged gospel managed to hold on through the 1940s, despite taking a battering from such grim realities as aerial bombardment and such crudely functional developments as mass aerial transport. In the end however, a faith that was corroborated principally by the airplane's lack of usefulness could not survive the resolution of the Aviation Age in purely practical terms, as a boon to commercial interests everywhere as well as a neat way to link Australia to Moscow. Just as important, whereas everyone could share the dream of aviation, only those who could pay the fare flew in the sleek new planes (so much for the gospel's promise to foster greater equality). Still, the disappointment barely registered, because no sooner had aviation had been stripped of its spiritual significance than we rushed to affix the gospel to the next bright hope on the horizon, space exploration.

There were important differences, however, for instead of brokering a new era of peace and enlightenment for mankind, space seemed to offer humanity the chance to start over elsewhere, to begin anew and learn from our past mistakes. Casting an eye over the space literature of the sixties and seventies, you see this confirmed in a most graphic fashion. The literature positively teems with images of neopastoral bliss. I cannot count the times I've seen artists' illustrations of astronauts tending fruit trees and vegetables in lunar biospheres, or sharing verdant domed gardens with a variety of birds and beasts. If the Aviation Age imagined a Heaven on Earth, the Space Age dreamt of the floating equivalent of the "Citie on a Hill." Then, too, a new emphasis on freedom entered the mix of flying and personal transcendence, and with it came the idea of finding deliverance through being liberated from the clutches of gravity, just like the mythical Daedalus when he flew from his Cretan prison. As the astronaut Wally Schirra once enthused:

> *Feeling weightless . . . it's so many things together. A feeling of pride, of healthy solitude, of dignified freedom from everything that's dirty, sticky. You feel exquisitely comfortable . . . and you feel you have so much energy, such an urge to do things, such an ability to do things. And you work well, yes, you think well, without sweat, without difficulty as if the biblical curse in the sweat of thy face and in sorrow no longer exists. As if you've been born again.*

In spite of these twists and embellishments, echoes of the old faith continued to crop up here and there, notably in the writings of the space colony guru and Princeton physicist Gerard O'Neill. In 1981, in a prophetic production called *2018: A Hopeful View of the Human Future*, O'Neill argued that space flight would eventually ease the population crisis, solve the energy problem, end international conflict, and usher in a period of "perpetual plenty." O'Neill should have been born a Russian, as the Soviets were far more mystical about space than the Americans and less troubled about harnessing technology to a religious millennialism—whether drawn from Russian Orthodox spirituality or the revolutionary dogma of atheist communism. As it was, the most astonishing thing about O'Neill's predictions is that they were published when most of the Western world had already given up on Space Age dreaming, feeling that space exploration and colonization were less a cure for society's ills than a means of avoiding them, or at least distracting our attention from them. Astronauts nibbling on thousand-dollar tubes of exotic snacks in space did not sit well with an American society struggling with urban crime and racial tensions, social injustice and rural poverty. Besides, the Space Age had already resolved itself with the Shuttle, a spacecraft whose principal virtue was not that it pioneered new frontiers but that it came home to roost.

The latter-day gospel of space flight came to naught. But it left us with a legacy we are not entirely able to shake off. The Aviation Age we could file away quite happily because, for all its mundanity, air travel actually did shrink the world: it waged a war on time and distance and won it. The Space Age, by contrast, only made us exquisitely aware of how little conquistadorial headway we could ever hope to make on a galactic scale. Though, at first, the rapid development of space technology fueled our dreams, the more we knew the less possible it all seemed, until, through the workings of some strange inverse law, the Space Age ended up demonstrating the limits of technology to create a new Eden. In spite of all the bullish talk of cosmic mastery and neoparadisiacal colonies, space continued to elude us and to preserve its essential mystery.

The problem, at root, was that despite claims to the contrary, the age of space exploration was unlike any other era of exploration. For years, space visionaries followed Arthur C. Clarke in casting space travel in the mold of the "great voyages of discovery" that had given Europeans dominion over new lands (and peoples), opened up new markets, and brought them unimagined wealth. Space travel, Clarke had suggested, could do the same, but for the whole of mankind, leading humanity to a "greater Renaissance." Taking the maritime metaphor out for a run in his book *The Enchanted Loom*, NASA physicist Robert

Jastrow wondered when the "great voyages" would begin. "I have a vision of black-hulled ships," he wrote, "taking flight from their parent stars to move out into the Galaxy. No crews walk their decks; the hulls are silent beyond the quiet rustle of moving electrons. But each ship is alive. Swiftly it speeds to the rendezvous with its fellows. Now the star travelers wander together through the void, driven by the craving for new experiences." This imagery is so seductive that it belies the daunting sense of scale that even a dream of space exploration must confront. It's the problem with seeing the Moon, for example, as a sort of Ascension Island roughly midway between continents that might someday trade with each other; the exponential increase in the space between planets, and finally stars, turns out to be where the loose historical metaphors of the space visionaries break down.

As Philip Morrison's quirky 1968 film *Powers of Ten* guilelessly demonstrates, this inflationary expansion takes immediate effect once you begin zooming upward from the Earth's surface. Through a succession of simple images, each on a scale differing from the next by a factor of ten, the film recedes from a couple of picnickers sprawled out in the sunshine to arrive at an impersonal image of the entire known universe. The jolt lies in how quickly the measure of man is dwarfed into insignificance. Within two frames, the picnickers disappear and, within six, the frame that contained them is filled by the Earth's disc: increase the magnification by another two factors of ten and our home planet is just a spec among thousands amid the starry firmament. The ludicrous distances involved in space travel were something the visionaries could gloss over for only so long. Mars alone would take almost a year to reach, Pluto more than twenty. In addition, it was rapidly becoming clear that the human body was not built to endure the various strains of space travel. By the time Jastrow wrote up his seafaring vision in 1981, the conquistadorial dream was fast fading; the reason his decks are empty and his hulls silent is that his ships are no longer fitted for human passengers but for intelligent machines.

And yet, it is precisely because the "elsewhere" of space resists being conquered—and therefore being known—that we can still project our various longings onto it, as if it were no more than a blank screen. For this reason, when I think about space I often think back to a balloon reconnaissance experiment I took part in at school in London when I was just old enough to appreciate that the world extended beyond house and garden. My entire class spent a day writing letters to imaginary readers, describing our lives and our families, our hopes for the future and the antics of the household pet. Then we taped our epistolary efforts, complete with name and address tags, to the ends of balloon strings and launched our helium-filled envoys into the skies. After that, we waited, hoping, I now see, to get a foretaste of the meaning of destiny.

Every day that followed the "launch," I would picture my name-tagged balloon—my very own spacecraft—journeying to distant climes, buoyed by my fervent desire that it should find its way into the hands of a friendly stranger. Just imagining such an encounter filled me up somehow. Although I didn't understand the sentiment at the time, I felt empowered, enlarged; I'd be a force to contend with, a cause that produced effects. When a week or so later my mother summoned me to the phone to talk to a boy in Birmingham who'd found my balloon, I was wild with excitement. He told me about his family and his school and his older brother who was in the Navy, and all of it sounded as convincingly make-believe as any faraway fable I'd ever read. As for Birmingham (a city I now associate with tangled freeways and industrial grime), never had an unknown destination been rendered more exotic by the simple virtue of my never having been there.

Perhaps the allure of space and the desire for cosmic encounter merely replay in adulthood the child's wonderment at the size of the world that one otherwise outgrows—not because one ceases to delight in all things transcendent, but because the realm of transcendence tends to shrink as one matures. Like junkies who must perpetually up the dose of their chosen drug in order to hit the same high, adults in search of the emotionally gratifying feeling of enlargement that comes, paradoxically, as a result of contemplating things that dwarf us, must place themselves in ever more majestic and cowing contexts. The astronomer and space evangelist Carl Sagan, who died in 1996, had an innate understanding of how this equation worked, which is one reason he perpetually tried both in print and on television to wow us with scale and number—his legendary "billions and billions." As Keay Davidson, his biographer, points out, Sagan repeatedly sought to place his readers and viewers "in the same emotional state he had enjoyed all his life: the state of feeling childlike before unimaginable immensities."

Sagan understood, too, that our fundamental desire to hurl part of ourselves into the void was one wishful half of a boomeranging expectation that envisions something bouncing back—at the very least some intimated knowledge of elsewhere. Space travel certainly promised that much, but Sagan was too impatient for that and so he arranged for us to reach out across the galactic void and extend a collective, species-wide greeting to the stars, first with Pioneer 10, which bore a plaque announcing mankind's existence to the universe, then with Voyager, which carried a phonographic copper record containing aural and pictographic samplings of the best that Earth had to offer. Sagan's wife, Ann Druyan, called it "Earth's Greatest Hits." No one was under any illusion that these craft stood anything but the slightest chance of interception. Their purpose lay in reaching out.

Had Sagan lived to see NASA's 1997 Pathfinder mission to Mars (the space agency's greatest success in decades), he would have delighted in experiencing how the boomerang came back at last, for Pathfinder gave us our first real taste of virtual space exploration. We saw what its mobile rover saw as it bumped its way over the rosy Martian terrain. When it changed direction, we changed direction, and when it picked up a rock sample, we scrutinized it. In a sense, we wore Pathfinder like a virtual-reality glove.

Although Pathfinder seemed to speak of a coming Space Age we would experience vicariously, via remote probes and electronic communication, NASA never managed to follow up on the mission's success. At the same time, however, another kind of experience was taking shape on the internet, where the discovery of a new kind of deep space, cyberspace, offered people the chance to travel to strange new worlds and experience all manner of alien encounters—and not just with other people, but with avatars that could take whatever form their operators chose, gender hybrids, robots, and unicorns included. Suddenly it became possible to realize online what we could only dream of in the sixties: scanning the stars for E.T., messaging other solar systems, even building colonies on alien worlds.

The way such activities manifest themselves swings from the scientific to the dreamy and takes in everything in between. There are companies, for example, that will beam your e-mails to the stars, scientists who will recruit your PC into the search for alien life, and online communities that thrive on their membership's desire for otherworldly experiences. One enterprising company, Team Encounter (founded by Charles Chafer, a space entrepreneur with a privately funded rocket launch to his credit), is currently scouting online for subscribers willing to purchase virtual seats on its forthcoming Deep Space Probe mission. At fifty dollars a pop it's a lot cheaper than Pan Am's *Clipper* would have been, even if you only get to travel by proxy, courtesy of a cyber-message and DNA sample. Still, the mission does have genuine appeal, not least because the company plans to launch a real-life probe in 2005 that will be the fifth spacecraft ever to leave the solar system and follow the Pioneer and Voyager crafts into deep space, and because, taking a leaf out of Pathfinder's book, it will involve its virtual passengers in an ongoing and interactive online mission-control operation.

Meanwhile, the Texas-based company Celestis has been rocketing people's cremated remains into space since 1997. The company's canisters, stuffed with "personalized" space capsules no bigger than a lipstick container, orbit the Earth for a few years before reentering the atmosphere, where they burn up harmlessly. Celestis's chief point of interest, however, is that it has already dispatched a number of the Space Age's foremost thinkers to their starry Valhalla, among them, *Star Trek* creator Gene Roddenberry, Gerard O'Neill ("Your wish is fulfilled," wrote his family in tribute), and Krafft Ehricke, one of the original V-2 designers and a lifelong believer in mankind's eventual migration to the stars.

Even Timothy Leary—agent provocateur, space colony promoter, and mind-expander extraordinaire—availed himself of Celestis's service and had his ashes blasted into the skies on the company's maiden flight. It was a glorious finale for someone who in life had frequently attempted to levitate off this planet using any means available, usually hallucinogens. Though we'll never know exactly why Leary pledged his dying allegiances to Celestis, I like to think that he was tickled by the company's promise that on his eventual return to Earth, he would come back "blazing like a shooting star."

Of course, the virtualization of space does not herald a new Space Age, nor even a Space Age reborn. If anything, it signals instead the subsuming of one age by another, the Information Age. Ten years ago, few people would have guessed that the internet's electronic counterpart to outer space would be the new vessel of promise into which we'd pour our extraterrestrial hopes, much less have predicted the various ways in which online activities would provide a range of "off-world" satisfactions. But will info-space continue to answer to our emotional needs ten years from now?

The odds are that we will have moved on. It seems to be a recurrent tendency among us to mistake bursts of rapid technological advance for the means by which we will achieve transcendence. In recent years, nanotechnology, cybernetics, and bioengineering have all been greeted with a kind of messianic fervor, just as the Space Age was in its day. What they have in common is that they are coming technologies; they sit halfway between being merely imagined and being fully realized, and into this gap rush their prophetic champions, determined to see in them a promise that goes beyond the capacity of what mere technology can deliver, something unattainable and utopian. Once their potential is resolved, however, it's another story. Already the internet has been stripped of much of the idealization that was wired into it only a few years back. It's no longer magical, but everyday. We've learnt that its businesses aren't immune from market economics, and dreams of achieving greater self-realization in a disembodied Nirvana have been trivialized by porn-site chat rooms and instant messaging.

What this entails for our post–Space Age dreaming remains unclear. Perhaps the allure of outer space will finally be dispelled as a result of being accommodated on the internet. Or perhaps we'll simply pick up our extraterrestrial dreams and sow them elsewhere, just as we reinvested the winged gospel in space flight once aviation showed itself to be spiritually bankrupt. Then again, maybe mysticism will prevail and the vast constituency of people who believe in UFOs, and who are living so determinedly through a Space Age that never happened, may end up carrying the day. Whatever transpires, one thing we can be certain of is that the dreams themselves will not simply disappear: as long as we continue to be human, we will continue to hunger for space.

CHAPTER 2

ONE SMALL STEP

I am surely not alone in wondering from time to time what became of the Apollo astronauts. At the end of the sixties they were among the most famous people on Earth, supercelebrities who shook hands with religious leaders and stood shoulder to shoulder beside heads of state. Their pictures were plastered all over the place, and to space enthusiasts far and wide their every word seemed to carry a mysterious import. To add to their fascination, we were privy to the most intimate details of their lives.

The astronauts were the ultimate modern heroes. When, years after they were introduced to America as model Eagle Scouts—brave, trustworthy, clean, reverent, and all the rest—we learned of their predilection for fast cars and fast lives, for strong drink and weak women, their stature was not diminished, but enhanced. For, in truth, nothing could sully them: what read as delinquency in, say, your regular rock-star rebel, was just more evidence of their abundant bravery. The astronauts, it seemed, had been touched by angel dust. Everything they said and did, every public speech and official appearance, every roguish folly and impish misdemeanor, and every whimsical tidbit reported by the press confirmed them as a breed apart. These were men who had the "right stuff," the steely nerves, quick-fire responses, and necessary swagger that allowed them to perch atop towering rockets that blasted them clean off the face of the Earth.

I still remember their faces clearly, as they appeared on the front pages of newspapers and the covers of magazines, grinning heads craning out from the turtlenecked metal rims of their white space suits, helmets tucked under their arms. Neil Armstrong always managed to look beatific, as if he'd already spent a lifetime touring the astral planes, while Jim Lovell was his opposite, fleshy faced and earthy—the kind of guy who in another life might have felt quite at home running a small-town grocery store and passing the time of day chatting up the locals. Then there was the hawklike Gene Cernan, as flinty-looking as the moon rocks he collected with Harrison Schmitt. Schmitt was the first scientist in space and, along with Cernan, the last man to walk on the moon. All of them were heroes of my childhood dreams, fearless warriors of comic book proportions who had traversed the unknown and inky realm I thought of as Outer Space.

Where other children collected baseball cards, I collected pictures of astronauts, patiently cutting them out of magazines and pasting them into a scrapbook alongside images of rocket ships and lurid artists' renditions of other worlds that I'd X-Acto'd out of Explorer Series books. Fantasy and reality were seamlessly blended together in my imaginary constructions, with the astronauts providing the unspoken link. Thanks to them, I believed passionately in our spacefaring future; we would all glide between the stars, float in microgravity and holiday on the moon: where the astronaut-pioneers led, the rest of us would follow. Nor did my parents find the astronauts any less laudable. To them, they were rare and precious reminders that when humanity determined to do so, it could surpass itself.

Then suddenly, the astronauts disappeared.

Although my memory has no doubt squashed together a train of events that unfolded over a sensible period of time, it still seems to me that one day we were marveling at how men walked on the Moon and the next we'd forgotten all about it. I didn't understand then about budget cuts and retrenchment, or the allure of executive jobs in finance and industry, and I certainly didn't see how people who'd been figureheads of the most dynamic agency in the world could be soundlessly absorbed into its bureaucratic ranks. All I knew was that the astronauts had gone.

In the years following, occasional news from the gloaming to which they'd retreated offered little in the way of hope. That Neil Armstrong had become a recluse was one shocking revelation. Buzz Aldrin's decline into alcoholism was another. I never bothered to check the reports from the rumor mill, and for all I knew they were greatly exaggerated. The point is that they were believable. It made perfect sense that in the absence of a space program committed to sending men back to the Moon, or even to Mars, the next obvious frontier, the astronauts should slip into a kind of mourning, withdrawing as J. G. Ballard became fond of repeating, into "mysticism and silence."

When I finally came to meet three Apollo astronauts, more than thirty years after the first Moon landing, the experience was somewhat surreal—like encountering a clutch of Magritte's bowler-hatted businessmen floating in a coffee shop. I was in Los Angeles on a muggy weekend in June 2000, working on a story for a British newspaper. The venue was the Beverly Garlands Holiday Inn, a plasticky hotel in North Hollywood, built smack up against the freeway, and the event I was covering was a "celebrity and collectors show." A few weeks earlier I had received a publicity flyer listing the various stars who would be there and I had been stunned to see astronauts' names among them. I knew they were big crowd-pullers on the private lecture circuit, but it struck me as bizarre that they should participate in a show that brought together fans and their idols for a weekend of contrived intimacy and a spot of honest trade. Here, there would be no speeches required of them, no display of support for this or that space policy, and no platform for the airing of new schemes or old grievances. At the same time, the commercial incentive that might motivate some faded celebrities seemed irrelevant. All the astronauts billed to attend the show had done well for themselves since leaving NASA; Walt Cunningham had gone into banking, Edgar Mitchell was head of a research institute in California, and Dick Gordon had become president of an engineering company in Los Angeles. Some need other than poverty had brought them to what I couldn't help feeling would be a tawdry affair.

Arriving at the event, I simply followed the crowd, thin at first, as it funneled through a labyrinth of small rooms crammed with vendors of movie memorabilia and then fanned out into a large ballroom where it swarmed and buzzed. The ballroom was where the stars were stationed for the duration and, unlike the dealers' rooms, it had atmosphere. Troy Donahue, the Leonardo DiCaprio of his day, was there, still lean and twinkly-eyed in his sixties, and from *The Exorcist*, a buffed and businesslike Linda Blair. Across the room I spied David Hedison, star (under the name Al Hedison) of the original Fly movie, and onetime heavyweight champ Leon Spinks, who sat beside his publicist grinning his endearingly toothless grin as he scoured the room for boxing fans who might remember the day he snatched the world title from Muhammad Ali. Lending glamour were veteran Bond girl Lana Wood and Lee Meriwether, the former Miss America who played Catwoman in the sixties Batman movie. All were happy to sign autographs for a fee.

From behind rows of trestle tables the stars sold mementos from their once illustrious careers—publicity shots, lobby cards, magazine cuttings, and film stills. To drum up business, they would turn on the charm and as they affected to share reminiscences, starry-eyed fans fished in their wallets for money: ten dollars for a head shot, fifteen for a film still, and another fifteen for an autograph. Although one or two of them—such as Lee Meriwether—were there to raise money for charity, most seemed to be lining their own pockets, cashing in on the trade in popular memory.

Once I found my bearings, I began casting about the ballroom in the hope of sighting the astronauts, but they didn't appear to be there. I backtracked through the rooms full of dealers, past huddles of pale, earnest movie fans, and there was still no trace of them. For a wild instant I convinced myself that they'd pulled out of the event, sent their apologies and stayed at home, or simply changed their minds. And then I spotted the sign. Tacked onto a wooden pillar outside one of the smaller conference rooms across the lawn from the ballroom was a scraggy piece of white card and on it was written in black marker pen, Walt Cunningham, Dick Gordon, and Edgar Mitchell. There was no mention of astronauts and no mention of Apollo—just the names. To my surprise, I felt a surge of excitement. Like the movie buffs in the ballroom, I was about to meet my heroes.

To be famous is to always be meeting people who already know a great deal about you, and it was no different with the astronauts and me. I knew that Dick Gordon had flown on Apollo 12 with Alan Bean and Pete Conrad. The mission had been a relaxed affair, the relieved exhalation that followed the nail-biting technical balletics of Apollo 11. There had also been a lot of joshing among the crewmates—all the schoolboy enthusiasm behind the moon shot erupting suddenly as the nerviness associated with procedures-never-before-tried evaporated. Walt Cunningham had had the distinction of flying with Wally Schirra on Apollo 7, the first of NASA's three-man missions and the flight immediately after the tragic fire that killed Virgil "Gus" Grissom, Roger Chaffee, and Edward White on the launch pad. And Edgar Mitchell had accompanied Mercury veteran Alan Shepard on Apollo 14. The two of them got lost in Cone Crater; unable to find the rim, they had panicked and their pulses had raced at 130 beats a minute. Now I was ready.

The mood in the conference room could not have been more different from the fun and games in the ballroom. It was as somber as being in church. The three astronauts sat at the far end of the room behind a long table covered in white cloth and mounted on a low dais, while autograph hunters, entering from the opposite side of the room, queued reverently in single file as if waiting for a benediction. I looked on as each was granted a solo audience, during which hands were shaken firmly and heads nodded in smart pseudo-military bobs. Checks for astonishing sums of money changed hands, since the astronauts' fees were far higher than those of the stars. One man who had brought along a small library of NASA pamphlets—the genuine articles, all dog-eared and yellowed and with zany sixties graphics on the covers—got each of them signed by all three astronauts, running up a bill approaching $1000.

The atmosphere, however, was unaccountably heavy, which puzzled me momentarily until I realized the cause: it was clotted with respect. Everyone was talking in hushed tones and smiling self-deprecatingly at everyone else. If you didn't know better, you would think you'd stumbled upon a meeting of the Supreme Court. And yet when the space enthusiasts weren't coughing frogs out of their throats, shuffling their feet or otherwise demurring, it was clear that they knew their "missionographies" back to front. Swapping little-known facts among themselves was part of the thrill of being there, and a few of them even attempted nervous conversational sorties while the astronauts signed their photographs and booklets. For their part, the men of Apollo were as happy as lambs to be quizzed about their working lives in such knowledgeable detail. Like the stars across the hotel lawn, they seemed visibly rejuvenated by the doting attention.

I waited in line and tried to formulate some questions of my own. Should I ask intricate questions that demonstrated how much I, too, already knew about their lives and work? Should I ask about the past or the present? Space politics or space policy? Then again, perhaps Dick Gordon would rather talk about the football team he left NASA for in a bid to follow up one dream come true with another. As the line before me got shorter and shorter, I found that the only question taking shape in my mind was "What was being in space really like?" So I asked. Though I can't say quite what I was expecting to hear, I knew I was after something satisfying, something—maybe a revelation—to appease thirty-odd years of curiosity. Instead, I was told: "Of course, being in space was a startling experience, but we were primarily there to work." Or: "We were lucky enough to live through the Golden Age of space exploration." One of the astronauts sidestepped matters entirely: "Read my book. I go into that in some detail," he said.

I should have known better. For what could the astronauts possibly say that could successfully transport me there with them? What words would be adequate to describe what it was actually like to drift under the starry canopy of the universe thousands of miles above the spinning earth without leaving their gravity-bound hearers disappointed and uncomprehending? Better to dodge the question. Better to operate on autopilot and dish up tired, predictable fare instead.

When, I wondered, did the astronauts stop trying?

Though I now barely remember the rote exchanges I witnessed that day, one odd detail has stayed with me—the way Walt Cunningham's wife, Dot, took a fifty-dollar bill from the outstretched hand of a fan. As she plucked the note it made a crisp noise of the kind you hear when bank tellers do their impatient second count of a wad of bills. I was instantly reminded of Tom Wolfe's account of the trials endured by the astronauts' wives: always having to perform like public figures, always having to smile, to be gracious, to put a brave face on things, to mouth the party line. It wasn't that the Cunninghams needed the money. Walt's banking career had seen to that. But that fifty-dollar bill was her due.

In retrospect, I'll admit to having been a little starstruck meeting the astronauts, even as it saddened me to think they'd been so starved of public attention that a celebrity show could salve their egos: Had the importance of their work faded so much from our minds that, like forgotten movie stars, they somehow needed to bask in their own mythology? At the same time, I felt that they were too good for the company they were keeping. Whereas stars of stage and screen were destined to fade, weren't history makers part of the living present? History makers get decorated and commemorated and memorialized. They become part of the permanent fabric of things. The problem was that even as I argued myself out of sorry conclusions, I sensed that in the category confusion I was fighting there lurked some deeper truth. The astronauts of Apollo were, in fact, just like movie stars; they burned brightly in the glare of publicity when they were offered good parts to play, and then, when the roles dried up, so did they.

If the thinning gray heads and leathery complexions bothered me, it was because the simple truth of the astronauts' natural progress into old age seemed a shorthand for the withering of everything they stood for; and if they went, then so would my dreams. It's probably just as well that today's astronauts do not invite the same order of investment. Today's astronauts are like day laborers, competent but faceless scientists and engineers who are largely interchangeable with their colleagues on the ground. Nor are we much interested in the humdrum maintenance work they do, placing satellites in orbit, practicing docking maneuvers, and repairing telescopes. Since we do not idolize them, we won't resent their growing old.

Meeting Walt Cunningham, Edgar Mitchell, and Dick Gordon brought home other truths besides. For these astronauts, I now saw, had been immortalized in popular memory in the high flourish of their youth. Although it seemed otherwise (so much had we taken these men into our hearts), we knew them only through the filter of the mass media. They existed for us only on screens. Eventually, in a final transition familiar from the world of cinema, they became screens themselves—ciphers on to which we could project our collective fantasies about space. Even the astronauts seemed to sense this aspect of their own unreality. The twelve of them who walked on the Moon are members of one the most elite clubs on the planet, and yet privately they refer to themselves as the Order of Ancient Astronauts. This crypto-Masonic moniker may be self-mocking, but there's self-knowledge in there too, in that it acknowledges a certain melding of history and mythology, as if the astronauts had never been more than creatures of legend.

Sadly, the reality is no more cheering. Three of the twelve are dead and the club has long been defunct; since 1972 it has acquired no new members. In fact, it is not hard to imagine a near future in which there will be no one left who has walked on the Moon. Then, after a few more decades have passed, the once remarkable feat of traveling to an alien world may perhaps cease even to elicit admiration, as it has already ceased to serve as inspiration. It will become a peccadillo of twentieth-century man, obsessed with making his way to places whose principal appeal was their seeming unattainability—Everest, Antarctica, the ocean floor, the Moon.

Then again, another fast-diminishing membership is the club of people who actually care.

Being of a certain age myself, it is easy to forget that for an entire generation the moon landings are already history. The marvelous contraptions that sent men hurtling into orbit are now museum pieces in front of which fathers give their sons impromptu lessons in American patriotism. With their thick metal husks—sealed on the outside with giant rivets and lined on the inside with flip switches—and their diving-bell portholes, they look as antiquated as anything dreamt up by Jules Verne. The engineers who designed them are meanwhile dead and dying, and the assembly plants and launch facilities that once made Florida seem a magical place to starry-eyed children and a crucible of futuristic fantasy to their parents have long been left to wrack and ruin. For the post-Apollo generation, the Space Age belongs unequivocally to the past. The question is how the children of the fifties and sixties came to set so much store by its aspirations in the first place.

Part of the answer has to do with psychology, for the era hitched its dreams to the coattails of a postwar optimism primed to soar into the skies at the slightest provocation. That humanity's hopes for a new era of peace and prosperity should feed off the promise of human expansion, space colonization, moon bases, starships, and interstellar travel seemed as natural as believing that washing machines and food blenders made for a happier domestic life. The wisdom was beautifully naïve and firmly rooted in the collective postwar weariness of the world; by breaking free of the Earth, the thinking went, humanity might break free of its primal nature—namely its proclivity toward self-destruction—and realize its true destiny as a unified species. All this idealism effectively hinged on making a break with gravity, as if weightlessness were a direct correlate of true liberation.

Another factor that gets overlooked is how aggressively space exploration was marketed to an initially skeptical public. A Gallup poll conducted in 1949 showed that the vast bulk of Americans dismissed out of hand the idea that rockets bearing anyone more plausible than fictional heroes like Buck Rogers could reach the Moon by the year 2000. Yet within six years, as a result of the concerted efforts of a loosely related group of science fiction writers, rocket experts, space artists, popular science writers, and visionary military men, public opinion had completely turned around. By the time Stanley Kubrick's *2001: A Space Odyssey* hit cinema screens in 1968, there were few people left who thought to question the now famous scene in which, via a deft match cut, a bone hurled into the air by an early ancestor becomes a revolving spaceship. Once the Moon looked to be a given, it became much easier to view interplanetary travel, space stations, vacations in microgravity, as predestined—prefigured, as Kubrick saw it, in the very birth of technology.

For decades, the space culture was saturated with fantasy, and there was precious little reality to encourage anything more. The balance began to shift after World War II, when the performance of the V-2 (V for *Vergeltung*, the German word for retaliation) seemed to justify the enthusiastic outpourings of more peaceable rocket scientists. But the first public intimations that a new mood of can-do optimism was afoot came with the appearance in 1949 of *The Conquest of Space*. Written by expatriate German rocket scientist Willy Ley and lavishly illustrated by Chesley Bonestell, *Conquest* explained the "how to" of space travel in simple terms to nonspecialist readers while encouraging them to let their imaginations run wild over Bonestell's lush yet astronomically accurate alien landscapes.

A year later, moviegoers thrilled to George Pal's *Destination Moon*, a film that set new realist standards in the depiction of space travel. And in 1951 Arthur C. Clarke published *The Exploration of Space*, a book that struck a note of such reasoned confidence, and with such eloquence, that the road map to the stars laid out in its pages was one NASA's project managers would later faithfully follow. Clarke acknowledged that space exploration would be "difficult, dangerous and expensive"; nonetheless, the course he plotted for its accomplishment steadily built expertise as it went along, progressing from suborbital test flights to orbital flights, and then from circling the Moon to landing on it. After that, said Clarke, who knew how far we might go? We'd visit the planets, build bases on the Moon and on Mars, and then make our way to the stars. We would be "the discoverers, not the discovered."

Slowly the emphasis changed from what was possible to what was probable, and something like an organized space advocacy movement began to make its presence felt. By holding high-powered symposia, lobbying sympathetic politicians, and whipping the media into a pro-space frenzy, space advocates succeeded in building support for their cause both among the general public and inside the corridors of power. They had one aim: to ensure that space travel was seen as a practical goal for humanity.

Anyone who remembers the barrage of articles that *Collier's* magazine threw at a space-hungry public in a sustained PR campaign that lasted for two years would know that resistance was more or less futile. The first installment of the now famous eight-part series on space travel ran in 1952 under the banner headline "Man Will Conquer Space Soon: Top Scientists Tell How in Fifteen Startling Pages." On the magazine's cover a winged rocket was depicted discarding its fiery second stage as it sailed over the Earth's horizon. On the inside pages, a lead article by Wernher von Braun, the German rocketmeister who would eventually mastermind the American space effort, described an Earth-orbiting space station that served as a hub for space taxis and shuttle vehicles and whose steady rotation generated artificial gravity; space medicine expert Heinz Haber explained the challenges relating to human survival in space; and Harvard astronomer Fred Whipple discussed space-based astronomy. Other editions promised such tantalizing exclusives as "Man on the Moon: Scientists Tell How We Can Land There in Our Lifetime" and "The World's First Space Suit: How and Where We'll Use It."

The *Collier's* series launched von Braun as space exploration's man about town, and he was swamped with requests to appear on radio and television. In 1954, he was recruited by Walt Disney to be the linchpin of a documentary series on space travel that Disney was producing for ABC but also using to promote his new California theme park. The first program, called "Man in Space," aired in 1955 to an audience of millions, and its great achievement was to make space travel appear completely feasible to those who would eventually end up paying for it. Against a backdrop of animated sequences of rockets launching and landing—and tracing perfectly arched trajectories through the starry skies as they did so—von Braun claimed it would be possible to build and test a "practical passenger rocket" within the next ten years. In "Man and the Moon," screened later the same year, he ventured further readings of the scientific runes, this time concerning the construction of space stations and the building of a lunar orbiter.

Von Braun's seemingly realistic projections helped shape the expectations of the crowds who poured into Disney's Tomorrowland to ogle the missile-shaped, finned rocket (still a close cousin to the V-2) designed by Ley and von Braun that stood to attention outside a futuristically curvy space-port. Tomorrowland tapped knowingly into the nascent culture of consumption by presenting all its futuristic fare as being almost within our grasp. Visitors could actually taste the future here. Just as important, the smoothed-out life the future promised became thrillingly palpable as they rode on all-aluminum passenger trains and Fiberglas boats and cruised down an Autopia freeway. Better yet, on the Rocket to the Moon ride, visitors could sit in vibrating chairs and watch the Earth recede from them as they drew closer to its spookily barren satellite. Who wouldn't find that empowering?

Still, all this pro-space rallying of public support took place in the complete absence of any kind of commitment from government. And as Robert Truax, president of the American Rocket Society and commander of the Navy's Bureau of Aeronautics (and space activist extraordinaire), was fond of pointing out, it developed in the absence of any concrete rationale. Yet the American people bought into it, in part because whichever way the space advocates presented space travel—as the last frontier, the new frontier, or the final frontier—it was always a metaphorical extension of the American West. First, a handful of brave pioneers would chart routes through unknown and perhaps dangerous new territory, and then the colonists would follow, a trickle initially, and begin homesteading on the edge of the known world. In time, that trickle would become a stream and eventually space, like Texas, California, and New Mexico before it, would become theirs. Little wonder that when Gallup took the temperature of public opinion in 1955, nearly 40 percent of those polled believed that rockets would transport men to the Moon within fifty years. However, Gallup never asked whether there was actually a reason to send out the scouts.

That reason presented itself in unambiguous terms on a single night in October 1957 when the Soviets hurled a 184-pound satellite called Sputnik into orbit around the Earth, wowing the world with their wizardlike mastery of the heavens. As if to mock how sleepy the U.S. space program was by comparison, the bleeping ball of metal actually passed twice over the American continent before it was detected. Meanwhile, like a bad coincidence, on the ground, a scale model of the Navy's ill-fated Vanguard rocket, which had been slated to achieve in the near future precisely what the Soviets had just accomplished, was literally buzzing around Capitol Hill offices in a vain attempt by its proponents to impress the power brokers.

In the months afterward, Americans put themselves through a gauntlet of emotions. They felt humiliated and cowed and they pointed fingers of blame in every direction. Then, like the proverbial sleeping tiger awakened by a rival, America bared its teeth. In no time, polls were attesting to a new spirit of self-sacrifice abroad: people were ready to do whatever it took to better the Russians and defeat the menace of communism. Before the year was out, Texas Senator Lyndon B. Johnson was already talking about a "race." The following spring, Wernher von Braun successfully launched Juno rockets that carried scientific payloads into orbit; even Vanguard finally lifted a satellite into space; and NASA, an evolutionary offshoot of NACA (the National Advisory Committee for Aeronautics), was given official blessing. The rest, as they say, is history.

Looking back at the space race today, it is impossible not to marvel, still, at the heights and the speed to which technology can rise when it is driven by ideology. With the Apollo program, in particular, a whole new world was conjured into being. Beginning with a new iconography in which everything was larger and louder than life, massive rockets, tall as apartment blocks and as ill tempered as the old gods of war, took fiery leave of their launchpads and ripped through the skies. As if that were not spectacle enough to sate the appetite of a carefully nurtured Space Age voyeurism, Americans were treated to the suspense of countdown, the set-piece drama of Mission Control and the marvel of the space suit—itself a small spacecraft. With the novelty of ground-to-space communications, a beguiling new language was born, instantly enriching our vocabulary with such tech-savvy terms as "CapCom," "EVA," and "translunar injection burns." But the pièces de résistance were the live telecasts of astronauts fooling around in microgravity, brushing their teeth, somersaulting, and clumsily aiming for their mouths as they squeezed the tubes of goo they called space food.

It was wonderful theater. And behind the scenes (behind the screens) was another story—in fact, a better story, although not one that either NASA or its Soviet counterpart wished to play out on the public stage. This story hinged on the very concept of a race, specifically on the idea of exertion, which is endemic to any contest. To put it bluntly, at every stage of the space race, both sides were extending themselves fully as they strained to obtain the leading edge. Every launch, every newly modified vehicle, every differently staged rocket, and every virgin orbit perched on the vertiginous edge of what was possible; all of it was the most that could be done, impetuously tried at the very earliest moment.

Nowhere was this truer than in the Apollo program. In the buildup to the climactic moon landing of Apollo 11 in 1969, successive missions were one-off stepping-stones leading to the single mission that would do it all and then more. There were no second chances, not least because Congress had been sharpening its budgetary knives for some time and public opinion was beginning to waver (although Americans remained excited about space, they were less than thrilled with the $24 billion being lavished on Apollo). With this noose around its neck, threatening to tighten at the first sign of failure, each Apollo mission bore the weight of the entire space effort. No wonder heavy sighs of relief accompanied every incremental notch of success: the first docking of the lunar lander, the first lunar orbit, and of course, the first moon landing. Small wonder, too, that Michael Collins, circling the Moon all alone in the command module Columbia, was able to think of little else other than mentally preparing himself for the grim possibility that he might have to leave Neil Armstrong and Buzz Aldrin to die in the Sea of Tranquillity. It was not a decision he needed to actively take but one he would have to endure. Since no one knew for certain whether the Eagle had the wherewithal to make it back from the lunar surface, Collins sweated out his ordeal doing the only thing that remained in his power to do—testing his own resolve.

The irony is that the moon landing and moon walk, which took NASA to its absolute limits, was both the making and the breaking of the Space Age. Resources, skills, technology, and sheer hubris were stretched to a maximum and then applied with laser-beam precision to bringing off the feat of Apollo 11. For a brief, shining moment, NASA had the whole world in its thrall. There were men on the Moon, and it had taken less than ten years to get them there. It was glorious, it was momentous, it was breathtaking; and then, with an almost scandalous alacrity, it was over.

It is hard to say which is more astonishing: the fact that the Space Age turned the corner so abruptly or that the general public barely cast a backward glance of concern. The one exception was NASA's wing-and-prayer management of Apollo 13, a mission that went dangerously awry after an oxygen tank exploded on the way to the Moon, ripping open part of the service module and imperiling Jim Lovell and his crew. The ensuing drama (improvised, desperate, and according to many commentators, NASA's finest hour) revived a flicker of interest, but the play for our attention had already been lost. Norman Mailer, in Houston to watch the first moon landing, recorded the precise switchblade moment. It came, amazingly, as reporters filed out of a live telecast of the first moon walk in droves: already bored with footprinting and flag planting, they weren't going to hang around to watch Neil and Buzz collecting rocks. What happened?

Although I was only five at the time, I retain a vivid picture of where I was and how I felt when Neil Armstrong bounced about in the lunar dust to plant the American flag on an alien world. Not long before then, my parents had finally bought a television, plopping it right at the foot of their big double bed in our suburban London home. In those early days of black-and-white, when quiz shows and talent contests dominated proceedings, my after-supper treat was to nestle down beside my mother, head propped up on elbows, and glut myself on television. While I have no recollection of most of what I watched in those early years, I have the distinct memory of being awestruck by two things—the moon walk and *Star Trek*, with the one leading, as I saw it, inexorably to the other. When it came to space, fantasy and reality marched to the same beat. But then everybody brought at least a little wishful thinking to the moon walk, and that's where the trouble began.

The problem was that reality could not sustain the burden of expectation it was intended to carry after that momentary exultation opened so many hearts to little flutters of hope. Watching the grainy footage, one knew that one was witnessing one of the twentieth century's defining moments, even if exactly what it portended remained foggy.

The confusion came later, when people wanted to assimilate what they had just seen. From within the heart of the establishment where military, industrial, and political interests accommodated one another nicely, an official version of the moon landing quickly took shape. It was a victory, a national triumph, and one in the eye for communism. This, of course, is the version of events bequeathed to history. Open almost any book on the space race and you will learn that the Eagle's touchdown was the showstopper that capped a race for ideological supremacy between two superpowers at loggerheads politically and given to displays of technological braggadocio such as those that terrified the world during the Cuban missile crisis of 1962. Occasionally, it is presented more colorfully, as the final thrust in a bout of cosmic jousting, the posturing behind which was inherently medieval. I cannot help but think of Nikita Khrushchev in this regard, getting drunk as a feudal lord and dancing on the table every time the Soviets scored a point against capitalism (which happened more frequently than the history books let on). But the official story is not the whole story, because the space advocates had primed us to expect something else and to view the moon landing not as a grand, sweeping end, but as a new beginning.

From the start of their campaign the space advocates dangled the Moon before us as the warm-up prize for our efforts at interplanetary travel. After that there would be bigger planetary prizes, until eventually we'd travel to the stars and the whole galactic treasure trove would be ours for the taking. The Moon was always just the first leg of our journey into space. The feeling, in short, was today the Moon, tomorrow Mars. With Apollo 11 making the first step look so smooth, the question on everyone's lips was: What next?

Arthur C. Clarke was the chief architect and foremost exponent of this kind of sky's-the-limit thinking, not to mention the most prolific. Between publishing *The Exploration of Space* in 1951 and taking up his front-row seat to salute Apollo 11, he penned a half dozen books extolling the virtues of space exploration and noted that, all in all, there were now some four thousand more available on the subject. In *The Promise of Space*, a book that appeared in 1968, just a year before the moon landing, it is possible to get the gist of Clarke's project just by glancing down the contents page. Here Clarke blithely skips (and these are his own subject heads) from "fantasy to science," "man in orbit," "the birth of Apollo," "the lunar colony," "paths to the planets," "the commerce of the heavens," and "other suns than ours" to end up with "to the stars," setting out the Order of Things with a confidence reminiscent of God planning the six days of Creation. Note that attaining the Moon is scheduled somewhere in the infancy of our space-faring adventures.

Clarke has always had the extraordinary ability to make space travel seem an altogether straightforward affair. There's a sleight of hand involved, of course, but Clarke spins so beguiling a web of intrigue that it generally goes unnoticed. In *Promise*, for example, he lists a practical itinerary of our off-world requirements for atmosphere, gravity, and water, enumerating the preconditions for human survival on other planets as if traveling to them called for little more in the way of advance planning than a Boy Scout expedition. Next, he unwraps the science of rocketry—the big numbers, the specialist language, the complicated engineering—in terms of such cozy familiarity you can almost hear the reader's happy sigh of comprehension. Finally, at the point where Clarke knows his readers have relaxed sufficiently into the picture, accepting its wild schemes as mere extensions of everyday engineering, he reels them in to share his armchair fantasies as equals. Imagine a near future, he says chummily, in which "any amateur astronomer" (no special skills required, you understand) could turn a telescope on the Moon and survey the twinkling night lights of our lunar settlements.

It is easy now to accuse Clarke of making space travel look too simple, only it wasn't obvious at the time. Besides, the imagery of the moon walk played directly into the hands of its romancing interpreters in that it patently seemed to promise so much more than a triumph of state-sponsored technology. It could be used to summon up all manner of sunny vistas—a new beginning, an evolutionary portal, even humanity's rebirth—for there was Neil Armstrong, the new Adam, tethered to the known world by nothing more than a length of artificial umbilical cord, talking about satisfying the "deep inner soul" of humanity. It was as if the giant leap for mankind genuinely belonged to us all and there wasn't a single soul on the planet who couldn't justifiably take pride in it. And yet impressionable minds, filled with Clarke-like imaginings, were busy projecting even then. After all, no image is better contrived to symbolize the simple joys of progressive achievement than that of first steps tentatively taken. If people's hearts swelled with hope, it was largely because they were certain the next steps would soon follow.

Reality proved very different. The American program never got past the Moon's first base—a feeble effort by cosmic standards, like chucking tin cans across the backyard—and even then homesickness prevailed over the imperative to press onward and upward. Images of our lush fragile globe beamed back from afar made cooing, protective converts of the most forward-thinking rationalists, and before long many of these had swaddled themselves in Gaia and environmentalism. Exploration was out and conservation was in. Worse still (at least for those of my generation who had imbibed Space Age dreams along with our mothers' milk), space itself was internalized, its dark brooking depths becoming little more than a poetic analogue for the uncharted continents of the human mind. Within less than a decade of landing on the Moon, all our outward-bound aspirations had more or less turned in on themselves.

To add to this irony, the principal people we have to thank for this unexpected legacy are none other than the astronauts.

"The vast loneliness of the Moon up here is awe-inspiring," said Jim Lovell, during a live broadcast from Apollo 8. Then, barely missing a beat, he added, "It makes you realize just what you have back there on Earth." With these words Lovell set the tone of premature nostalgia that would characterize all manned missions to come. In its most visceral form, such longing for home led Russian cosmonauts aboard the Salyut space station to play recordings of Earth sounds—thunder, rain, birdsong—whenever the monotonous hum of the fans in their electronic equipment got them down. "They were like meetings with Earth," one of them confided in his diary.

From Apollo 8 onward, it became increasingly clear that what most preoccupied astronauts was not the Moon but the Earth. Frank Borman, Jim Lovell, and Bill Anders were the first crew to slip into lunar orbit and give themselves up to the pull of the unknown, and the strange world they circled clearly fascinated them. It was like "plaster of Paris," said one. Or, "like dirty beach sand with lots of footprints in it," said another. They also beamed back descriptions of the far side of the Moon, whose round visage, locked away from us in a gravitational stranglehold, is completely invisible from the Earth. Anders compared it to a sand pile that kids had played in for a long time. "It's all beat up," he said, "no definition. Just lots of bumps and holes." And yet even as the astronauts eagerly soaked up sights never before witnessed by human eyes—the more magnificent for having been familiar from a distance and yet for so many centuries unresolved in their full and very foreign detail—their hearts hankered for home.

What captivated them most were not the wonders of the proximate world, gray and barren beneath them, but the beauty of the far-off one they had left behind, the "light beyond our lights," as the poet Archibald MacLeish sentimentally described it. Mushy comments like Lovell's were soon a dime a dozen. In fact, years later, Frank Borman was still reeling from the experience. Recalling the way the Earth distinguished itself against a background that—let's face it—offered plenty in the way of competition, he remarked, "It was the only object in the entire universe that was not either black or white." Instead, it was a deep sea blue, wreathed in delicate whorls of white. With the sun behind it, it was iridescent—a shining, spinning disc suspended against a backdrop of velvety black. In short, it was difficult not to imbue the planet with exemplariness.

Bill Anders took hundreds of photographs of the Earth and from every which angle; floating on its ownsome looking like an opalescent marble, peeking up over the Moon's dark horizon to scatter rays of Earth-shine, or setting down behind its lackluster satellite for a brief "night." Many of these images would become lasting icons of the environmental movement. As bywords for Gaia, emblems of California's Whole Earth movement, and metaphors for basic human value, they injected into the ordinary course of human action an appreciation of longevity and process.

They also renewed a sense of responsibility toward our common stewardship of the Earth's bounty, and in fact one of Anders's photographs was adopted as the flag of the first Earth Day. As Apollo 9 astronaut Russell Schweickart, an early proponent of planetary consciousness, saw fit to remind us, "That little blue and white thing" he was lucky enough to gaze down on like a guardian angel was everything—"all of history and music and poetry and art and death and life and love, tears, joy, games." In effect, the astronauts of Apollo collectively redefined the moon shot for future generations as the gestalt-shifting moment that gave us singular insight into the fragility and preciousness of our home planet. As Dick Gordon confided to me on that hot Los Angeles day, "People are always asking what we discovered when we went to the Moon: what we discovered was the Earth."

Whether or not the astronauts intended their impromptu revisionism of space exploration's outward-bound rhetoric is neither here nor there. The point is they couldn't help themselves. At a distance of 250,000 miles, the Earth looked small enough to cup in the palm of a hand. Floating alone in the dark void like a misplaced Christmas bauble, it appeared in need of protecting, cherishing. It was hard to believe that the planet could be home to thousands of millions of people, harder still to acknowledge that they were heedlessly poisoning its atmosphere and defiling its seas. For the first time mankind was able to stand outside of itself and turn a cold eye on its own innermost contradictions. As purveyors of the new knowledge, the astronauts were aggrandized by the act of traveling upward, their thoughts at once elevated and rarefied. They'd become privy to the vantage point of God.

Almost all the Apollo astronauts were religious men (so too, for that matter, was most of the NASA establishment). They carried Bibles and communion wafers into space, recited prayers in their capsules and modules, and gave thanks to God each time they were safely delivered home. It was only natural that they should begin to see themselves as Heavenly Messengers, duty-bound from on high to bring mankind to its senses—or, as Buzz Aldrin, himself a Presbyterian elder, had it, "awakened once again to the mythic dimensions of man." The most poignant message, however, came earlier, when the crew of Apollo 8 began their Christmas Day broadcast with "In the beginning, God created the Heavens and the Earth." Here were men who had journeyed farther from our origins than anyone before them, and what affected them most was that prehistoric moment, lost in time's deepest archives, of when we came to be. Even the ascending saints, it seems, could be humbled.

Yet, even allowing for the triumph of religious sentiment over rational observation, to leave matters here misses the larger point about the influence that position exerts over perception. Because if the psychologists are right, we turn to creation myths whenever known reality stops. As we reach out to touch the unknown, we simultaneously grasp for some reaffirmation of who we are and (only then) extend the limits of our consciousness. What the astronauts were reminding us of as they read aloud from the opening verses of Genesis was that the boundaries of our identity ought not to stop with family, or town, or faith, or nation-state; we were one species, and perhaps it was not ridiculous to suppose that there was such a thing as one global soul. From here, everything else flowed: Gaia, designer Buddhism, transcendental meditation, the international peace movement, environmentalism, antinuclear protests, tree hugging, and rebirthing.

Of these, Gaia's specific debt to the Space Age is the most striking. James Lovelock, the British atmospheric scientist and father of the

Gaia hypothesis, first developed his idea of the Earth as a self-evolving, self-regulating system while working for NASA in the late sixties, devising experiments to detect life on Mars and studying Apollo photographs of the Earth. In 1979, when Lovelock first ventured into print with his thesis, he defined Gaia as "a complex entity involving the Earth's biosphere, atmosphere, oceans, and soil; the totality constituting a feedback of cybernetic systems which seeks an optimal physical and chemical environment for life on this planet." His notion of the Earth as a living being struck a chord with a wide range of nature lovers, from indigenous cultures who thought of the Earth as a sacred spirit to mystics who sought the "oneness" in nature and environmentalists who were all too aware of how delicate was the balance of equilibrium in a complex system: cut down a rain forest in one part of the globe and you create a desert in another. It was the scientific community that gave Lovelock—and Gaia—a hard time. In an interview with Salon.com in 2000, Lovelock described his lifelong battle to win scientific acceptance as "a bruising experience."

Gaia, of course, is as well-known as it is popular, but how many people have heard of Noetics, brainchild of Apollo 14 astronaut Edgar Mitchell—a man who is better known for having been admonished by NASA for conducting an unauthorized ESP experiment with four friends on the ground? Mitchell was not the only astronaut to be profoundly and lastingly altered by the experience of going into space: Apollo 12 veteran Alan Bean has, over the decades, painted dozens of moonscapes, mixing moon dust and bits of charred Apollo 12 heat shield into his paints to lend true grit to his scenes of astronauts standing tall in the Ocean of Storms. Russell Schweickart became a vocal champion of Zen Buddhism and New Age cosmic consciousness, while Story Musgrave, a polymathic maverick who was recruited by NASA in 1967 and was still flying the Shuttle almost thirty years later, claims to have heard mysterious music in space. "It was noble, magnificent music," he told space.com reporter Richard Macey in February 2000, adding, "I was a little on the margin . . . I was walking the edge." Only Mitchell, however, founded his own school of spiritualism.

Making the most of his spiritualized perspectives on space, Mitchell incorporated them into the thoroughgoing alternative knowledge system he calls Noetics. In a recent public lecture, he recalled his moment of revelation:

> *From the vicinity of the moon on the way home I had a sense of awe at the wonder of the universe and sensed an interconnectedness that was beyond my previous experience. Perceiving the separate galaxies and galactic clusters and stars and planets but knowing that somehow they are interconnected—and feeling a sense of wonder and joy and buoyancy associated with that insight—I came to realize that our story of ourselves as told by both science and our religious cosmologies was incomplete and flawed and that we needed a new story to answer the questions in the space age of who we are, how we got here and where we're going.*

It was in order to write that new story that in 1973 Mitchell founded the Institute of Noetic Sciences, a nonprofit organization that conducts and sponsors research into "consciousness and human potential." Based in California's Marin County, home of hot tubs and Rolfing, the institute, whose name derives from *nous*, the Greek word for intuitive knowing, has a finger in several metaphysical pies. It administers the Temple Award for Creative Altruism, presented annually to three generous souls "whose lives and work embody the inspirational light of unselfish service motivated by love." It organizes regular educational seminars, ranging from the usual paranormal and esoteric staples exploring consciousness, healing, and spiritual alchemy to such worldly topics as "The Energy of Money" or "Becoming a Practical Mystic," and it sponsors large-scale international conferences.

Among the various publications to have emerged from these conferences, many reflect an interest in the power that mind can exert over matter, including *Spontaneous Remission: An Annotated Bibliography* and *Science Within Consciousness*. What supporters of Noetics are seeking to build is an empirically based body of knowledge pertaining to the realm of subjective experience. To the reductionist models of materialist science, they wish to add holistic models. To science's deterministic explanations, they add teleological or purpose-recognizing ones. At root they believe that Noetic knowledge is not new knowledge, but a rediscovery of the esoteric core common to all world religions. Through Noetics, they argue, we may better understand our spiritual nature. After an hour or so spent browsing the institute's website (which, incidentally, has become the bulletin board for a Noetically-minded community that currently numbers 50,000), I came away feeling as though I had just shared a congenial tea with Mary Baker Eddy and Buddha.

What are we to make of Noetics? On the one hand it's pure 1970s California, worldly, pragmatic, and yet thoroughly esoteric. It is also fundamentally inward-looking. In line with the teachings of the Human Potential Movement and Werner Erhard's "self-actualization," or EST seminars, both of which sprang up along the shores of Marin County at much the same time, its principal compass of concern is the individual. The idea that individual human beings are universes unto themselves, miniature versions of God's grand creation, has roots that stretch as far back as the Middle Ages. Then, natural philosophers exploited the analogy between microcosm and macrocosm in order to underscore their belief that humankind was an integral part of God's design, the rightful heir to some spark of the divinity that resided in the heavens above. In the context of the waning Space Age, however, the notion of a correspondence between biology and cosmology acquired a new twist. Now the vital link that needed to be established was less the correspondence between big and small, than that between the inner and the outer.

In Noetics, the all-encompassing void of outer space is a symbol

of the unconscious mind. Succeed in penetrating one and you penetrate the other—except in our case, our inability to plumb the alien
depths of the cosmos matched our basic ignorance about the nature
of mental power. The overall message was straightforward enough:
when we gaze out into limitless space, what we are really reckoning
with are the vast, unmapped territories of the human psyche. This
was an ingenious way to assimilate the Space Age's essentially
expansionist ideals, compensating us for the fact that we would not,
at least in the foreseeable future, become a space-faring species, colonizing new worlds, mining precious metals on the Moon, or tapping
cheap energy sources on distant planets. Physically, economically,
and technologically, deep space would remain off limits for a very
long time to come. Mitchell's achievement was to make peace with
the new reality: instead of conquering space, he enabled space to
invade us.

Mitchell's thinking recalls the mysticism of Andrei Tarkovsky's
cinematic space epic *Solaris*, which was based on Stanislaw Lem's
groundbreaking 1961 novel and released eleven years later.
Although it was immediately hailed as "the Russian *2001*," nothing
could be further from the truth. Unlike Kubrick, Tarkovsky has little
time for technology, and in *Solaris* he abandons the gee-wizardry of
revolving space stations and futuristic moon bases to focus exclu-
sively on the puzzling nature of reality and the limits of science. His
real subject, you sense, is space and mental health.

Solaris is an eerie film, more psychological thriller than science
fiction. We enter the scene after learning that a small team of astronauts that has been studying a strangely sentient alien sea has begun
hallucinating. As the waterworld the astronauts orbit swirls and
churns beneath their space station, ghosts arising from their inner
consciousness materialize before their eyes and shadow them
through their long, lonely days and fevered nights, driving them to
the edge of sanity. Although some kind of accommodation between
man and alien intelligence is eventually brokered (not by one of the

astronauts, but by the psychologist-hero who is dispatched to the space station to address the problem), the film hints, somewhat darkly, that by going into space mankind is defying some kind of unwritten law of nature. And there we come to the issue that lies at the very heart of the space effort, to wit: Is mankind's push into the cosmos the result of a natural drive—an urge as deeply embedded as the other basic impulses, for example, the sex drive? Or are we in our determination to fling ourselves off the planet contravening the very essence of who we are?

Sometime in the near future a strange thing begins to happen: children start developing stunning powers of mind. Confounding everything we know about human development, they're able to move objects through the air by effort of will alone, to see through walls and read their parents' thoughts. Soon the children begin to change. Without any need of expressing their emotions, their faces turn stony; without any need to see, their eyes turn blank, and babies remain in their cribs manipulating the world around them remotely. The parents are terrified, because they know that these children they no longer recognize as their own are forever lost to them. Eventually, the children metamorphose entirely, becoming points of light that fly up into the sky. Escaping the tyranny of matter, they abandon the Earth to unite with an alien Overmind in a universe of untold complexity.

In his 1953 novel *Childhood's End*, this is how Arthur C. Clarke pictured the next step in the evolution of humanity. It would be a painful step, justifying the separation anxiety that all parents feel about letting their children grow up. But, concludes Clarke, such a step is inevitable; as a species, we must let our future selves go.

Time and again in his writings, Clarke returns to the idea that space is calling out to us, beckoning us to our true fate like a benevolent siren. His other recurrent theme is that we are unable to resist its call. "It is often hard to avoid the feeling that we are in the grip of some mysterious force or Zeitgeist that is driving us out to the planets, whether we wish to go or not," he wrote in "Space Flight and the Spirit of Man." Published in 1961, this seminal essay represents one of Clarke's more impassioned attempts to prepare us for the coming changes and to warn us of the consequences of not heeding the call. The world is now "space conscious," said Clarke, but it is not yet sufficiently "space minded . . . [and] our entire culture will suffer from sensory deprivation if it does not go out into space." The implication is that instead of evolving like the children in *Childhood's End*, mankind will somehow wither and atrophy if it fails to rise to the challenge.

You can imagine (indeed, you can practically hear) the murmurs of approval that resounded in Space Age circles, where Clarke's novel acquired instant iconic status. Among the faithful, the very idea that we might shrink from the cosmic prospect before us and align ourselves with the forces of reaction was considered outright foolishness, like closing the door on an evolutionary portal. And yet to pass through that door entailed leaving part of ourselves behind. In a wonderfully perceptive, heart-on-sleeve account of the emotional impact of Apollo, written in the form of an extended personal letter to her eighty-year-old father, the Italian journalist Oriana Fallaci gives voice to this very dilemma. "On the one hand there was myself, the child who believes in the stars, and on the other hand there was you, the adult who believes in the Earth. . . . It was as if a war, a gulf, had opened between us." Others were less bothered by the inevitable rupture. Timothy Leary, for example, insisted that the Earth was a "nursery planet" or "womb-planet"—a place that mankind was obliged to grow out of if it finally wished to grow up.

Among space advocates it was taken for granted that going into space was akin to crossing an evolutionary threshold. As early as 1929, when the dream of space flight was still a twinkle in rocket scientist Robert Goddard's eye, Cambridge physicist J. D. Bernal was busy arguing that under the selective pressures of worldly limitation mankind must eventually split into two distinct species, Earthkind and Spacekind, and it was quite clear which had the evolutionary advantage. Later, once space travel was within realistic view, Arthur C. Clarke predicted that "expansion into space will produce a quantum jump in our development as great as that which took place when our ancestors left the sea." Rockets, however, and not air-breathing lungs would be the agents of our destiny. Imbuing these totems of progress with something approaching shamanistic power, Clarke wrote, "They can take us to that greater Renaissance whose signs and portents we can already see, or they can make us one with the dinosaurs."

Echoing Clarke, Wernher von Braun ranked the 1969 lunar landing as "equal in importance to that moment in evolution when aquatic life came crawling up on the land." Von Braun wanted us to recognize our space-bound surge for what it was: an adaptive development in human history. By responding to the calling of the stars, just as the land once beckoned our ancestors, we would transcend ourselves. What lay on the other side of the evolutionary leap, he did not say—wisely perhaps, given the lethal way in which his native Germany had recently assaulted Darwinism. But evolutionary ideas were already in the air, spreading like contagion. Just before takeoff, Neil Armstrong endorsed the notion that going into space was part of our genetic inheritance, a simple matter of programming. The astronauts were driven skyward "just as salmon swim upstream," he told the *New York Times*. Meanwhile, America's favorite futurist, Buckminster Fuller, happily chirped that Apollo 11 was "the dead center of evolutionary events."

Taking a somewhat cooler view of things was naturalist, anthropologist, and historian Loren Eiseley. In his book *The Invisible Pyramid* (1970), Eiseley agreed that what might be at stake in space travel was a matter of our long-term survival, and he argued that the motor behind our thrust upward was blind biological imperative. Removing all anthropomorphism from the picture, he compared mankind to a slime mold colony. In his opinion, we were just "spore bearers" compelled to spread our seed as far as we could. Eiseley was far from unique in taking this view; in fact, the term "seeding" is arguably the most overused term in Space Age literature, as though the Earth were a giant space-flower whose astronauts would one day pollinate the galactic bloom. But Eiseley gives the metaphor a new twist.

"Is humanity like some giant ripening puffball, feeling the mounting pressure of the spores within?" he asks, making deliberate play on the explosive sense of urgency that space advocates felt so keenly. Eiseley was fascinated by that urgency, and in an attempt to account for it he suggested that man is fundamentally a creature driven by "centrifugal tendencies"—consumed with a singular desire to launch himself upward and outward in search of new pastures. Given our relentless depletion of the Earth's resources, he argued, this imperative to hurl ourselves into space was as critical as survival itself. History, Eiseley concludes, is an "invisible pyramid." From the very beginning of time, all of it, the entire history of civilization, has been secretly enslaved to the monomaniacal purpose of constructing the means for mankind to leave the Earth.

Despite the slime mold comparison—which rather undercuts the sense of grandeur with which Clarke (who clearly felt that entering space was somehow ennobling) and others wished to imbue the subject of space travel—Eiseley was every bit as much the evolutionary determinist. Within a decade or so, however, as it began to look as though mankind's achievements in space might fall far short of expectations, it became clear that evolutionary theorists would need to work harder to justify their grand theories of human development. At first, some of them responded by merely shouting more loudly. Buckminster Fuller, for example, penned an essay called "The Universe Is Technology" in 1978 in which he simply continued to insist on our evolutionary leap. After reiterating the idea that space exploration was as natural to us as "a child running around on its own legs," he ingeniously salvaged our failure to colonize other worlds by styling the Earth itself as a settlement. "We are in space and have never been anywhere else," he rhapsodized. "We are already a space colony."

Over time, merely insisting on the leap was not enough. Since the eighties, evolutionary justifications have themselves had to evolve, adjusting (unlike Fuller, who was clearly in denial) to that fact that space exploration began and ended with the moon landings. Since we do not inhabit the outposts of the solar system and will not embark on such a presumptive conquest in the foreseeable future, the Space Age Darwinists have had to shift gear. Now they argue (pace Edgar Mitchell) that the evolutionary adaptation that came with Apollo occurred on the level of consciousness. It still happened, it's just harder to see.

In a book called *The Global Brain: Speculations on the Evolutionary Leap to Planetary Consciousness*, published in 1983, eco-philosopher and fellow of the Institute of Noetic Sciences Peter Russell offers a prime example of this shift, and of the intellectual contortions that it appeared to call for, since the book is nothing if not inconsistent. First Russell argues that the Space Age launched us into an era of accelerated mental development and heightened self-awareness. Later, he suggests that what the moon shot ultimately represented was Gaia extending her nervous system outward, seeking contact with other Gaias (there's even a diagram in the book showing Gaia's tendrils—magnetic lines, perhaps?—swirling around Jupiter and Saturn). Finally, Russell ventures the theory that "human society grows like brain tissue." The first stage is a proliferation of cells, and the second is a phase of growing interconnectivity—a process, he says, whose importance was underscored by those astronauts who briefly glimpsed the planet to be a single, complex system. In the end, Russell's goal seems little different from that of religious philosopher Pierre Teilhard de Chardin's in that his planetary consciousness anticipates the eventual formation of a "social superorganism"—a kind of Noosphere with bells on.

One of the more unusual places the evolutionary argument surfaced at the height of the Space Age, when our advancement still seemed self-evident, was in a slim volume called *Space Age Management* by James Webb. Little read outside of business and management circles (in part, no doubt, because it is exceedingly dull), the book, published in 1969, has barely made a mark in the literature on space. However, the ideas it contains are both important and radical.

James Webb was NASA's administrator throughout the sixties. Handpicked by President Kennedy in 1961 to preside over Mercury, Gemini, and Apollo, he was then at the pinnacle of a power-track career that had taken him from the military through law school into government and thence into industry (with a return to the Marine Corps during World War II sandwiched in). Webb's first period of government service saw him running Harry Truman's budget department and then serving as Under Secretary of State in the State Department. Then, when Dwight Eisenhower took office in 1953, he slid comfortably into a senior executive position at the Oklahoma-based oil company Kerr-McGee. That was where Kennedy found him. Thus, at the age of fifty-four, Webb found himself back in government, overseeing the nation's space program. He was the chief coordinator, supreme planner, and all-powerful decision maker of everything to do with space. He politicked, jostled, coaxed, and cajoled for NASA in Washington. He controlled the awesome budgets, dispensed contracts to the aerospace industry, and imposed impossible deadlines on everyone. He stood, in short, precisely where the buck stopped, and it was on the back of the superlative performance he choreographed that he wrote his book.

Space Age Management articulates nothing less than a new

domestic politics for a technological era. Among its key recommendations, Webb insists that science and technology should be fully integrated into the social infrastructure and that trustworthy leaders be put in place who understand that a society's "goals, projects and systems must be viewed as interdependent elements." In this way, he says, you build a highly "adaptive" society, capable of organizing and reorganizing itself so as to maximize widely diverse resources, but ultimately coordinated by a group of management executives in organic flux. Like a rapid-response squad, such a society can instantly react to changes in the national and political environment. Not surprisingly, Webb's blueprint for this flexible, cooperative, and yet competitive new society was NASA under his own administration. There he had achieved a satisfying integration of man and machine and an equally gratifying blurring of the boundaries between production, exchange, and consumption. The astronauts, moreover, as both system components and end-of-line commodities, were model citizens of the new technocracy. "There is no reason why we cannot do in other areas what we have done in aeronautics and space," he boasted.

Webb's paradigm for the rational administration of society was specifically designed for an evolving nation, one just coming to terms with its new powers and potential. But instead of treating the individual as the basic unit of perfectibility, Webb's social Darwinism focused on the fitness of the social organism. "Man's destiny is a product of his intellect." According to Walter McDougall, the Pulitzer Prize–winning chronicler of America's space program, what Webb envisioned taking place in American society was a "revolution from above."

Webb's vision of a fully integrated and systematized future won political sanction when, just moments after the moon landing, Richard Nixon told America that "for one priceless moment in the whole history of man, all the people on the Earth are truly one." The promise of space exploration, he implied, was that of reconciling differences, globally, as man and machine together claimed new frontiers. Nixon's speech communicated to the American people the idea that the pioneering spirit need not be celebrated only as a virtue of the nation's trailblazing past. It was alive and well and, more important, happily wedded to the new technological economy. At that moment, the push for colonization was just one step away. Few foresaw that it would never happen, that we would stand on the Moon but never possess her.

Webb was the last NASA administrator to reap the benefits of unfettered optimism. Even in the years immediately following his tenure, reality was having a hard time keeping pace with expectations. While von Braun and other space advocates continued to wax lyrical about evolutionary leaps and mankind's cosmic destiny, NASA was struggling to justify its existence in a post-Apollo climate, where budgets were tight and living standards were in decline. After Watergate and Vietnam, when public faith in the wisdom of government was at it lowest ebb, the agency was simply unable to weather the storm of protest against spending vast chunks of the federal budget on space. As a result, the Moon was abandoned. Manned space exploration was abandoned. And with the drive for reusability that resulted in the Space Shuttle, space was not colonized but routinized.

The Shuttle had neither the thrust nor the imaginative power to lift us up again, boosting morale, and making us believe in a brighter Space Age future. And when Challenger exploded in 1986, sending schoolteacher Christa McAuliffe and six others to their untimely graves, NASA lost what little public support had lingered on. The agency has never recovered. Nearly two decades on, its guilt persists over the revelation that the disaster could have been avoided. So does public mistrust of the agency. Although NASA's former administrator Dan Goldin beat a path out of this impasse, promoting space as a place better fitted for machines than human beings, neither the government nor the public rallied behind him to supply the agency with necessary funds and (just as necessary) a popular mandate.

In little over three decades NASA has gone from being the brilliant and visionary new kid on the block, armed with a sacred mission and bankrolled to the hilt, to suffering a full-blown midlife crisis. NASA has become an entrenched bureaucracy, slow to move with the times, much less set an example, and it is widely criticized for squandering time and resources on the ever unpopular International Space Station, as well as for lacking a bold vision of our future in space. Notwithstanding the fact that its former Russian adversaries are now, technically, its vassals, it is the Russians who have been perceived in recent years to have made innovative headway in space—first through numerous missions of guile and endurance on Mir and, most recently, by engineering Dennis Tito's groundbreaking trip as the first space tourist (a trip the NASA leadership famously opposed, misjudging popular sentiment once again). To make matters worse, as its funding continues to spiral downward, NASA is now having to contend with aggressive start-up entrepreneurs launching their own satellites, planning new manned missions to space, and whispering that the bloated agency impeding their independent efforts ought to be scrapped altogether.

Nothing of the dynamism that Webb sought to cultivate remains. Perhaps the former administrator had the wrong management model in the first place? Or perhaps his ideas have simply had their day, just as the earlier management models associated with Henry Ford and Frederick Winslow Taylor had theirs. Either way, hierarchic, machine-like organizations, comprising thousands of components working toward realizing a common goal, are now outmoded. Lumbering dinosaurs in a world full of darting, nimble new-form creatures, they are not equipped to meet the demands of the new economy, assembling and reconfiguring themselves like quicksilver—with the synaptic efficiency of those communications companies that have lately effected their own quiet revolution, neither from above nor below but from what were once the sidelines.

Although we still live in a Space Age of sorts, its parameters have shrunk. What's more, this shrinkage has occurred as we've struggled to digest scientific evidence suggesting that the universe itself is far more extensive than was ever thought possible. It is true that NASA continues from time to time to launch probes off on long, indeterminate voyages to the outer bounds of the solar system and beyond, but these efforts are quickly forgotten. And although Mars continues to bait us, the unmanned vehicles that the agency periodically lobs over there have demonstrated an unruly tendency to crash or get lost. Even Robert Zubrin, the irascible president of the Mars Society, who for years has campaigned for a manned mission to the red planet, has been forced to scale down his plans and settle for a more proximate colony. At the time of this writing, the society's twenty-ton habitation module—a lonely metal tin that sits on the rim of an impact crater in the Arctic's Devon Island—awaits its summer crew of would-be astronauts. In operational terms, the Space Age now extends no more than 300 miles or so above the surface of the planet to embrace the congested zone where satellites buzz, space stations float round in dreamy circles, and the unblinking eyes of a hundred scanners scrutinize every aspect of life on Earth.

Perhaps the Space Age's detractors were right all along when they insisted that space was no place for mankind—that our passage beyond the bounds of the Earth's stratosphere involved some kind of trespass. On the eve of the Rocket Age, C. S. Lewis set the critical tone. We did not belong in space, he argued. In Lewis's view, expressed in his 1943 novel *Perelandra*, the vast interplanetary distances were "God's quarantine regulations" designed to prevent us spreading "the contamination of our own corruption." Rather like a curse, Lewis's fears have to some degree been played out in reality, for many of the early astronauts appeared to experience strange withdrawal symptoms once they'd returned home. They had tasted the fruit of temptation and were forever changed by it. Dee O'Hara, a nurse working with the original astronauts, diagnosed the problem as "rage at having come back to Earth." Talking to Oriana Fallaci, she confided:

> *Do you know that for months John and Wally and Scott went around looking at the sky? You could speak to them and they didn't answer, you could touch them on the shoulder and they didn't notice: their only contact with the world was a dazed, absent, happy smile. They smiled at everything and everybody and they were always tripping over things. They kept tripping over things because they never had their eyes on the ground."*

Describing a similar kind of space sickness in his poem "Home," the poet John Witte writes about a maladjusted astronaut returned to Earth to find that he has been drained of all strength. He can no more lift a bunch of flowers given to him by a child than raise his head off his pillow where he is "pulled down by the gravity of a dream." Formerly he had been as a god: "He lifted a building in one hand, a pencil in the other." But now, reduced to a state of infantile helplessness, "he spills milk on his shirt" and "his fork slips clattering on the plate." He is totally ill equipped for dealing with the ordinary burdens of daily existence, which seem to him to represent the weight of the world. The irony that animates the thinking behind Witte's poem is that so much about space flight infantilized the astronauts: the squeezy play food and the umbilical cords required for EVAs, the carry-cot chairs found in Russian Soyuz capsules, and the diapers that astronauts and cosmonauts alike were obliged to wear inside their space suits. The implication that's hard to resist is that the much vaunted rebirth of mankind glimpsed through space travel is in truth the fast track toward senility.

In a collection of short stories, written over two decades but published in 1988, two years after the Challenger disaster, J. G. Ballard takes such morbid thinking to its logical conclusion: his astronauts are not just senile, they are, for the most part, dead. Even the title of his book, *Memories of the Space Age*, suggests burial. In many of the stories Earth-orbit (for practical purposes, already the limit of our Space Age reach) is a dead zone that locks the decaying bodies of deceased astronauts into a holding pattern around the Earth. Ballard's characters are obsessed with these "orbiting biers." In "Cage of Sand," the dying inhabitants of an Earth ravaged by imported Martian viruses mark time by the biers' bright passage overhead; and in "The Dead Astronaut," the biers burn up in the atmosphere like shooting stars only to deliver the astronauts' remains into the hands of relic hunters, avid for trophies of a once glorious past. One story, set in the wild heart of the Amazon jungle, features a Kurtz-like character who tricks the natives into forming a cargo cult devoted to the worship of an astronaut who fell to Earth in the jungle. In their innocence, the natives eat the deified astronaut, believing that by so doing they are incorporating his spirit into their bodies. But, explains the story's narrator, what they are really ingesting is the twentieth century's "psychopathic projections."

Never one to miss a cultural beat, Ballard was quick to put his necromancy to service in subverting some of our more cherished Space Age assumptions. "If the sea was a symbol of the unconscious," he says, "was space perhaps an image of unfettered time, and the inability to penetrate it a tragic exile to one of the limbos of eternity, a symbol of death in life?" And again, in a grim story that sees the straggling remnant of mankind wrestle hopelessly with a mysterious sleeping sickness, he says, "Could it be that traveling into outer space, even thinking about it and watching it on television, was a forced evolutionary step with unforeseen consequences, the eating of a very special kind of forbidden fruit?"

Squared up against the real world, Ballard's sense that space travel is, at root, an "evolutionary crime" has been sadly borne out, and not just by Challenger—which looked so much like a retribution for our sins. For even if we allow that *going* into space confers some evolutionary advantage on the species, *remaining* there is another story. To the extent that human biology is simply not suited to microgravity, there are real "punishments" involved in long-duration missions. Even relatively short stays in space can produce profound changes in the body, consistent with what NASA euphemistically terms "space adaptation syndrome": a loss of red blood cells, a reduced ability to exercise, a diminishment of bone density, weight loss, cardiac arrhythmia, even a lengthening of the body. In short, months and years in space compromise our physical integrity and frazzle our psyches. As Ballard might see it, our hubris gets repaid in withered muscles and weakened bones.

Somewhat surprisingly, in the face of this brutal reality, the interplanetary imperialists (Robert Zubrin among them) continue to spin tales of seeding and conquest. Driven by visions of our eventual apocalyptic collapse, or in some cases merely by the nagging insistence of the superego, they remain determined to effect our expansion across space, imagining us colonizing the planets as we go. What these would-be conquistadors fail to understand is that a fundamental component of the attraction of space exploration is precisely its impracticality. That impracticality, in turn, preserves dreams (like Carl Sagan's, for example) unsullied by the messiness of actually colonizing the universe. The perversity of this story is that, without commerce, space cannot be explored; but by making the magical mundane, the original hunger is diluted. Mammon, of course, is no friend to purity, but purity doesn't send 200 tons of structural steel into orbit.

In any event, to all but a few acolytes, the clarion calls of Zubrin and his kind have begun to sound shrill, not least because amid all their showmanlike rallying, urgency, and polemic, a more pedestrian language of the Space Age has entered common usage. For the most part, this language belies the destination-focused rhetoric of would-be cosmic colonizers: the term "spaciness," for example, signifies placelessness. In an enjoyable offbeat study called *Late for the Sky*, cultural historian David Lavery devotes a whole chapter to what he calls space talk—namely, the language that describes the various means by which we may leave Earth without actually going anywhere. We can trip and fly, get spaced out or high. It is no accident that the terminology of the Space Age and that of the drug-infused counterculture of the sixties coincide; both, Lavery contends, share a profound aversion to gravity, to the stay-put forces that underwrote a postwar society which wanted a place for everything and everything in its place. There could be no social evolution in such a society, no new things coming into being.

Contemporary society, by contrast, owes much to the Space Age's approval of displacement and dispersion, to the idea that the uprooted can thrive as well as the rooted. We are far more comfortable these days thinking of space as both every-place and no-place, rather than as something stretching throughout the universe in all directions that we might claim like land and then hedge with arbitrary frontiers. It is taken for granted, too, that space can be internalized, becoming a frame of mind, or indeed that the mind may be accorded its own space in cyberspace. The only conception of space that somehow runs counter to these post–Space Age constructions is the idea of enchanted space—the kind of space that is still alive with the possibilities of alien encounter.

CHAPTER 3

FOREVER ROSWELL

The town of Roswell, New Mexico, has neither international airport nor domestic terminal. Instead, a single landing strip, at one time belonging to the military, fetches up unceremoniously in front of a squat building that has been rebuilt for civilian travel. To get there, you have to hop on a small sixteen-seater that takes off from Albuquerque and then coughs its way across the parched deltas and dark scraggy dunes of the southwestern desert—a flame-colored landscape so bleakly empty and mysteriously shadowed it could almost pass for the dusty plains of Mars.

Like many visitors, I was traveling to Roswell because I wanted to see for myself the town where a flying saucer piloted by three humanoid creatures purportedly fell to Earth in 1947, swiftly becoming the subject of a government cover-up. I wanted to take the temperature of the place, visit the International UFO Museum, and talk to people who were there when the incident happened. I didn't have any expectation of getting to the bottom of things, but I did want to understand the peculiar blend of superstition, mysticism, fundamentalist certainty, and antigovernment sensibility that made Roswell tick. I sensed that if I was looking for reasons that the Space Age failed us, giving rise to a thriving subculture aimed at undermining it—an anti–Space Age, if you will—then this remote little town in the middle of the desert would offer plenty of scope for speculation.

I cannot say precisely when or how the crash at Roswell first impinged on my consciousness. But somehow I had absorbed the salient details of the case—Area 51, Hangar 18, Jesse Marcel, something about an autopsy. I even had a mental image of a swollen-headed and bloated corpse on the mortuary slab. I knew these elements of the Roswell story the same way that I knew that ships disappeared in the Bermuda Triangle, or that an oversize primate called Bigfoot roamed the forests of northern Canada: through a passing acquaintance with junk culture. I did not yet know, however, how seriously ufology buffs treat the crashed-saucer story. It is the preeminent case in their field, the only time officialdom has ever admitted to owning a flying saucer—never mind that the admission was retracted almost as soon as it was made, or that, as some commentators have argued, it was itself a cover-up, dreamed up by military bigwigs wishing to put people off the scent of classified experiments in Cold War technologies.

Once I decided to make Roswell my business, it quickly became clear that there was no single coherent crash story. Instead, competing stories circulate simultaneously through a body of literature built on the back of leaks, rumors, testimonials, and hearsay. Before long, I found myself bogged down in conflicting accounts of what happened and in spiraling explanations that attempted to reconcile inconsistent testimony. I grew suspicious of people's motives (witnesses *and* chroniclers) and frustrated not so much by the lack of evidence per se as by the self-reinforcing convictions of people for whom evidence was beside the point. Trying to pare down the story to its barest bones, I realized that even the basic facts—such as what time the UFO was seen, on what day, and where it landed—cannot be established with certainty. In spite of all this, in the telling and retelling of increasingly elusive, ever shifting events, the crash story has actually won supporters, even as it has failed to notch up one iota of credibility.

In 1994, as a direct result of being lobbied by Roswell's more vocal supporters, New Mexico Congressman Steven Schiff asked the General Accounting Office (the investigative arm of Congress) and the Air Force to search all Roswell-related files for any mention of the crash incident. The official response was negative: there was never any mysterious crash, and the Air Force did not have in its possession the mangled remains of a UFO or the pickled bodies of space aliens. Of course, no response could have better pleased the conspiracy theorists; their paranoid logic construes every denial as further proof of a cover-up. But neither has it made a dent in Roswell's marketability. Roswell is famous the world over. It has brand recognition. In the last few years alone, it has lent its name to a variety of commercial ventures, including a video game about FBI agents hunting down invading aliens, a feature film starring Martin Sheen, and a prime-time television series premised on the idea that the aliens did indeed land, bringing with them leathery pods containing unruly creatures bearing a curious resemblance to human teenagers.

Like De Smet, South Dakota, where *Little House on the Prairie* author Laura Ingalls Wilder grew up, or Gettysburg, Pennsylvania, Roswell has become a magnet for people who wish to possess a piece of a legend. Believers will cross continents to visit the crash site, fifty miles out of town, where they can stare in puzzlement at an unremarkable patch of rocky scrub (the all-important evidence having been hurriedly secreted away by government agents) and wonder at the meaning of it all. It's hard to tell what they take away from the experience, above and beyond the visceral satisfaction of being there, with its connotations of communion and mysterious auras. But these people are seekers and seekers always find. Perhaps they discover a sense of community through forging bonds of shared belief with others. Or perhaps they find some kind of resolution, imposing onto the empty site, as only faith can do, a full and portentous meaning.

Roswell has had an interesting time adapting to this year-round traffic in pilgrims. The local population is predominantly fundamentalist Christian and, as much out of secular conservatism as religious scruples, people are leery of being invaded by what they see as a bunch of weirdos with a blasphemous take on the cosmos. They don't want to live in UFO Central. Yet at the same time, they are pragmatists. Making a decent living in remote regions of rural America has always been tough, and tourist revenues, which now account for more of Roswell's total annual income than either farming or manufacturing, offer a welcome respite from the constant struggle. For the most part, the people of Roswell have squared away their dilemmas by biting their tongues, tolerating the tourists, and quietly pocketing the money.

Or, in some cases, not so quietly. During the celebrations of the fiftieth anniversary of the crash in 1997, when Roswell was overrun by tourists, a wily rancher by the name of Hub Corn began promoting his own crash site, thirty-three miles west of Roswell. For fifteen dollars per head, Corn, who has since shut down operations, would usher visitors onto his land and lead them along a winding trail to a barren spot where they might ponder the mysteries of the cosmic unknown. Borrowing freely from the Kubrick-Clarke style guide, he erected two huge granite monoliths at the entrance to his trail. He also moved to the crash site a large boulder whose hand-carved inscription proclaimed the place to be a "Universal Sacred Site." Hub Corn may be a straw-chewing hick with a soft spot for kitsch, but like all good entrepreneurs he has an intuitive grasp of what people want. In this case it is confirmation—which presumably explains why he went out and bought for the family Suburban a vanity license plate that reads "BELIEVE." His homemade monuments assured people that Roswell was indeed a holy town, the birthplace of a fundamental transformation in human experience whose full implications we have barely begun to fathom. "We Don't Know Why They Came," said Corn's boulder, "We Only Know / They Changed Our View / Of the Universe."

By and large, Roswell caters to the needs of its visitors more directly, with a perpetual round of talks and lectures as well as two museums of ufology, the larger of which operates a research library and education program. But the high point of Roswell's outreach activities is the annual UFO Encounter Festival. Taking place in July—the month in which rancher Mac Brazel first stumbled upon mysterious crash debris strewn over one of his fields—the festival draws together mystics and curiosity seekers for a weeklong celebration of all things alien. By inviting a host of *Star Trek* actors to headline its various events, the festival organizers inject a little levity into things, putting the call out to science fiction junkies yearning for some live action as well as to hard-core believers. I timed my visit to coincide with the festival, hoping to glimpse Roswell at its most open—hoping that UFOs would be very much the order of the day.

Before leaving home, I booked a motel room, touched base with the festival organizers, and sketched out an itinerary for the first few days of my stay. What I had not anticipated was that I would emerge from Roswell's airport into the pounding desert heat to find myself stranded in a more or less empty parking lot. There were no buses, no taxis, and no signs of life. Accordingly, I adjusted my mental picture of how small an American small town might be. In the distance, I could discern some low-lying buildings, which I took to mark the outskirts of the town, but I was reluctant to risk walking in stifling conditions that made heat-wave trickery as likely to account for appearances.

In the end, I got a ride into town with an elderly man who introduced himself as Trinny (short for Trinidad). He was picking up his brother-in-law, a loquacious character called Clovis Torres who was returning to Roswell after several years to attend a high school reunion. When I mentioned my interest in the UFO Festival, Clovis

launched into confessional mode. He told me that he had grown up
with no television, no radio, and no newspapers and that he'd had no
idea of the events that formed the basis of the Roswell myth. Later,
when he was acquainted with the story, he asked his mother for his
late father's diary, thinking that his father, a military man whom he
recalled as having known some of the players involved in *L'affaire
Brazel*, might have mentioned so strange an event. While there was
nothing of substance in the diary, on one of the blank pages at the
back, his father had written the name Jesse Marcel and the words
Patterson Air Base. For readers not fully conversant with Roswell,
Jesse Marcel was the army officer sent to recover the crash debris
from Mac Brazel's land, while the Wright-Patterson Air Force Base
outside Dayton, Ohio, is one of two contenders for the high-security
location where the crashed saucer is supposedly stored. The other is
Area 51 in Nevada.

Clovis's story was the first of many, since everyone in Roswell
seemed to have a tale to tell. It was as if all of the town's old-time
residents couldn't help themselves when it came to feeding their own
bit of intrigue into the mix, just to stake their piece of belonging.
Clovis's story was also typical in failing to add anything of substance.
It offered up a little mystique while explaining nothing, and it per-
petuated the he said/she said culture of gossip on which Roswell
myth-mongers thrive.

Trinny and Clovis dropped me off at the National 9, a run-down
motel just north of Main Street, Roswell's principal drag. The book-
ing office had a sign up over the front desk that read, "Roswell, New
Mexico—They Will Return." Beneath it was printed an oval-shaped
alien head with dark, slanting eyes—large, almond-shaped lozenges
that looked like the radiation symbol but with its bottom limb missing. Roswell's aliens belong to that species of extraterrestrial that has
come to be known in UFO and abductee circles as the "Gray." The
Gray, whose doe-eyed visage gazes out from the cover of Whitley
Strieber's best-selling abduction memoir *Communion*, has become

mainstream culture's generic alien. It has eclipsed the scaly lizardlike creatures that stalked the B movies and cartoon strips of the fifties, and that more recently took the villainous role in the 1996 movie *Independence Day*, and it has displaced the ubiquitous Little Green Men. It's as if, by unspoken consensus, the Gray has become the public mascot around which people who reject Space Age rationalism can rally.

Personally, I've always been struck by the way that the Gray, with its large wobbly head, sunken eyes, and truncated body, resembles the human fetus, though I have no idea what to make of this unlikely association, save for the fact that both represent a kind of undifferentiated homogeneity. However, the late Stephen Jay Gould once suggested, with reference not to aliens but to Mickey Mouse, that we are hard-wired to respond favorably toward creatures that exhibit "neoteny," the state of showing the characteristics of juveniles within species. In Mickey's original *Steamboat Willie* days, he possessed a much longer snout and a larger body in relation to his head: in short, he looked a lot like a mouse. By giving him a shortened snout, big eyes, and a (relatively) larger head, Disney intuitively tapped into our programmed response to anything that reminds us of human babies. In the case of the Gray, which is by no means entirely friendly, the large heads and appealing saucer eyes certainly make the species less threatening than the lizardlike aliens of old. Perhaps times are changing and we're feeling rather more well disposed toward otherworldly visitors than we used to.

Even by small-town standards, Roswell proved something of a backwater. Shabby old Main Street provided the sum total of what action the place had to offer. Strung out with cheap motels, family-style diners and a few dozen down-at-heel stores, it presented clear signs of the economic desperation the town has suffered over the years. The crucial downturn took place long ago, in the sixties, when the Walker Army Air Base was decommissioned and Roswell's population suddenly plummeted. Roswell has never recovered from the disappearance of the base, which issued the famous press release about having "captured a flying disk," only to deny it twenty-four hours later. Its population hovers around the 45,000 mark, while unemployment refuses to ease below 7 percent—high even for today, but disastrous in the nineties, when the rest of the country was experiencing unprecedented economic growth. I tried casting Main Street further back in time, into the prosperous fifties, when it would have been bustling with pert military wives and its stores would have been freshly painted and prim. But I just couldn't see it. Neither could the makers of the TV movie *Roswell*, starring Martin Sheen, since they filmed their civic scenes in a more picturesque town in Arizona. Thus on the eve of festivities, I concluded that tired, depressed, and anonymous-looking Main Street was beyond repair.

The next day, it was transformed.

Overnight it had morphed into a buzzing town center. All the stores were open and enjoying a brisk trade, and the sidewalk was thronged with a holiday crowd of people wearing shorts and eating ice cream. Many had driven in from out of state, from Arizona, California, and Texas, to enjoy the carnival spirit, munch on fresh roasted corn, and spend their money on an assortment of alien knickknacks. You couldn't walk more than five yards without encountering a street vendor or having printed matter thrust into your hands, sometimes by aliens on roller blades. That first day, I picked up flyers for an alien comedy show, for an all-singing, all-dancing spectacular called *Roswell: The Musical*, and for an organization that went by the tantalizing name of Alien Resistance HQ. A special festival supplement that came with the *Roswell Daily Record* gave a more comprehensive listing of the week's events, including an alien parade, an alien costume contest, an alien treasure hunt, and an alien chase. A roster of bands was scheduled to play at the open air stage on Pioneer Plaza, while Neil Norman and his Cosmic Orchestra, an outfit, I later discovered, that wrote and performed soundtracks for science fiction movies, was to play at the Civic Center.

Later that day, I visited the Civic Center for the official opening of the festival and snooped about the main hall, taking things in. It was crudely divided in two by a huge floor-to-ceiling curtain so that one half, decked out with arts and crafts stalls, resembled a church social, while the other half, windowless and dimly lit, masqueraded as a lecture theater. Here, a host of speakers invited to expound on matters esoteric—everything from crop circles and cattle mutilations to UFO defense programs—would have to compete with the noise of the fair, not to mention the lines of Trekkies wanting autographs from Tuvok, *Star Trek*'s only black Vulcan and one of the chief heroes of the *Voyager* series. In the foyer, Dutch and Japanese television crews were filming Roswell's cowboy-handsome mayor, Bill Owen, enthuse about the tourist industry (which the town is so assiduously courting) and the movie industry (which has done so much in recent years to boost popular interest in aliens). I managed to join them in time to hear the mayor commend those "who come to Roswell to have some of their questions answered," before a skimpily clad and impressively muscled Spice Williams, who played Vixis, sidekick of the evil Klag in the movie *Star Trek V: The Final Frontier*, cut the ceremonial ribbon and greeted fellow space cadets in fluent Klingon. For the uninitiated, this sounds much like a dog barking up a piece of bone.

The carnival atmosphere had not abated one bit by the time the alien parade kicked off on a blazing hot afternoon two days later. If anything, the town was in danger of overdosing on the otherworldly. On Main Street, in particular, there was no escaping the aliens. Green felt specimens crammed shop windows, inflatable Grays tethered with string flew from higher stories, and all kinds of weird life-forms paraded about the place sporting the latest in latex fashions. There seemed to have been an invasion of children with pea-green faces and springy antennae, and even Roswell's spherical street lamps were kitted out with alien eyes. The parade would have to struggle to hold its own against these exuberant background attractions.

Stopping off for a drink at a roadside stand, I got to talking with the proprietor, a retired naval intelligence officer by the name of Patrick Jennings. Assuming I'd found a kindred spirit, someone who didn't take all this too seriously (he was, after all, wearing a baseball cap sporting the slogan "I love aliens—they taste just like chicken!"), I ventured an observation on the nature of credulity only to find that I was addressing a believer. The saucer story was beyond doubt true, Jennings told me, making sure to add that when he was in the Navy he'd been involved in quite a few cover-ups himself. I asked why he thought it was necessary to keep things of evident national interest from the nation, and in response he trotted out the usual military guff about not wanting to cause mass panic. "People would think that our weapons would never work on them," he explained. This last statement was so far off my radar that I could only shrug, but what Jennings said about panic has a bizarre precedent. In 1938, Orson Welles famously modernized H. G. Wells's *War of the Worlds*, adapting it for radio and updating the Martians' landing site to Grovers Mill, New Jersey, for added effect. Broadcast nationwide the night before Halloween, the radio show caused immediate uproar on the East Coast, with scores of people evacuating their homes and arming themselves against the poison-gas-spreading invaders.

The alien parade was a drab affair that did not merit its top billing. Much more entertaining was the alien costume contest held at the Museum and Art Center, where there were awards for the cutest, scariest, and funkiest aliens. One wobbly toddler in a Dracula cape and big ugly felt head had the audience hooting because he kept trying to pull out one of his eyeballs. But he lost first place to a shiny blue bug child who squeaked, "Take me to your leader." Looking around the hall, it was clear that people were having a rib-ticklingly good time. Whether they took the fun and games with the proper pinch of salt, however, it was impossible to tell. I had made a mistake with Patrick Jennings. So why shouldn't there be many more people in Roswell who were happy to make light of Mac Brazel's discovery in the interests of tourism, while all along believing in its essential truth? There was certainly enough incentive to warrant such pragmatic double standards; after all, according to the Chamber of Commerce, for an outlay of $33,000 in festival funding the town expected a return of $2 million. Then again, if the people here really did believe that the aliens have landed, their convictions would hardly put them on the margins of American society. According to a poll conducted by *Life* magazine in spring 2000, their view is shared by 30 percent of the nation's population.

Back at the National 9, feeling in need of a few pointers, I sought out Horace and Becky, a couple I initially got to talking with because they were as mystified as I by the fact that frosted doughnuts were the only foodstuff available at breakfast. Becky, who'd grown up in Roswell, wasn't exactly put out, more dismayed, by all the UFO paraphernalia surrounding us, and she made a point of telling me that she did not believe in space aliens: "I believe in a Christian universe where God created man and woman." Her husband's thinking was more along lines I felt comfortable with. "People are just looking for something to believe in," he said. "They're searching. They want to know where we came from, where we're going, and what purpose we're here for." Horace and Becky gave me the names of some of Roswell's oldest and most well connected residents. They'd be believers, the couple cautioned, but they figured that by talking to them I would get a good idea of the climate of thought that characterized Roswell in the aftermath of the cover-up and which in some quarters persists to this day. It was thus that I found myself interviewing Ruth McPherson, who co-owned Cobean's, the town's stationery supplier. The conversation we had was bewildering, with my being at a loss much of the time to understand the link between the question I'd asked and the answer it received. Still, if I am to convey anything of its interest, I need first to sketch out the basic sequence of events that have persuaded so many people of the government's skulduggery.

. . .

It all began one summer's night in 1947, when rancher Mac Brazel came across a mass of glinting debris. He didn't think to report his find until a few days later when, running errands in nearby Corona, he happened to hear local gossip about people seeing flying saucers. There were rumors, for example, that Dan Wilmot and his wife watched from their porch one night as a mysterious glowing disc zoomed out of the sky overhead making a swishing sound and then disappeared over the horizon. As an aside, it is worth noting that much of America was in the grip of a flying saucer craze that summer. In June, Idaho businessman and pilot Kenneth Arnold had reported seeing a family of strange V-shaped objects that skipped across the sky like saucers skimming water. The story made sensational headlines across the country, and there followed a spate of sightings, which reached almost epidemic proportions on the West Coast.

Back in Roswell, Mac Brazel went straight to the sheriff, who immediately contacted officials at Walker Army Air Base, informing them that there was something they might want to look into. The base put one of its intelligence officers, Major Jesse Marcel, on the case to arrange the recovery of the debris. Along with a small detail from his department, Marcel examined the scattered materials in Brazel's field (for reasons I will come to, this field has not been designated the official crash site) and took a few pieces home for further investigation. Some of the debris he recovered appeared to be of very thin sheet metal, but Marcel claimed that he could not scratch it, cut it, or tear it, and when he folded it up it instantly sprang back into sheet form. He also picked up some charred rods that bore hieroglyphical inscriptions. At the air base, Marcel's seniors were equally mystified. The debris did not come from anything they recognized as their own, nor did it bear a resemblance to anything Russian they'd managed to intercept. Thrilled at the prospect of being the first unit to ground one of the discs so much discussed in the papers, base commander Colonel William Blanchard put out a press release saying that the army had captured a flying saucer.

On July 8, the story made the front page of the *Roswell Daily Record*, and from there it was wired to agencies across the country. Excitement spread like a contagion. All day the phone lines in Roswell were jammed, and Sheriff Wilcox boasted that he received three calls from London, one of them from the *Daily Mail*. The debris, meanwhile, had already been flown to Fort Worth for further analysis, paving the way for Brigadier General Roger Ramey, the Air Force commander there, to pour cold water on the whole affair. This he did the next day when, speaking from Texas, he informed reporters that the debris belonged to "a harmless high-altitude weather balloon." Ramey went on to suggest that Jesse Marcel may have failed to recognize the debris for what it was, since mixed in with it were "the crushed remains of a ray wind target."

As far as the public was concerned, that was that. But in Roswell, a complex alternative story would be pieced together over the years, based on the individual testimonies of people who claimed to have seen or heard something they should not have seen or heard, or to have participated unwittingly in a brutal and unsavory cover-up. Jesse Marcel, now deceased, was the first to break his silence after being coaxed out of the closet in the late seventies by UFO researcher Stanton Friedman. Marcel claimed, among other things, that the weather balloon debris that appeared in newspaper photographs after General Ramey went public with his disclaimer was not the same debris that he had examined. He would have known a weather balloon anywhere, he said. Then there were various stories about recovered aliens. Some people swore to having seen the three Grays in question at the crash site; others, like the wonderfully named Thaddeus Love, claimed to have transported them from one secret hideout to another. Glenn Dennis, then the town mortician, says he received anonymous inquiries about the availability of three small caskets. And one former

Walker pilot by the name of Oliver "Pappy" Henderson waited until he was an old man before admitting that he flew the bodies to the Wright-Patterson Air Force Base via Fort Worth.

After years of silence, literally dozens of Roswell's longtime residents joined the party; one of them is Ruth McPherson.

Cobean's Stationers was set back from Main Street in one of those narrow buildings that seem to extend backward forever. At the rear of the shop, in an elongated storeroom, an island of desks pushed together served as a makeshift office. Ms. McPherson, a trim seventy-something with wiry white hair, sat at one of the desks. "The people involved in the case were thoroughly reliable, and I have no reason to believe they'd put anything over on anyone," she was saying. "The government, on the other hand, has lied to us before, so why not in this instance?" Ruth had little trouble choosing whom to believe and the issue of evidence was, for her, neither here nor there: "I didn't see it. But I don't know how electricity works either," she said. Ruth had known Dan Wilmot. He was a man of great integrity, she told me; "a leader in our church and a leader in the community." His word could be trusted. She also knew Pappy Henderson and his wife from church. "He told his wife, Sappho, what had happened, but instructed her not to repeat it to anyone until he was dead." I didn't press her on which of the Hendersons turned whistle-blower, since alternative accounts had Pappy spilling the beans after reading about the Roswell incident in a tabloid magazine years after the event, when he was comfortably retired in California. Instead, I asked why the military officers didn't get to talking among themselves about the bodies, but Ruth was insistent that officers were under "strict orders" not to talk. "It would not be the first time the government has deceived us," she went on. "First they denied finding anything at the crash site, then they came out with a story that it was a mannequin, not a body." Why bother with the mannequin story at all? I asked. To which Ruth retorted: "Why don't we get some money back from the taxes we've paid all these years?" I took her to mean that either way government was inscrutable and nefarious.

Ruth McPherson confirmed what I have long suspected about believing in irrational things, and that is that such beliefs seldom stand alone. Instead, they are cushioned within a coherent system of thought. In her case, a readiness to assent to the most outlandish stories from the lips of friends and neighbors was a direct measure of her dislike of government: one conviction accounted for the other. Interestingly, this is a form of believing that does not require any seeing, empirical proof being superfluous to the if-x-then-y loop of reasoning that takes us from government secrecy to alien visitation—or for that matter, from pyramids to aliens, crop circles to aliens, or the limitations of modern science to aliens. Nor does it require the usual insistence that causes precede effects. Thus, instead of positing a cover-up to demonstrate government duplicity, Ruth's belief in the duplicity is, ipso facto, evidence of a cover-up. Similar errors in reasoning—formally called "affirming the consequent"—are commonplace among conspiracy theorists invoking cover-ups to explain everything from JFK's assassination to the terrorist attacks of September 11, 2001, but the art of turning conclusions into premises finds some of its most fertile ground in the otherwise dry soil of Roswell.

Ruth McPherson was nonetheless right about the government's record of lying about military activities in New Mexico. Beginning with the decision in 1942 to develop an atomic weapon at Los Alamos, secrets large and small have been concealed across the state. Even the testing of the A-bomb in 1945 in the desert only a couple of hours' drive away from Roswell was blamed on the explosion of a weapons depot. At Holloman Air Force Base in nearby Alamogordo, reconnaissance balloon flights took off for decades without the public knowing. Nor was the public informed of the regular test launching of rockets at White Sands, most notably the series of V-2s that were requisitioned from Peenemünde and shipped into New Mexico after the war on more than 300 railroad cars. Wernher von Braun and the team of World War II German scientists who developed them were not long in following, and soon they themselves were quietly busy developing and testing the Redstone rockets that NASA would eventually take an interest in. The government also consistently denied the existence of a cache of nuclear weapons in the Manzano Mountains near Albuquerque. Also near Albuquerque, in 1957, the Air Force mistakenly unloaded a hydrogen bomb 600 times more powerful than the bomb dropped on Hiroshima. Although catastrophe was averted and no one was injured, the military kept the affair hushed up for almost thirty years.

Then there are all the backpedalings and smoke screens associated with the Roswell incident itself. In 1995, in response to the request made by Congressman Schiff for a thorough investigation of all files relating to Roswell, the Air Force reclassified the debris found on Mac Brazel's ranch as a top-secret reconnaissance balloon designed to spy on Soviet nuclear testing and ballistic missile launches as part of Project Mogul. For obvious reasons, Mogul was not something the military wanted to shout about in 1947, and so it came up with the weather balloon story. Then, in 1997, the Air Force offered yet another explanation. In *The Roswell Report: Case Closed*, a serious production of 217 pages, it admitted that there was a link after all between the Walker Army Air Base and Wright-Patterson in Ohio. However, it was not the link ufologists wished to see confirmed. Apparently, in 1959, a captain named Fulgham, who was based at Wright-Patterson, was participating in a high-altitude balloon flight near Roswell, when his balloon and its 900-pound aluminum gondola crashed. Fulgham suffered a severe head injury in the accident, and by the time he was taken to Walker for treatment his head was badly swollen: his eyes appeared sunken, his face puffy, and his skin yellow. All in all, the report concluded, his head resembled "the classic science-fiction alien head." When Fulgham was flown back home, even his wife failed to recognize him. Now the Air Force was arguing that, despite a discrepancy of twelve years, this event became entangled in people's minds with Mac Brazel's story.

If only the Air Force had left matters there, hanging unresolved on this rather creative note. Instead, it went on to say that there had been another crash near Roswell in the late forties, this time involving a balloon carrying research dummies. These were the mannequins to which Ruth McPherson referred so dismissively. At this point it becomes hard to deny her cynicism a certain warrant, since dummies are simply too close to bodies to allay the suspicions of minds tuned to conspiracy. Even so, I couldn't help feeling that her mistrust of government had as much to do with a sense of principle as betrayal. As such, it was of a piece with a characteristically western slant on the U.S. Constitution, which cherishes the freedom of the individual above all else and construes government involvement in the daily lives of the people as meddling. Libertarians typically think this way, mistaking a lack of accountability for the independent spirit of pioneering, but then so, too, do the paranoid doyens of America's far-right militias, who blithely ignore the numerous structures that governments put in place to create and protect societies, which actually nurture individual freedom, in order to sustain their belief that government strength derives, above all else, from an ability to keep secrets.

The trouble is that conspiracy is so seductive. On top of the moral indignation it encourages as a proper response to the trespassed rights of the people, it offers other benefits. It spins a web of beguiling explanation around everything that defies comprehension (which is why you often get aliens and crop circles and Elvis lumped together), and it invariably lays the burden of responsibility elsewhere. In so doing, it perpetuates the myth of an inclusive us: "we," who are common victims together, dupes one and all of a higher-level deception but with the potential to unite as brave seekers after truth. Hence conspiracy's universal taunt—the truth is out there.

Nowhere in Roswell is this conspiratorial stance more plainly exploited than at the International UFO Museum, which took over the old Plains Theater on Main Street in 1997 and turned it into something resembling a police incident room crossed with Dr. Strangelove's nerve center. It even has its own towering map of the world mounted along one wall and dotted with little flashing lights indicating those places where close encounters of the first, second, and third kinds have been reported. To tour the museum you progress through a series of chapel-like alcoves where you can learn all you ever wanted to know about the 1947 crash, and if you're still hungry for information you can fill up on such subjects as "crop circles: phenomenon or hoax," "space and our universe," or "ancient cultures and their connections to extraterrestrial life forms." All the alcoves share the same aesthetic, with photographs, press clips, scrawled notes, and copies of leaked security documents tacked to the wall alongside maps where significant locations have been highlighted in red marker pen. It's straight out of *Columbo*, with the result that walking round the place you feel embroiled in an ever deepening mystery. Anyone paying close attention, however, will notice that in the alcove devoted to Jim Ragsdale's story, the museum does in fact suggest that at least part of the mystery has been solved—the part that answers what fell out of the sky. But it is not a solution that will satisfy anyone outside the UFO fraternity.

New Mexico truck driver Jim Ragsdale came out as a witness in 1994, when he was dying of cancer and determined not to go to his grave without first telling his daughter what happened to him back in 1947. He warned her that she'd have a hard time believing what he had to say, and then he told her that he had actually seen the UFO everyone had long been speculating about come down. Screeching and trailing flames, it had come plowing through the trees, sheering off their tops, before crashing into a huge rock near the Capitan Mountains, where Ragsdale, only twenty-two at the time, was camping with his girlfriend. Then there was only darkness and silence.

"Scared but curious," Ragsdale later told ufologists, he and his girl-friend set off to explore the wreckage. What they found was a banged-up disc, some twenty feet across, that was hissing steam through a jagged hole ripped across its side. "I looked inside the hole," said Ragsdale, who claims to have climbed into the craft, "and inside, there was a chair that looked like a throne. It looked like it was made of rubies and diamonds. There were other little chairs, four or five, and a lot of instruments on a panel. There were also the little people, four of them. They looked like midgets, about four feet long. Their skin, if it was skin, was sort of gray and when I touched one of them, it felt like a wet snake." There was more: stuff about collecting a large sackful of debris, about the girlfriend dying in a mysterious car crash a few weeks later, and about Ragsdale's house being ransacked for evidence by "men in black." But I was no longer concentrating. All I could think of was whether Ruth McPherson could possibly hate the government enough to believe this Tolkienesque yarn, complete with space goblins and magic stones.

For its part, the UFO Museum was persuaded by Ragsdale's story, since it fit with other evidence (including the testimony of two Franciscan nuns—read: unimpeachable) that had persistently foiled experts precisely because it pointed to a crash site near the Capitan Mountains. The museum, however, is far from unbiased in its views. Founded by Walter Haut, the Walker officer who wrote the original press release claiming that the Army had captured a flying saucer, and Glenn Dennis, the local mortician who'd been guardedly quizzed about funeral caskets, it is a sanctuary where believers may congregate without fear of being persecuted by rationalists, outraged Christians, and other debunkers.

The day I visited, for example, I overheard a woman discoursing loudly on the nature of our relationship with aliens. "They gave us Stealth technology, satellite technology and microchips, and in exchange they're taking our children," she was saying. When she noticed that people were listening, she went on: "They don't want our planet though, because we're just a speck in the universe, a joke to aliens, an infant race. We live in a three-dimensional world, while they live in four dimensions." Then there was Bob White, who is a familiar figure in esoteric circles. For some years now he's been touring the paranormal festival circuit exhibiting a hunk of metal that looks like a pinecone. White insists that it fell off a departing UFO and further claims that Los Alamos National Laboratory geologists are lying to him about its true chemical composition. No one giggled in disbelief as they listened to White, who'd set up shop at the museum for the duration of the festival. Nor was anyone smirking at the stories about strange sightings that were being traded across the floor like stocks and shares. Instead, people formed long queues at the museum shop to purchase the latest ufology had to offer in the way of books, pamphlets, and research papers. This was serious business. Serious enough to net the museum more than $1 million a year, most of which gets plowed back in to the organization, especially the library, which houses more than 3,000 books and 40,000 documents.

To a large extent, Haut and Dennis view themselves as crusaders. They established the museum to spread the word, as it were, and they stand staunchly by the Ragsdale story, championing the spot that the trucker stumbled upon, fifty-three miles northwest of Roswell, as the official crash site. Haut, now in his seventies and still barrel-chested, has a tendency to get impatient with those who mock. "I get fed up with folk who think we're just rubes down in New Mexico who wouldn't know an airplane from an umbrella," he told me. Dennis is more sanguine about criticism, much of which he says comes from local church leaders convinced that he and Haut are simply there to blow smoke and make money. "We didn't want a carnival in here," he insists, "which is why we registered the museum as a nonprofit organization and built the library."

Dennis is an interesting figure, not least because he did not go public with his personal story until 1990: "If I'd have told earlier, people would have thought the undertaker had sniffed too much formaldehyde," he jokes. But his main reason for delaying, he says, was not wanting to embarrass his children. When he finally made his confession, he found himself caught between his father's paranoia ("what troubled him most was the idea that someone would shoot me") and his mother's superstition ("she thought I'd finally gone over to Satan"). How Roswellian, I thought. Then Dennis appeared on the television show *Unsolved Mysteries,* and overnight he became a minor celebrity. When I was interviewing him, Spice Williams, *Star Trek*'s favorite Klingon, interrupted us to gush over how wonderful it was to meet him. "I just play in science fiction movies, you live it," she cooed. And a couple of years back, internet millionaire Joe Firmage, who has written at great length about his own mysterious conversations with what he calls "beings of light," flew Dennis and Jesse Marcel Jr. (who glimpsed the famed wreckage as a six-year-old boy) out to his home in California just so that he could shake their hands.

Dennis's story is almost as incredible as Jim Ragsdale's. Also twenty-two in 1947, and freshly graduated from mortician's school in San Francisco, Dennis took a job at the Ballard Funeral Home, where he claims to have received an anonymous call quizzing him about embalming techniques and asking if three small caskets were available for immediate collection. That same day, Dennis says he responded to an emergency call and drove an injured airman to the Walker infirmary, which was, unusually, under heavy guard. Before he'd begun to formulate so much as a casual inquiry, he was escorted off the base, but not before a nurse whom he knew intimated that something very strange was afoot. A couple of days later, she contacted Dennis and divulged the whole story, telling of top-secret autopsies and bloated alien bodies. After that, the nurse disappeared mysteriously, never to be seen again.

Dennis doesn't like talking about the events of July 1947, having had too many unhappy encounters with reporters who jump down his throat if he so much as changes an adjective in his story. He has written up his experiences instead. Nor has Dennis been given an easy ride inside the ufology community, where his testimony has met with a mixed response. It's inconsistent, say some ufologists—and those are the kind ones. Yet irrespective of whether or not his story is true, irrespective even of whether or not it is *thought* to be true, going public with it has transformed Dennis's life beyond all expectation. Compared with the quiet and uneventful retirement a mortician might typically lead, Dennis, now in his late seventies, finds himself in the thick of a thriving enterprise. Nearly 200,000 people visit the International UFO Museum annually, and many of them consider him a celebrity. They'll swoop down on him, peppering him with questions or demanding his autograph, as soon as he steps out of his office. He is regularly invited to appear on television or to take part in radio shows about the Roswell incident, and he is always busy either organizing or participating in conferences about ufology. Plunged into activity, controversy, authorship, and community, his life has been given new meaning.

The mortician's experience made me curious to discover more about his peers. Were their lives similarly enriched by their ufology affiliations? Were they, too, enjoying the incalculable benefits of greater self-realization? After a couple of days spent tagging along with the contingent of hard-core ufologists who had come to Roswell solely to give or attend talks at the Civic Center, I decided the answer to these questions was yes and yes. It was all a matter of degree.

Technically speaking, there is no such thing as a career ufologist, although Glenn Dennis comes close. Ufologists are hobbyists. They collect and swap information about sightings and compile detailed case notes, and their filing cabinets bulge with transcribed interviews with people who've had strange sightings and stranger meetings. The more articulate among them write and publish books, many of which become best-sellers, and virtually all of them produce papers for peer review and distribution. Ufologists tend to be bookish. They value the medium of print—its indelibility, its power to testify, the way it acquires bulk and sway. Although there are exceptions. Peter Davenport, for instance, who pressed a business card into my hand after one of the talks at the Civic Center, operates a UFO telephone hot line out of Seattle. Or Dennis Balthaser, who hosts one of a number of Roswell-related websites dedicated to the higher purpose of selling videos. There are also clubbable, organizational types who set up and run UFO societies such as MUFON (Mutual UFO Network), FUFOR (Fund for UFO Research), and BUFORA (British UFO Research Association).

What unites them all is their sense of mission or purpose, their belief that in making a lot of noise about UFOs they are performing a public service. Quite what that public service might be depends on whom you talk to. George Fawcett, who has spent more than fifty-five years studying UFO phenomena, thinks of himself and his comrades as "pioneers and freedom fighters." Dennis Balthaser conducts his online UFO business under the moniker TruthSeeker, and Stanton Friedman, the Roswell specialist most determined to winkle some sort of confession out of the military, sees himself as an esoteric sleuth, committed to exposing a "cosmic Watergate." Peter Farley, on the other hand, an Australian-born ufologist who now lives in New Mexico, considers himself more a man of the people. His protest against cover-ups dripped with the indignation of the betrayed masses. "If people steal our history, they steal who we are," he told me.

The ufologists I met in Roswell seemed preoccupied with the neurotic tics of corporate professionalism: with proper titles, business cards, and status. Those with Ph.D.s invariably let you know they have Ph.D.s. Kevin Randle, Ph.D., author of a best-selling book about the Roswell incident, includes his academic credentials in his byline in the local paper. Perhaps there's a little of the big-fish-small-pond syndrome at work here, but such overt concern with form can

backfire, especially when the seriousness of the prefix is entirely
undone by the waywardness of the job description. Dr. Steven Greer,
for example, the founder and director of the Center for the Study of
Extraterrestrial Intelligence, has a penchant for conducting study sessions in open fields by flashlight. The same goes for Steve Kates, a
self-styled investigator of aerial phenomena who goes by the name
Dr. Sky.

Any affiliation to science, though, however tenuous, curries favor
within the ufology community. Engineers, geologists, and physicists
who come on board are embraced with particular enthusiasm, and
UFO sightings reported by military men, pilots, or astronauts (Mercury astronaut Gordon Cooper being the latest to venture into print
with such revelations) are treated as somehow more objective. And
Stanton Friedman, bearded, bushy browed, and looking every bit the
nuclear physicist he once was, ceaselessly parades his scientific pedigree before anyone who will listen.

Even those talks purporting to be scientific were no such thing.
Ron Regehr, for example, a retired engineer who I'd spotted at Friedman's talk because he was wearing a T-shirt proclaiming "End UFO
Secrecy," lectured about the need for governments to join forces and
build a UFO detector. He said that UFOs had been haunting American nuclear-testing sites and he cited Department of Defense documents, released under the Freedom of Information Act, that report
repeated UFO penetrations back in the 1970s of high-security ICBM
bases and nuclear weapons storage areas. Apparently the CIA has
long been concerned about such infiltration and the U.S. Space Command is now planning defensive strategies in preparation for the possibility of war in space. Atop this garden-variety UFO paranoia was
layered Regehr's science—or rather his so-called science—popularly
known as the New Physics. Newly fashionable among science fiction
writers and a handful of rogue physicists with New Age leanings,
such as Jack Sarfatti, the New Physics is all about UFOs causing
"plasma ionization of the air" and using "gravimagnetism" and

"zero-point energy" to effect faster-than-light travel. It is rapidly acquiring a substantial fringe following. Indeed, when I later looked up these exotic birds on the web, I found that there exist several organizations uniquely dedicated to improving the links between ufology and science via the New Physics.

There is the National Institute for Discovery Science (NIDS), founded and funded by wealthy Las Vegas hotelier and businessman Robert Bigelow, whose company Bigelow Aerospace seeks to promote space tourism. NIDS also invites people to report UFO sightings, which it then promises to investigate using a team of private detectives. Another outfit is the International Space Science Organization (ISSO), founded by Joe Firmage, the former CEO of the internet consulting company USWeb and author of an esoteric door-stopper titled, improbably, *The Truth*. These days Firmage, whose Mormon values hold faith with a resplendently populated universe, is committed to researching new propulsion technologies and to turning the fledgling ISSO into a large-scale experimental research center in the process. Both NIDS and the ISSO are keen to publicize their science connections; Firmage, for example, recently joined forces with Ann Druyan, Carl Sagan's widow, to launch One Cosmos, a multimedia science company founded to rival Space.com. This was a genuine coup, since Druyan is widely seen as the keeper of the Sagan flame. One Cosmos, however, was felled almost as soon as it raised its head above the dot-com parapets, becoming an early casualty of the 2001 crash. Bigelow, meanwhile, is buddies with Harvard psychiatrist John Mack, probably the most highly placed academic to support the reality of alien abductions. Mack has distinguished himself in the field of ufology by proposing the idea that alien visitors are in fact our time-traveling future selves come to save us from our own folly.

I also came across a bizarre collective calling itself Stardrive. Effectively an archive for existing New Physics research, it offers rogue cosmologists tripping on wild post-quantum imaginings easy access to papers on such cutting-edge topics as "torsion in superstring theory," "anholonomic geometrodynamics," and "Stargate portal connection engineering and the missing cosmological mass enigma." One of Stardrive's stated goals, under the organizational impetus of Project Star Force, is "to make *Star Trek* real." Having learned this, I was finally able to square the circle between the ufologists in their makeshift lecture theater at Roswell's Civic Center and the warp-drive obsessed Trekkies on the other side of the curtain. The twain met, because each group longed for the realization of the other's wishful thinking.

But was there any substance at all to the New Physics? I asked science fiction writer Gregory Benford. Benford is also a physics professor at the University of California, Irvine, who happens to sit on the review panel that vets proposals submitted to NASA's Advanced Propulsion Program—a forward-looking though meagerly funded effort ("NASA spent a hundred times more on the space station's toilet," he told me) to investigate such far-out things as antimatter drives, magnetoplasma rockets, and—Benford's own baby—electromagnetic beam propulsion. According to Benford, "The New Physics is only new to ufologists, but zero point energy and the Casimir effect that's behind it are hardly new to physicists. Gravimagnetism, however, is new to me. In fact, it doesn't make much sense, because gravity and magnetism are two completely separate field theories and there are no effects I know of that can use a magnetic force to counter gravity." Benford likens today's ufologists to those nineteenth-century spiritualists who were forever grabbing at the scientific fringes, scavenging for respectability: "They would quote mathematical papers investigating the fourth dimension, because they believed that spirits lived in a higher dimension, which was how they could appear and disappear like phantoms. The spiritualists attempted to scientize the afterlife. Now they want to justify faster-than-light travel. The same tropes appear again and again."

There were other talks at the Civic Center about crop circles and cattle mutilations and how Eschelon communications satellites are in fact a super-secret spy system. Peter Farley talked about alien visitations past and present and the role that these visitors play in the global conspiracy known as the New World Order, and Peter Davenport talked about his own sightings in Baja, Mexico, and about the day-to-day travails of running the National UFO Reporting Center. In short, there was no science to be had then, and there is no science today. As I now glance at a list of forthcoming UFO Museum lectures, I notice that among a raft of personal talks promising to divulge intimate details of contact experiences, there are to be lectures on "UFOs and the Psychic Sasquatch," cryptography and remote viewing, Area 51, and a 1951 incident known as the Lubbock Lights—another apparent Air Force cover-up.

Across the square from the Civic Center lies a gateway to another world. To reach it, you don't have to negotiate gravity fields or Stargate portals and you can leave your stun gun at the door. The world I refer to is contained in a low-level building that houses Roswell's Museum and Art Center. It is part of the same pale concrete complex as the Civic Center—just one hundred yards away but a whole cosmos apart. Outside it, a spindly-legged rocket launcher stands about twenty feet tall announcing the Goddard Planetarium and the set of galleries devoted to Robert Goddard, the eminent founder of American rocket science. Barely anyone stops to take a closer look at this metal contraption, which looks as though it would be hard-pressed to launch a shuttlecock. And yet, beginning in 1930, its maker spent over a decade living in Roswell, building and test-launching a series of liquid-fuel-propelled rockets just to prove that space flight could be something more than a Jules Verne fantasy.

When I visited the made-to-measure replica of Robert Goddard's workshop, faithful down to the last lathe and the American flag flown above the doorway, I was one of only two people there—rather amazing, considering the number of tourists in town and the permanent crowd coursing through the Civic Center. The workshop, as artifact entire, was a surprisingly evocative place. Aside from the absence of workmen and the noise of work, the only thing missing was the smell of grease and spent explosives. Everything else—the bare wooden workbenches, the rows of drill presses, the tooling machinery for cutting and shaping sheet metal, the walls lined with every size of saw and chisel—spoke of a tinkerer, someone who thought with his hands and who made things happen. And yet Goddard didn't look the mechanic. A looped reel of black-and-white film, screening continuously in one corner of the workshop, showed him to be a small, balding, slightly stooped man with a sunken chest. He looked utterly cerebral, though his appearance was partly the result of the tuberculosis he developed as a teenager.

The film was vaguely comedic. Rough cut, fast moving, and jerky, it was almost Chaplinesque, and it showed Goddard and his regal-looking wife, Esther, out in the field watching rockets firing, not firing, or diving into lame projectiles that collapsed under gravity's pull. Although you might not guess it viewing this film, Goddard launched his first rockets long before the cameras began turning. While studying for his physics degree at Clark University in Worcester, Massachusetts, where he later taught, he would regularly sneak off to his Aunt Effie's farm to set off his homemade rockets, traipsing all over her strawberry plants as he did so. During World War I, he developed bazooka rockets for the U.S. Army to use against German tanks, then later, with support from the Smithsonian, he began firing rockets on the outskirts of Worcester. It wasn't until 1926, after many trials and much error, that he launched his first successful liquid-fueled rocket. It flew to a height of forty-one feet, and to Goddard's romancing eye "it looked almost magical as it rose."

Goddard decamped to Roswell after an embarrassing midair explosion involving one of his rockets frightened Worcester residents out of their wits. Instantly the local press was on his back complaining, but the reporters' real crime was in resurrecting the "Moon Man" sobriquet that the *New York Times* coined back in 1920, after Goddard published *A Method of Reaching High Altitudes*—the pamphlet in which he first proposed that powered rockets fired beyond the Earth's stratosphere might be capable of reaching the Moon. Goddard hated being called Moon Man. Besides, he was beginning to resent his academic duties for taking him away from his real work. So when Charles Lindbergh managed to help secure Guggenheim funding for him, he seized his opportunity and left. In Roswell, where the weather was almost always favorable for launches and the locals minded their own business, Goddard thrived. He experimented with various design problems, trying out different metals, different fuels, and different cooling systems; he fooled around with the arithmetic of propulsion, the chemistry of combustion, and the use of airtight chambers; and eventually he launched 18-foot rockets that flew to heights of 9,000 feet.

On the flickering screen in the corner of the workshop, Wernher von Braun, who curiously never lost or downplayed his German accent, was paying tribute to Robert Goddard, calling him his "boyhood hero" and praising his singular achievements. The setting was an open-air ceremony held in 1960, before a gathering of assorted dignitaries, to place a marker on the spot that launched the world's first liquid-propelled rocket, firing it into the bright sky. From the jerky amateur footage shot at Goddard's Eden Valley testing ground, the looped reel jumped forward in time to a confident Apollonian moment, when it had become clear that a direct line could be traced from Goddard's experiments on his Aunt Effie's farm to the moon landings. What the film blithely skipped over were the war years—in a sense, the missing link. In 1939, Goddard, who was growing increasingly concerned that the German scientists he had corresponded with in peacetime were up to no good, called on Army officials in Washington and showed them some film Esther had shot of various test launches. "We could slant it a little," he explained to the assembled generals, referring to direction of the launch, "and do some damage." But the generals only smiled benignly, thanked the missile man, and sent him on his way. Of course, Goddard (who ended up spending World War II designing experimental airplane engines for the Navy) was proved right about rockets being able to do damage, but not before the Germans had rained down a thousand V-2s on London. Perhaps it was just as well that Goddard did not live to see the V-2s that the Americans requisitioned from Peenemünde fly over New Mexico's domed blue skies. He might have felt a twinge of paternal guilt. But as fate would have it, he died of throat cancer just days after Hiroshima was bombed.

Later that evening, my last in Roswell, I caught up with Peter Farley and Ron Regehr at Applebee's, a noisy chain diner up near the National 9. I was still full of enthusiasm for Robert Goddard when I joined their table. Did they know that a rocket he launched in 1929 was the first to carry a scientific payload—a barometer and a camera? I asked. And wasn't it amazing how Goddard's Roswell rockets largely anticipated in technical detail the German V-2s, down to the inclusion of fin-steering, gyroscopic control, and power-driven fuel pumps? The ufologists were polite enough, but I could see that they weren't really interested in rocket science. Or at least, they were no more interested in it than I was in finding out whatever became of the Sumerians, whether or not Atlantis really existed, and which of the world's most magnificent monuments might be reasonably attributed to the handiwork of Von Daniken–style ancient astronauts—all of which was on the table for discussion. It was as if we'd got on different trains somewhere in the 1940s, one marked Roswell and the other marked Space Age, and progressed on parallel tracks, never meeting, never even having to acknowledge that the other's world existed. I was unable that evening to divert talk to issues that interested me: the complete lack of hard evidence that argued for the existence of UFOs, say, or ufology's ongoing and dependent relationship with known technology—from the sightings of phantom airships through dirigibles and ghost bombers to Stealth-like saucers. But I excused myself from their company only when Peter Farley began telling me in all seriousness that he had met the earthly representative of the Galactic Federation, that I had been abducted many times without my knowing it, and that I probably had a microchip implant embedded in my brain, just behind my left ear.

Afterward it occurred to me that Roswell and the Space Age did in fact intersect, but only to trade hostages. Leaving aside for a moment the question of evidence, hidden or not, and parochial concerns about cynical profiteering, an awful lot of people believe the saucer story. Fanning out in great radial sweeps from a core group in Roswell, via the conduits of organized ufology and out into the free-for-all forum of the world wide web (on a recent search on "Roswell and aliens," I summoned up more than 37,000 sites), is a large-scale community built entirely on a pyramid of rumor and gossip. It is as if the Roswell incident has been ushered into existence by a collective and determined effort of will. The question is why. What needs are being satisfied by believing in Roswell? And what psychosocial function do visiting aliens perform?

If Peter Farley and Ron Regehr are representative of the constituency of believers, and I think they are, then Roswell is not an isolated belief. It fits in with a broader willingness to embrace the idea of ineluctable mystery, with ancient Sumerians or Mayans or Egyptians, and with crop circles and channeling. I suspect that people who like mysteries, people who wish to preserve a domain of knowledge that lies beyond science's reach, never got caught up in the currents of excitement stirred by the Space Age proper. Rockets were too cold, too clinical—their magic a trick of appearances, not a matter of essential ineffability. Besides, rocketry relied on a conception of space that was equally unappealing: outer space was a void, a nothing, a realm bereft of sense and sentience that had so little claim on existence it required a bunch of physics equations just to conjure it into being. More than anything else, a belief in space-faring aliens rejects this styling of space as a no-place. It speaks of a desire to reenchant space, to reinstate it as a higher realm—if not exactly Heaven, then at least a vital place where we might commune with someone or something other than ourselves.

In light of the recent and staggering success of filmmaker Peter Jackson's adaptation of *The Lord of the Rings*, one might be forgiven feeling that among the episodes of the sixties that are relevant to this story is the blossoming of an extraordinary literary genre—the complete creation of fantasy worlds—where magic actually worked. I don't mean to suggest that Tolkien wrote the first fairy tales; it's actually far more interesting than that. What he did—reportedly because he felt cheated that the Anglo-Saxons did not have a mythic history comparable to that of the Greeks and Romans, the Hindus, or even the Scandinavians—was to create a complete and consistent mythos from scratch. As others have said, this is comparable to Homer's having to write the entire corpus of Greek myths, from creation onward, in order to then write *The Iliad*. For many Tolkien fans, this is the enduring charm of Middle Earth: not that the plot is anything special, or the characters, but that it is so complete, right down to Elvish language and dwarfish runes. Everything and everyone, the mundane and the supernatural, has its place in Middle Earth—in an ordered universe credible enough to command what Tolkien called "Secondary Belief."

The significance of this is in the timing. Although Tolkien wrote and published *The Hobbit* in the 1930s, and *The Lord of the Rings* in the 1950s, they didn't become a commercial phenomenon (in the United States anyway) until their publication in affordable paperback editions in 1966. And by 1969, they were the greatest cult success of all time, not only because of their own popularity, but because they gave birth to an entire genre of world-creating fantasy that attempted to conjure up what Tolkien himself once described as a wind blowing from beyond the world, something felt but unseen. Those dates are—and I don't see this as coincidental—almost exactly synchronous with the "return to earth" of the Space Age and the beginning of the modern boom in pop-cultural ufology.

Of course the Space Age in its own oblique way also posed the question of where mankind stood as a species in the order of the universe. I say oblique, because it was implied rather than overt, though it was not so invisible that it escaped attention. In a short story called "Surface Tension" written in 1952, the Catholic science fiction writer James Blish neatly allegorized the problem by positing the existence of a microscopic mankind whose universe is a droplet of water. These beings inhabit a world where they are continually taunted by the idea that something more might lie beyond the meniscus above them, over which shadows sometimes play and through which occasional muted sounds, seemingly from a world beyond, reverberate. To explain away these puzzling phenomena, they invent a whole mythology that imagines a higher world, a realm of spirits in the sky who will wreak terrible punishment on any human who dares to penetrate the mystery of what lies above and beyond. It is only a matter of time, however, before hubris triumphs over superstition and a crew of restive humans builds a "space ship" that will shoot upward and probe the unknown. Risking life and limb—and near drowning—Blish's "spacefarers" eventually penetrate the meniscus of the water droplet, only to discover the egregious extent of their own insignificance. They are not alone, but they are of no consequence. They are literally beneath notice.

Perhaps Blish, his Catholic sensibilities inflamed, wrote this story as a riposte to those Space Age philosophers who insisted that transcending the physical bounds of our world was somehow synonymous with transcending human nature. Not that they envisaged attaining anything so lofty as a state of grace, but they certainly spoke in grandiose terms of humanity entering a new era through the conquest of space—an era in which mankind would clearly see that its destiny was a matter of unifying as a species or else self-destructing. The break with gravity did not produce the desired result, but that did not snuff out the hopes embodied in the Space Age: hopes of making contact with superior civilizations, of attaining greater self-realization, and of understanding our true cosmic status. These hopes are now more alive than ever, although they manifest themselves in unexpected ways, Roswell among them. In some ways, Roswell symptomizes how the Space Age itself crash-landed. The idea that "little gray men" literally fell to Earth is the perverse fulfillment of a Space Age desire to realize a greater community of mankind by discovering our own place within a greater community of species. It further suggests that while our small planet may, in the cosmological scheme of things, be a nowhere place, it is nonetheless someplace worth visiting. Like the *Star Trek* fans who continue to yearn for the drama of encounter, Roswell believers are caught up in a fictitious space opera born of a Space Age that never happened.

As my plane tilted up and over the town I was leaving behind, I scanned in vain for a glimpse of one of twelve missile silos built outside Roswell in the early sixties to house the 75-foot-long Atlas F. This missile, an extremely expensive surface-to-surface ICBM that used liquid oxygen for fuel, just like Robert Goddard's more volatile productions, was for a short while the most sophisticated weapon in America's Cold War arsenal. But it was soon eclipsed by the Minuteman. In fact, the Air Force phased out the Atlas F so rapidly that all of Roswell's silos—themselves costing several million dollars apiece—were decommissioned in 1965, only a year after they were completed. The silos had been nothing but trouble anyway; about 185 feet deep, they suffered water-pump problems from the start and never really worked properly. And in 1961, a 24-ton crane used to lower steel into holes in the ground plunged into one of the silos and burst into flames. Six men died in the accident and fourteen others were injured.

Today the abandoned silos are rapidly appreciating in value because of their historic significance and limited supply and because there will never be any more built. One by one they are falling into private hands. Some are being used as homes and others as storage facilities, but two of them have met with a more interesting fate. In 1997, movie special-effects whiz John Farhat, in partnership with UFO whistle-blower Bob Lazar—a physicist who has charged the government with holding nine UFOs near Groom Lake, Nevada—purchased one of the Roswell silos for their company Terraform Inc. Their idea is to create a self-contained subterranean environment that can duplicate the ambient temperatures, pressures, and atmospheric and chemical conditions on Mars. Once converted, the facility will be available to scientists interested in studying a real-time analysis of the Martian ecosystem.

Meanwhile, in December 1999, another Roswell silo was transformed into the launch and command center of an advanced laser beam called the Starlite, designed to transmit personal messages into deep space. Owned by a consortium of laser scientists and communications companies calling itself Messengers Laser System, the Starlite fired off its inaugural round of digitally coded interstellar greetings on New Year's Eve 1999 to the rousing overlay of kettledrums and horns from Richard Strauss's *Also Sprach Zarathustra*, best known as the theme to *2001: A Space Odyssey*. It was quite a spectacle. The heavy steel doors covering the silo were flung open so that they stuck out of the ground like standing stones and the powerful green laser, bright and bold against the night sky, rose in a solid column of light from the depths of the silo to connect heaven and earth like a Biblical covenant. Not since the Voyager probe left Earth in the seventies has mankind been able to send customized messages to the stars. And at such a bargain: for a mere $9.95, anyone can pen an e-mail message, hit the send button, and know that his or her words will hop from cyberspace into deep space, where they will travel for all eternity. "The Starlite can serve as Planet Earth's beacon to the Galaxy, letting whoever is out there know we exist," runs the advertising patter produced by Messengers Laser System.

They may be gimmicky, yet both these ventures hint at the emergence of a different kind of Space Age, one in which not only rockets but travel itself is redundant. Instead of going to Mars, we simply re-create Mars here, simulating the subtlest of its atmospheric nuances. In the 1978 space thriller *Capricorn One*, Peter Hyams made just such a simulation the basis for a grandiose deceit. At a time when public confidence in NASA was at a low ebb, his movie had the agency's chiefs faking a mission to Mars and then plotting to kill off its "astronauts" before they made it home. One has the feeling that for Hyams the very idea of a Martian simulation was as repugnant as the conspiracy designed to hide it: both represented a betrayal of our Space Age idealism. For this reason, the movie is somewhat at odds with today's appetite for theme park culture. Anyone who has noted the rise of EPCOT centers, Biosphere 2s, and heritage sites like Historic Williamsburg or the Jorvik Viking Center at York, in Britain, could have predicted that the coming of a Theme Park Mars was just a matter of time: if we're quite happy to let simulation and "infotainment" stand in for history, why should it not also substitute for other realms of human experience, the futuristic and imagined among them?

More radical still, because it represents another level of abstraction, is the idea embodied in the Starlite of a Space Age in which exploration is replaced by communication, and in which all the central themes animating the Roswell saga—a desire for enchantment, of wanting and yet fearing to make contact, of getting space to resonate with the spiritual side of ourselves—may be satisfied by proxy. Instead of sending flesh-and-blood emissaries into space, we could beam up avatars, digital doppelgängers that will speak our minds, relate our history, or demonstrate our science. We can talk to the stars in strings of ones and zeros and scan the skies for similar signals sent our way from afar. In space, as on the ground, the new currency will be information.

CHAPTER 4

SPACE FOR RENT

The day I became a citizen of Alphaworld I reinvented myself entirely. I changed my name, transformed my appearance, and stepped into a climate of perpetual sunshine—a place where I would be judged neither by age, gender, nor race, but by words and deeds alone. Thus it was that with the greatest of ease, and using no more than a few moves on the keyboard and some judicious clicks of the mouse, I was ready to begin a new life in a new world.

At first I barely recognized myself; for while I was able to express my thoughts and feelings with little difficulty and make myself understood to other people, I felt no particular affinity for the clumsy-looking and cartoonishly curvaceous avatar that was meant to be me. All around me, in formal gardens and town squares, along riverbanks and even in the streets, other avatars were clumped together in conversational huddles. I thought about joining them, knowing that each of them was simply an on-screen representative of a flesh-and-blood keyboard operator like myself—I could even follow their discussions, courtesy of the typescript running beneath the visuals. But a deep self-consciousness came over me. The self-possession I took for granted in the "real" world had temporarily deserted me, to be regained only later and largely through the building of relationships with other cyber-citizens.

In any event, I had more pressing problems to deal with, such as the fact that I seemed unable to walk in a straight line. Like a toddler experimenting with her newly discovered legs, I would totter about uncertainly and then stumble, never managing to take more than a few steps before either falling or bumping into something. Here was a virtual world that was, in almost every way that counted, faithful to the laws of physics, and yet in it I had no more motive competence than an infant. I kept walking into walls instead of through doors. I needed to work on my mouse control so that my avatar could move gracefully and not race forward in herky-jerky steps, or sway like a drunk, and I had to learn how to steady my hand, since one reckless sweep of the mouse a few inches across my desk could move me hundreds of feet across Alphaworld.

For those who've never tried it, joining a cyber-community is easy. You simply log on to the internet, enlist the help of a search engine like Google, and, in this case, type in Alphaworld. If you then click on the Alphaworld home page, you can download the virtual-world software, install it, invent a character for yourself, and leap recklessly into cyberspace; the directions are on-site and surprisingly straightforward.

I had wanted to call myself Omega when I first logged on. To a "newbie" suffering from dread of exposure, the name seemed to offer a mask of impregnability. But another Alphaworld citizen had already thought of using that "handle," or online pseudonym, forcing me to think again. In view of my intent to dabble in virtual space exploration and join a hardy group of pioneers rumored to be building space settlements on Mars, I decided to call myself Percival, in honor of Percival Lowell, the American astronomer who at the end of the nineteenth century believed he could see canals crisscrossing and girding the red planet—ferrying, or so his romantic imagination suggested, precious water supplies from the poles directly into the hands of a desperate and dying civilization millions of years more advanced than our own.

Having settled on my nom de plume, I discovered that my wardrobe of personal identity, pulled from a menu on my tool bar, extended to roughly two dozen avatars. Delving into this virtual closet, I found that I could manifest myself on-screen in the form of a T-rex or a Raptor, a robot or Bunnyman (a creature resembling those bandage-wrapped mummies that scared the wits out of nubile Egyptologists in 1940s horror movies). Alternately, I could choose from an array of buff, ponytailed, Lara Croft imitators and Ray-Ban-wearing musclemen.

Thrilled at the prospect of being able to change appearance at will, I began trying on one avatar after another, essentially making a fool of myself in full view of other citizens. (It pays to remember that in Alphaworld anyone can see you if they happen to be in your virtual vicinity; which is to say, if your avatar appears on their computer screen). "Somebody keeps changing avs," announced one citizen, adding, ". . . lol" (shorthand for "laughing out loud"). And indeed, I did look ridiculous. Morphing from Bunnyman to businessman to miniskirted babe and back again, I appeared, unintentionally of course, to be preening. Even more interesting, as if to underline the momentousness of such fundamental transformations, each time I underwent an electronic shape-shift my name tag would be pictured on-screen, hovering (in an empty speech bubble) over a small heap of blackened dust of an appearance and texture no different from the residue one might find in the bottom of an alchemist's crucible. This was rebirth indeed.

Assuming an alter ego in Alphaworld required more of me, however, than simply choosing a new name and form; I needed to master a small repertoire of personality traits and gestures. So I set about experimenting with the assortment of emotions or "emoticons"— visual representations of emotions—that AW (Alphaworld) citizens routinely use as communicative shorthand. From the tool bar I began by selecting the simplest of these, a turn. Instantly, Percival executed the 180-degree revolution that serves to indicate that you are paying attention or listening to someone else. Next, I clicked my mouse on the "happy" icon and watched Percival bend his head, snatch a fist down toward his body, and then high-five, looking for all the world like a self-satisfied American teenager. "Angry" was more demonstrative still. My avatar placed both hands over his ears and then proceeded to sway up and down, bending and swinging from the waist in a contortion of rage. As Percival, I could also wave or bow (which seemed friendly enough), jump (in a celebratory fashion), fight (using a *Matrix*-inspired martial arts routine), and dance. This last was hilarious, and I found myself laughing heartily as Percival leapt, pranced, and spun, throwing his arms about in genuine ecstatic abandon. By now, I didn't care who was watching.

At last, I thought, feeling pleased with the manly avatar I'd chosen, I was ready to teleport beyond the AW Gate, where newbies find not just their feet but their hearts and souls, and enter Alphaworld proper. Only when I did so, I found that I'd suddenly turned into a woman. This was the first but by no means the last time my expectations would be foiled.

Alphaworld lays claim to being the first true cyber-community, in the sense that it offers people the chance to interact with others in real time within a 3D virtual world so vast that if it were scaled up to size it would, at 165,603 square miles, exceed the land area of California. In fact, Alphaworld has a notable predecessor in Habitat, a crude and somewhat two-dimensional online world created in 1985 by a couple of Lucasfilm games designers. After running for a while on a commercial U.S. server, Habitat acquired 500 or so regular "players" (it was always part game, part community) whose banter appeared in speech bubbles suspended over the heads of their cardboard-cutout-like avatars. Then in 1990, Habitat was bought by Fujitsu and given a Japanese-language interface; relaunched in Japanese five years later, it has since found a constituency of 18,000 users. Still, even today, Habitat's virtual environment is nowhere near as sophisticated as Alphaworld's, where lush green pastures encircle stunning cityscapes and forbidding fortresses perch on hillsides overlooking lazy, meandering rivers. In Alphaworld, moreover, it is not only possible to walk, talk, and, yes, even fly, but you can build and own property, make and break the law, fall in and out of love, interact with a living, breathing multi-user community, immigrate, change your sexual identity, and become a public figure—all within the space of a week, if you so choose.

Alphaworld was launched in 1995, by Activeworlds.com Inc., a Massachusetts-based company that designs 3D computer worlds for the purposes of education, training, and publicity for such clients as Boeing, Siemens, Juno, and Cornell University. In no time Alphaworld acquired a raft of enthusiastic and highly committed citizens who busied themselves building additional worlds. To date, more than a million people have downloaded the Activeworlds browser, a small one-megabyte package that delivers an entire universe or "metaverse" to your laptop. They have also placed more than 74 million objects (houses, bars, schools, monorails, police cars, caves, education centers, galleries, theaters, roller coasters, you name it . . .) in a host of new worlds that includes a virtual Yellowstone Park and an all-American small town called My-Town (a world that discomfitingly recalls the eerie perfection of *Pleasantville*), an ultra-realist version of urban Britain called England World, and the feudal Japan of Samurai. Among those worlds where imagination reigns more completely, Honeywood is populated by a bounding variety of strange animal hybrids, while Scrumpy offers up a medieval fantasy landscape featuring turreted castles, armor-clad knights, and distressed damsels.

While it is possible to visit Alphaworld for free as a "tourist," you can assume the full privileges of citizenship—such as building rights and the ability to whisper to specific individuals as opposed to being obliged to make public pronouncements whenever you open your mouth—only by immigrating (and at twenty dollars a year, immigration is cheap). When I became Percival, I therefore acquired much more than a new identity; I acquired a new country, a new home. Like any nation-state that desires the happiness and well-being of its citizenry, Alphaworld insists on a code of conduct that ensures that people treat one another with respect. You are instructed, for example, upon immigrating, not to insult tourists or other citizens and to refrain from expressions of bigotry or racism, hatred or profanity. Racial, religious, and ethnic slurs are prohibited, as is cyber-sexual behavior in public meeting places. The use of capital letters while communicating is considered shouting and is to be avoided at all times. "Flooding" (the continual posting of repetitive text) is likewise frowned upon.

As far as content is concerned, AW citizens are explicitly asked not to display material that contains nudity or pornography or that qualifies in any way as lewd or obscene, and should you attempt to promote violence, cruelty to animals, or any other illegal activity, or else post information about assembling bombs and other weapons, you will get unceremoniously booted out, to be readmitted only after demonstrating due penance. These rules have been refined over time by Activeworlds' designers and overseers (characters designated as Caretakers or Peacekeepers). In fact, just as in the real world, the rules assumed their final form through application, since criminals needed to be punished and victims hollered for justice. At the end of 1995, for example, less than a year after Alphaworld was opened to the public, an AW citizen known as Agent Rookie produced an online report describing a wave of terror perpetrated by a gang of cyber vandals led by one King Punisher. The gang had taken to looting and destroying property, by exploiting a weakness in the Activeworlds software that allowed it to claim other citizens' property as its own, and to issuing bare threats whenever anyone had the gumption to challenge it. What's more, its members were difficult to identify because they'd somehow discovered how to pass themselves off as other citizens.

King Punisher and his gang would recruit AW citizens into their "order" by stealing their passwords (blackmail, in other words), and then together they'd roam the virtual worlds looking for rich pickings. Agent Rookie infiltrated the order but was found out, becoming for a time the target of hate e-mail. But then, in a surprising turn of events, King Punisher denounced his own gang, claiming that he had never intended to do more than form a building coalition. He had lost control of things, he explained, when the gang had fallen under the sway of a swindler known as Atomic Jello, who had coerced members into adopting a rape-and-pillage ethos. From now on, King Punisher said, in a new mood of atonement, he would go by the name of Pharaoh and pursue a path of peace. That Christmas, Activeworlds fixed the software problems that had allowed King Punisher's gang to vandalize property and steal identities, restoring to Alphaworld its original neo-Edenic purity. Not long afterward, Agent Rookie posted a coda to his original report, saying that he had spotted Pharaoh out and about among the various worlds, asking citizens to forgive his former transgressions.

Passions tend to run high in cyberspace whenever wayward members of close-knit communities, such as are found in 3D worlds like Alphaworld, Vectorscape, and Britanniaworld, and in multi-user domains, or MUDs, see fit to misbehave. MUDs are two-dimensional worlds—that is to say, they are conjured up in typescript alone. Because MUDs have no avatars or other visual representations of persons or place, they exist as environments largely as a shared fantasy of their users. In many ways, they are more risqué than their 3D counterparts, because by imposing no limits on the imagination they free individual users to experiment with a range of inner voices.

Indeed, some MUDs actively encourage a kind of social promiscuity. This can be disconcerting to the casual browser who might search for MUDs online and innocently join BatMUD, for example, one of the oldest and more socially complex MUDs, only to find themselves being indelicately propositioned by a hedgehog on a magic carpet. Needless to say, this no-holds-barred approach to human interaction is not to everyone's taste.

Misbehavior is a problem because "cybernauts" expect online worlds to be somehow better than the real world. Cyber-communities are almost without exception idealistic, seeing themselves as places of free and open public discourse, on the model of the ancient Greek marketplace, or agora. They encourage diversity and experimentation, free speech and protest, and they aim to bring out all that is best in us, at least according to classic democratic principles. In their desire to evolve social complexity at great speed, such communities will encourage the people who participate in them to risk more than they might otherwise risk, to be more playful, more open, more "out there." Thus you'll find that trust is more readily extended between cybernauts than in the real world, where commerce among strangers rarely involves emotional disclosure.

Unfortunately, the price of this idealism is vulnerability. More than anything else, it is cybercrime that shows just how fragile such communities really are, how quickly they can devolve into anarchy and how hard it is to prevent social trespass, or indeed, emotional hurt. As a measure of the genuine pain wrought by cyber-crime, one need only look at the stream of articles, all of them anguished and moralizing, that flowed from the academic "e-press" after a notorious "rape" took place in LambdaMOO (a MOO is netspeak for a MUD that is object oriented).

The incident occurred in 1993, when a LambdaMOO user calling himself Mr. Bungle joined a gathering of people in the LambdaMOO "living room" and, using a "voodoo doll," forced two users of indeterminate gender to perform lewd sexual acts and to indulge in violent self-mutilation. Everyone present was horrified when Bungle's vicious text appeared on their screens, as it seemed clear that a terrible violation had just taken place. Now it's true that MUDers tend to indulge in outlandish role-playing, assuming the personae of wizards, aliens, starship troopers, or strange man-beast hybrids such as "squirriloids" in order to meet, greet, dispute, and, in some of the more zoologically oriented MUDs, rut. But Bungle managed to cross some invisible line. Although the only physical contact between him and his "victims" was an exchange of electronic signals, most LambdaMOOers agreed that the victims' integrity as individuals had been compromised, and the victims themselves, seeking redress, wanted Bungle booted out of the MOO. One of them even called for his "virtual castration." The ensuing debate brought about the rapid fragmentation of a formerly tight community along lines that seemed non-negotiable. There were those who felt that a "rape" in cyberspace should be treated as a real-life felony, and those who quite simply dismissed the incident as a nonevent. Like many crimes, and even more legally actionable injuries—think libel—the taking was of something immaterial. But the pain was indeed very real.

My own limited exposure to Alphaworld suggests that law and order have continued to prevail since the defeat of King Punisher. But then, my judgment ought not to be viewed as definitive, since I was never more than worryingly incompetent in my daily dealings in Alphaworld. Much of the time I found myself unable to execute the simplest of tasks.

One day, for example, I fell out of the Orbiting Space Station on Mars. I plummeted to the ground to find myself unhurt but in the middle of a vast tract of yellow desert, empty in every direction of any sign of human habitation. I tried numerous times (and failed) to take tours of Mars from various of the colonies' space-ports. I was forever walking into walls. In worlds like Yellowstone or My-Town, I fell into rivers.

At the same time, bumbling around Alphaworld was an experience so complete, so utterly engrossing, that it had a profound effect on my non-virtual life. Like imbibing too much of a good wine, Alphaworld is intoxicating to the extent that one experiences a kind of hangover upon returning to the real world. On several occasions, I found myself in the company of real, flesh-and-blood folk, waiting for them to zoom toward me at high speed, like avatars. Sometimes, I found myself looking out of the window fully expecting to see any one of a number of now familiar virtual landscapes stretching out into the distance beyond. Mercifully, I am able to report that I have not yet attempted to fly offline.

For all its out-of-this-world satisfactions, my frustrations with Alphaworld, particularly in my desire to build on Mars, were legion. For one thing, Mars is a lonely place. Often I was the only colonist there, taking solitary monorail journeys across the planet's vast canyons and soaring mountain ranges to visit empty motels and research labs or to stumble over the airlocked entrance to someone's private underground bunker—the kind of building that has been explicitly designed to keep intruders, like me, out. At one point, I seriously considered building a hut right next to the famous "Face" in Cydonia, thinking that by squatting there some enterprising traveler would eventually find me, much as if someone on a camel would be bound to come by were I to pitch up a tent beside the Great Pyramid of Giza.

As if to compensate for the shortage of companionship, there is plenty of information to be had on Mars. Within minutes of arriving for the first time, I'd located the Travel Bureau and found detailed explanations of Martian geography as well as information about how the transport system, comprising both rail and rocket, worked. I also learnt that the All-Mars Council handled global affairs, among them terraforming, and that the first settlement and first Martian government had been established in Amazonis Planitia. In fact, when you teleport to Mars (teleporting—that wonderful Space Age conceit—is not only possible in AW, it's the fastest way to get anywhere), you arrive in Amazonis to encounter remnants of the Mars Gate Land Rush. No doubt intended to evoke memories of California's Gold Rush, this consists of acres and acres of empty, paved-over land, claimed but now abandoned by Mars Gate Homesteaders. To the casual visitor who has come to expect highly developed central districts, like those found on other AW worlds (My-Town or England World, for instance), this first impression is disheartening. But Mars is different. The interesting sites are often out in the regions where serious Martians have built cities or opened up scenic landscapes, and it is necessary to persevere if you wish to reach them.

Near Elysium, an AW citizen called Paul has executed, to use the proper AW terminology, some attractive Martian "builds," including mountains, a lava lake, craters and a riverbed, even a series of caves complete with treasure hunt; while someone called Canopus has constructed an underground city, domes and escarpments, bridges, tunnels and reservoirs. I decided that I wanted to meet Canopus. Perhaps it was his (or her) airlock that I'd stumbled upon earlier. But before tackling Mars in earnest, I needed to learn how to build.

Building is why many AW citizens remain loyal to Activeworlds for years on end: you can chat online almost anywhere these days, but building up communities from scratch, using bricks and mortar and toil and sweat, is still a rarity. Building, however, is much, much more difficult than it looks and, as such, every garden villa, public square, bus terminal, or strip bar serves as yet another reminder of the commitment that AW citizens bring to the business of residing in an alternative world.

My first attempt at building was, well, disastrous. I had begun by picking an appropriately stocky and thickly muscled avatar for Percival's initiation into the world of construction, and I'd confidently called up the Building Tutorial pages. "First find empty land," I read in the introductory paragraph, and off I trotted to a desolate spot, cleverly (or so I believed) monitoring how far I'd strayed from the road outside the building school. "In order to start building there has to be at least one object at the site already; this is called a 'starter object' or 'seed.'" I cast about for a seed object, but since I was already on empty land, I had to make my way back to civilization to find something to "copy." I found a tree. Copying the tree, I carefully dragged its duplicate back to my plot, but when I clicked off the cloned tree in an attempt to leave it there, it disappeared. I repeated this process at least three times before I realized that my plot was actually on someone else's estate. To make any seed object stick and build anything of my own, I would have to build somewhere more remote.

Two hours later (real time), I had succeeded in carving out a piece of turf that measured one-tenth of a square mile and that was partly paved with grass and partly paved with stone. Although it also had a piece of roof tile poking out of it at an irregular angle, attempting to pass itself off as a wall, I felt a profound sense of achievement. In order to "claim" a piece of land in Alphaworld as your own, you have to cover it completely with your own objects; leave even a tiny spot bare and other people will be able to put stuff there that you will never be able to get rid of. This much I'd managed to do, but for the life of me I could not get a wall to stand up at the right height or angle; nor could I place a wall segment in such a manner that the whole length of its base met my floors. I ended up completely exhausted, long before I'd given so much as a thought to doors, windows, and such miracles of the building trade as roofs.

Afterward—in fact, after I'd read a kind of manifesto written by Moria, a designer of worlds who is the Creator and Caretaker of the AW world known as Colony Alpha—I understood that I was being too literal about things. It was not really necessary to build a hut on Mars in order to experience virtual space exploration; just being an AW citizen was to pioneer that new frontier. Whether or not you end up homesteading on its virtual virgin lands, Alphaworld offers up a 3D space that is genuinely elsewhere. Each and every AW citizen shares responsibility for the success of "living" there with others and for developing from humble beginnings a thriving community free from Old World (for which, read "real world") flaws and constraints. Better still, there are no natives with pre-existing claims on the place who have to be driven out. This is pioneering without bloodshed and hardship. And with the blood and guts taken out of it, what is left is the emphasis on social experiment: like outer space, cyberspace is a cipher for utopian dreams.

As Moria himself puts it:

> *I dreamed I saw a place where on a clear day you can see forever and ever, a dream true to your own wishes and desires in a dreamscape fit for all. In a world of fantasy, friendship and fun, where all those present can live in harmony, free from the strife and tension normally associated with the art of life. In a world where all are equal and where all desires are possible. In a world free from illness, death, and depravity, where truly all may live together in harmony, where none lack for company, friendship and love. A dream where we truly have the right and ability to create a future for all those present and where, by example, we can produce a collective spirit which can truly affect all those present by its goodness, truth and love for all time.*

Though not readily apparent from this passage, Alphaworld's idealism is not so much naïve as self-conscious; people seem to understand that both self-sacrifice and personal investment must be enlisted in the cause of improving society. Lest anyone forget this, they will be pulled up short by the AW citizen who actually goes by the name Idealist, and who, to the great enjoyment of whoever happens to be around, will wander the streets of Alphaworld spouting platitudes like "all of it would go away if religion was not even heard of," or "enough food, oil and travel money for ALL people." Irony without cynicism—it must be utopia.

To take the point further, reading postings in the Alphaworld newsgroups, I've noticed that the most common complaint is against citizens whose behavior has deviated from some kind of societal ideal: citizens who are too self-regarding, who won't open up their builds for public use, or who form alliances with one or two chosen cohorts but then shun everyone else. The griping and carping can be puerile, which is often though not always a reflection of the fact that a fair few AW citizens are still in their teens. But then plenty of teenagers in AW also understand absolutely the nature of the experiment at stake. One of them, SW Chris (actually, he turns twenty this year), responded to a questionnaire I posted in the newsgroups, which, among other things, asked whether the real world had anything to learn from Alphaworld. "To laugh at itself," he said. "AW is a mirror image of the real world, but things are a lot more compact. People from different cultures are put closer together, and it provides for some very interesting interactions. Sometimes people fight, but other times they get along wonderfully."

Peace, harmony, and understanding have been the mantra of so many for so long, that it is difficult to approach the impulse behind the sloganeering without seeing the entire history of countercultural hope and protest blur into hazy indistinction. But not too difficult. The utopian musings of cyber-gurus and the dreamy aspirations of citizens of cyber-communities are reflections, imperfectly refracted through two decades, of the drive, or perhaps I should say the crusade, that took place in the mid-1970s to win credence (and popular support and serious government funding) for space colonies.

The parallels are striking. It's not just that cyberspace has effectively replaced outer space as the new frontier, as the place where we might remake ourselves, begin anew, learn from our mistakes, and expand exponentially without ever exhausting the field of exploration. No, it's that cyberspace, like outer space, is not here. Just as thoroughly as breaking the bonds of gravity, venturing into cyberspace feeds a desire for escape, whether from the body, the family, the nation, or from mortal life itself. Somehow, once you're acquainted with the social experiments currently taking place in cyber-communities, the idea of sealing people into artificially constructed floating colonies far removed from the rest of the known world (but designed nonetheless to reproduce every feature of its physical aspect), seems positively ordinary. It was not always so.

"Here I sit in a patched-up mobile home on a lushly green field (mostly mesquite, Johnson grass and croton) at the end of a dirt road on the rural outskirts of a small town in Texas. A thick, forested fringe of cedar, oak and pine starts a hundred yards away to the east and north. A ranch with grazing cattle stretches to the west. My main companion is Ishi, the sole survivor of a small flock of guinea fowl I bought as chicks during the summer." These words come from the journal of Richard Crews, a modern-day Crusoe who has elected to maroon himself (more or less) on a twenty-acre plot of land outside Bastrop, Texas, there to undertake a grand experiment in self-sufficient living. The experiment was supposed to be collective, but from May 2001, when Crews first moved onto the site, until November, he was the sole resident of his "ecovillage." This diary entry dates from September, by which time Crews had put in a flush toilet, water, electricity, even a phone. He'd also acquired some solar panels, built a windmill on his roof, dabbled in hydroponics, and added gardening, composting, and recycling to his daily routine. It may not be much, but it's Crews's first step toward paradise.

Crews, who has long been committed to what he calls "ecological sanity," does not believe that he's abandoning the civilized world. Rather, he intends his efforts at creating a self-contained world to serve as an example to the rest of us as the only way that we might guarantee the very survival of civilization. While others are flocking to cyberspace to realize utopian dreams of community and explore what it means to build a "civilized" world, Crews still believes in the down and dirty that's involved in building colonies for real. He's a genuine seventies throwback. But what distinguishes his Space Environment Ecovillage, or SEE-1, from a commune, say, is that far from being an end in itself, it is only the first phase of an ambitious scheme calculated to take mankind to the stars.

The mastermind behind the colonization scheme is Marshall T. Savage, an African American fine arts graduate who in the early nineties remodeled himself as a scientific visionary and hatched an eight-step plan for migrating into space. Crews is one of a few dozen people for whom reading Savage's book, *The Millennial Project*, was a life-changing experience, and the SEE-1 colony over which he presides represents the project's modest beginning—a capsule world that aims to operate with complete autonomy. In time, SEE-2 and SEE-3 (to be built in progressively harsher and more isolated environments) will follow, before something to be called "Aquarius Rising" takes shape. This colony will be established on an isolated tropical shoreline site suitable for an ocean thermal energy plant and attendant "mariculture" facilities. "It will require millions of dollars and a community of thousands of people," says Crews, "and it will be a step toward a fully self-sustaining, floating ocean colony to be called Aquarius. This, in turn, will be a step toward even more isolated, self-sustaining colonies 'floating' (so to speak) in outer space."

Crews and his fellow devotees have banded together to form the Living Universe Foundation (LUF), a nonprofit enterprise dedicated to implementing the Savage plan. However, Crews, a psychiatrist with a Harvard M.D. whose wiry frame and cropped gray hair exude both health and energy, has taken his commitment to the next level. Having retired from private practice in the Bay Area's Mill Valley, where he also served as president of Columbia Pacific University, he packed his bags and moved to Bastrop to live out his "frontier dream" and become the LUF's first colonist at SEE-1. The decisive point for Crews came after Columbia Pacific was shut down in 1999 for continuing to grant students higher degrees after a 1996 review by the California Bureau of Private Postsecondary and Vocational Education deemed the courses insufficiently rigorous. It was a messy affair, though Crews will still defend the iconoclastic and alternative programs that the university ran.

Now, instead of battling the California judiciary, a "re-born" Crews spends his days mostly outdoors, building and gardening, fighting off unwanted swarms of grasshoppers, tending his fish tank and his guinea fowl, and dreaming of SEE-2. "I have a firm spiritual connection to the vision," he told me, "doing the best we can to salvage the species and rising to the challenge of the greatest frontier. We're at a very early stage of course, but then the millennium is young." In a world where instant gratification is the order of the day, Crews feels he has rediscovered the virtues of patience and the importance of distant visions. In his journal, he pays homage to the generations who came before us and gave their energies to building a better future, "that we might stand on their shoulders and see farther than they ever dreamed of seeing." His passionate belief is that we should do the same "because it is the greatest gift that we can give our children—to salvage and reconstruct the beautiful ecosystems of the Earth, and to move humanity forward to the 'high frontier' of space—to work toward raising Earth-born life off of this one fragile planet."

This, of course, is where dreams begin. Only in this particular case, it is where they end.

In the story of the rise and fall of the space colony, the name of one man stands out among all others: Gerard O'Neill. A charismatic public speaker, with the smooth good looks of a television soap star and an endearingly modish mop of hair, cut Beatles-style, O'Neill burst into popular consciousness in 1974 after publishing a visionary article in the journal *Physics Today* in which he outlined a scheme for human migration to the stars. The program relied on the construction of giant, rotating, tubular (or toroid, meaning doughnut-shaped) colonies in low Earth orbit, similar to the kind of structures that science fiction author Larry Niven later placed at the center of his *Ringworld* novels. Each "Island" habitat was to be several miles long, divided longitudinally into six regions (three strips of fertile farmland alternating with three zones of glass windows), capped by hemispheres large enough to contain mountain ranges, and shrouded within a petal-like array of strip mirrors designed to reflect sunlight into the body of the beast. In terms of both power and food consumption, the colonies would be completely self-sufficient. Moreover, they would be capable of supporting 10,000 people living in the kind of rational societies of which Earth-bound folk could only dream.

It was paradise regained, and plausibly so—at least for the few short years in which people marveled at O'Neill's skill in rolling together three cherished models of human development: the American model of settling a new frontier, the religious model of Christian perfectionism, and the evolutionary model that insists that speciation (the arising of news species) occurs more rapidly in isolated communities. As if to underscore the fact that O'Neill's colonies were progressive by any measure, NASA decided to fund them. From 1975 to 1979, the agency sponsored research into colony construction and the "mass-driver" technology this called for, and organized conferences and study groups to conduct feasibility studies and produce timetables and budgets. After the moon race of the sixties, NASA bigwigs rightly divined that space colonies had the potential to be the Big Idea of the seventies. And why not? It had, after all, been a Big Idea of the nineties . . . the 1890s.

At the end of the nineteenth century, Konstantin Tsiolkovsky, the self-taught Russian scientist who wrote pioneering works describing reaction motors, multistage rockets, and the production of artificial gravity and solar power, envisaged a future in which "millions of people" would be living in what he called "Mansion-conservatories" in the sky. "Who is there to stop Men from building their greenhouses and their palaces here and living in peace and plenty?" he asked, as he invited his readers to imagine flotillas of glassy cylinders, each of them 1000 meters long and 10 meters wide and designed to feed and house 100 people. Tsiolkovsky prophesied that there would be a "Great Migration" to the stars, led by settlers who were gentle, resourceful, hardworking, healthy, tough, and, largely, single. These settlers were "practically ideal men and women, angels in human form," and it would fall to them to point the way forward for the rest of us.

Already in Tsiolkovsky, you find two definitions of the colony existing side by side: first, the idea of a social elite removing itself, physically, from the undifferentiated mass of humanity, and second, the notion of the worker colony (termites come to mind), where individual will is subsumed beneath the interests of the collective. Tsiolkovsky's colonists, no matter how refined—how angel-like— their personal callings, were obliged to perform menial tasks, maintaining temperature and humidity control, recycling, gardening, cleaning, and superintending the safety and integrity of the colony, in a manner now reminiscent of behaviorist B. F. Skinner's 1948 novel *Walden Two*. The whole thing was a prescription for utopia, since Tsiolkovsky believed that by thus marrying elitism and selflessness "human society and its individual members become perfect."

Another early precursor of the O'Neillean colony was the Bernal Sphere, so-called after the hollow globes that J. D. Bernal described in 1929 in a short but extremely influential book titled *The World, the Flesh and the Devil*. Bernal envisaged these "spherical shells" in quasi-technological and quasi-organic terms. They'd be ten miles in diameter and made of the lightest materials, for instance, but they'd also resemble an "enormously complicated single-celled plant." Each sphere would be home to 20,000–30,000 space colonists, who, much as in Tsiolkovsky's Mansion-conservatories, would be kept busy with

power production, subsistence farming, and the necessity of enlarg-
ing the colony, perhaps by building out new sections of the globe in a
spiral form, "like mollusks." In a passage that reveals his own idealistic bent, Bernal predicts that in his spheres, "there would probably
be no more need for government than in a modern hotel."

Bernal's cryptic book title actually refers to the "three enemies of
the rational soul": the limits of earthly recourses, the limits of the
body, and the snare of unreason—all of which he thought it was
incumbent upon mankind to find ways of overcoming if it was to
keep to the path of progress. Bernal, it seems, believed in a kind of
triumph of the will. Distinguishing between two futures, the "future
of desire" and the "future of fate," he viewed our progress as being
from henceforward no longer dependent on physiological evolution,
but on "the reaction of intelligence on the material universe."

Bernal's notion that evolution could somehow be directed as a
result of migrating into space found plenty of echoes among
O'Neill's Space Age contemporaries. Dandridge Cole, for instance,
proposed building large-scale habitats in hollowed-out asteroids,
while Krafft Ehricke's outright rejection of our "planetary confinement" led him to fantasize about a greater tomorrow in which as
many people would be living off-world as on it. In a 1971 paper
titled "The Extraterrestrial Imperative," Ehricke, a German rocket
scientist who wound up working as a space systems scientist for
Rockwell International, painted the picture in vivid detail. "Space
cities with giant factories and food-producing facilities will maintain
their own merchant fleet of spacecraft, their own raw material mining centers on other celestial bodies, and be politically-independent
city-states, trading with Earth, forming new cultural cells of mankind
whose choice of living in space has increased tremendously, and
adding to the plurality of human civilization."

Proclaiming the evolutionary superiority of such societies was
just one step away. So, too, unfortunately, was misanthropy. "Perhaps," Ehricke ventured somewhat more tentatively at the end of his

paper, "as we place the extraterrestrial domain into the service of all people, we may be permitted to hope for the greatest benefit of all: that the ugly, the bigoted, the hateful, the cheapness of opportunism and all else that is small, narrow, contemptible and repulsive becomes more apparent and far less tolerable from the vantage point of the stars than it ever was from the perspective of the mudhole." Visionary utopianism or proto-fascism? It's hard to say, considering that before he joined Wernher von Braun's V-2 production line in Peenemünde (effectively gaining his ticket to the free world) Ehricke commanded a division of Hitler's tanks on the Russian front.

While Gerard O'Neill almost certainly read Ehricke's paper, he always maintained that his own commitment to the colony scheme arose after he and his engineering students, who together began modeling space colonies for kicks, realized that such structures could quite reasonably be built on a very large scale, using technologies no more sophisticated than those we already possessed. The one exception to this was the mass-driver, a kind of electromagnetic conveyor belt that O'Neill deemed essential for ferrying buckets of lunar raw material (much cheaper than exporting terrestrial raw materials) into Earth orbit, where it would be processed, then assembled into his basic cylindrical structures, each of which would have a structural mass roughly equivalent to that of a large ocean liner like the *Queen Elizabeth II*.

Where other schemes had failed to take off, for a wide variety of reasons, O'Neill's vision flew—with the scientific community, the public, and to a certain extent, Congress (O'Neill testified in a standing-room-only Senate hearing on the subject of space colonization in 1976). Unlike his contemporaries and predecessors, O'Neill actually sat down and bothered to work out the numbers, putting costs ($31 billion for Island One) and time frames (he proposed that Island One could be up and functioning between 1995 and 2010) into the mix. He was a media-savvy kind of guy: "He was on television all the time," fellow Princeton physicist Freeman Dyson has remarked. And he was the kind of figure to whom others readily attached themselves. In no time, therefore—even before he had expanded his *Physics Today* article into his book *The High Frontier* (1977)—he had succeeded in gathering around himself an entourage whose members can without understatement be called apostles. Indeed, there were times when O'Neill, succumbing to the spell of his own inspired leadership, would start referring to people as "believers" or "skeptics." Those who moved in the right direction from one camp to the other, meanwhile, he termed "converts."

In 1975, a core group of O'Neill's disciples founded L5, a society of pro-space activists dedicated to lobbying for the realization of the O'Neillean vision. (The L in L5 refers to Lagrangian points. At the end of the eighteenth century, French mathematician Joseph Lagrange discovered that there exist five gravitationally stable points within the force field created by any two bodies exerting a gravitational pull on each other. L5 is therefore the fifth such point between the Earth and the Moon and a favored location for the first space habitats.) L5 rapidly branched into a national organization with chapters springing up everywhere from Alabama to Seattle, replete with enthusiasts who saw in the space colonies program a chance to participate personally in the space dream—as opposed to merely being the spectators they'd been in the Apollo era. More than that, they saw the promise of the good life or, at least, an extension of the idyll that was American suburbia.

One of the most appealing features of O'Neill's colonies was their familiarity. Life up there would be just like life down here, only better. In his book, O'Neill insisted that the colonies "be as earth-like as possible," and he went on to elaborate a vision of middle-class utopia that assured readers that Island One's beauteous garden regions would be faithful re-creations of Provence or Carmel-by-the-Sea. His design, he said, "allows for natural sunshine, a hillside terraced environment, considerable bodies of water for swimming and boating and an overall population density characteristic of some quite attractive modern communities in the U.S and in southern France." Again, he stressed that many of the enjoyments of the early community would "be those which we would expect in a small, wealthy resort community on Earth: good restaurants, cinemas, libraries, perhaps small discotheques." Indeed, living in such a community "would be rather like living in a specialized university town, and we could expect a similar proliferation of drama clubs, orchestras, lecture series, team sport, flying clubs—and half finished books." The flying clubs were no casual afterthought spun upon the threads of a daydream, but were integral to O'Neill's vision. Although the Island One colonies would rotate to produce, centrifugally, an artificial gravity close to "Earth-normal" on the inside surface of the cylinders, as you moved up toward the axis of rotation, gravity would tail off almost to zero, allowing for such novelties as human-powered flight and low-gravity swimming pools.

Lest any of his supporters judge this vision of material abundance (luxury, by the standards of many) to be lacking in depth, O'Neill determined to make clear the link between good living and good management: "I think there is reason to hope," he wrote at the end of his book, "that the opening of a new, high frontier will challenge the best that is in us, that the new lands waiting to be built in space will give us new freedom to search for better governments, social systems and ways of life, and that our children may thereby find a world richer in opportunity by our efforts during the decades ahead." Here was O'Neill, the proud patriot, revamping America's founding mythology for a new era. Picking up on this theme only a few months later, Carl Sagan wrote approvingly of O'Neill's "space cities," referring to them as "a kind of America of the skies."

More important than resurrecting Tsiolkovsky's Christian perfectionism or Bernal's notion of choiceful evolution, and more important than even this deliberate evocation of America's pioneering past, O'Neill's colonies offered solutions to key problems that preoccupied people in the 1970s: raising living standards, protecting the environment, developing cheap, clean sources of energy, and allaying fears of a population explosion—fears that had been freshly stoked by Stanford biologist Paul Ehrlich's sensationalist best-seller, *The Population Bomb* (1968). Not least, they seemed to provide a way to move beyond the "limits to growth" scenario tremulously sketched out by the apocalypse-haunted denizens of the Club of Rome.

The "limits" argument had its origins in the Project on the Predicament of Mankind—an ambitious study into the relationship between population, pollution, food production, industrialization, and consumption of resources, undertaken in 1968 at the behest of Aurelio Peccei (an executive of the Italian corporations Fiat and Olivetti) by the prominent group of scientists who made up the by-invitation-only Club of Rome. After five years of research, the scientists emerged with a grim picture of a future in which each of the variables under study moved in the least helpful direction, so that food production fell as population levels spiraled and pollution rose as consumption increased, at the same time that the Earth's resources were dwindling to nothing. Eager to have these predictions confirmed, Peccei asked MIT computer scientist Jay Forrester to verify the mathematics behind the model. Forrester's conclusion, exactly what Peccei hoped for, was that the numbers spelled our doom. The Club of Rome delivered this bombshell in the full glare of media publicity, choosing a high-profile symposium at the Smithsonian Institution in Washington in 1974 as the platform for launching its surefire best-seller *The Limits to Growth*. With its no-hope argument (even if we repented of our growth-seeking ways, it was not clear we'd be saved), academic pedigree, and headline-grabbing launch, the book—which sold in the millions—scared the hell out of a lot of people.

In a lead article in *Science* published at the end of 1975, O'Neill confronted the limits argument head-on, claiming that manufacturing facilities in high-Earth orbit could build satellite solar power stations from lunar materials in order to supply cheap energy back to Earth. First, solar energy would be converted into electricity in space, then it would be beamed back to Earth as microwave energy and there reconverted into electricity. By year eleven, said O'Neill, energy flowing from L5 to the power grids on Earth could exceed the peak flow rate of the Alaska pipeline and by year thirteen, solar power plant capacity could meet U.S. needs. In one stroke, O'Neill thus provided his colonies with both scientific and economic justification. And to back him up, a group of engineers, sociologists, and economists who met at NASA Ames Research Center earlier that year to review O'Neill's energy production plans confirmed (even as they raised Island One's price tag to $140 billion) that "in contrast to Apollo . . . space colonization may be a paying proposition."

As a further consequence of his energy-production-without-pollution plans, O'Neill succeeded in forging an unlikely alliance between his pro-technology supporters and leaders of the environmental movement—a group that had not hitherto been noted for its support of the space program.

Stewart Brand, hippie holist, ex-cooperative resident, and publisher of the Gaia-inspired *Whole Earth Catalog*—an "outlaw information service" that promised its readers "access to tools"—was one of the first environmentalists to see how Island One technology could help achieve an alternative, eco-friendly lifestyle. And it was not just the idea of trapping solar energy that appealed to Brand and his readers; it was the idea of the space colony as commune. Here, after all, was a place where the 1970s idealization of the rural collective, with its grow-your-own-vegetables ethos of self-sufficiency and emphasis on conservation and recycling, found an echo in the high-tech visions of the scientific elite. In fact, in space you could go one better; you could grow you own vegetables not just without pesticides, but without pests, since bugs were one of the earthly evils that O'Neill suggested might be deliberately excluded from Island One, along with disease-causing bacteria and such undesirable features of the industrial world as cars and smog.

Best of all, O'Neill's vision seemed to promise that the Earth itself could eventually be returned entire to Gaia. In *The High Frontier*, O'Neill estimated that by 2050 there'd already be more people living on space colonies than on the Earth. Given more time, the relative population densities would become further skewed, eventually allowing the Earth to revert to a preindustrial idyll or garden reserve, "far more beautiful than it is now." What's more, it would be the space colonists themselves who would provide the stimulus for this marvelous transformation, because tourism from space "would serve as a strong incentive to enlarge existing parks, create new ones, and restore historical sights." Because these rather effete visitors (remember Tsiolkovsky's "angels in human form") would be intolerant of Earth's "dirt and noise," they would further encourage the cleaning up of remaining pollutants, allowing the air and rivers to breathe once again. Such would be the benefits of ecotourism from space.

All in all, concluded O'Neill, "the vision of an industry-free, pastoral Earth with many of its spectacular scenic areas reverting to wilderness, with bird and animal populations increasing in number, and with a relatively small, affluent human population, is far more attractive to me than the alternative of a rigidly controlled world whose people tread precariously the narrow path of a steady state society." Thus in one lovely sentence, O'Neill conjured up an image of paradise regained on Earth, just as it was in his heavenly colonies, and at the same time he (again) kicked down the limits-to-growth argument—just, it seems, to demonstrate how easy it was.

Brand (who, incidentally, is now a futurist in the Silicon revolution mold and who presides over a scenario-planning consulting company called Global Business Network) first met O'Neill in the mid-1970s at a sparsely attended seminar on space colonies that was part of a World Futurist Conference in Washington, D.C. Recalling the event recently, Brand told me, "No one knew of him or his idea, so a dozen of us watched him explain it. I was knocked out by the logic of his design solutions, and by him as a very smart, gentle soul. I talked to him there, and we became friends." Later, they flew into the Californian desert together to watch the first Shuttle land. For Brand, the immediate appeal of O'Neill's ideas was that it fit right into his own vision of technology as means to ends, or as Brand puts it, it was a "big clever tool!" Add to this O'Neill's emphasis on individuals in space and "it was a natural for Whole Earth."

Determined to do his bit to promote O'Neill, Brand edited a book on the subject of space colonies in 1977, giving O'Neill plenty of room in which to hang himself or triumph, as well as access to the wider community of environmentalists. In the introduction, Brand argued that space colonies were right in line with the movement's concerns: "They're so damned inherent in what we've been about for so long," he said, as if slapping his thigh in disbelief; artifice versus nature, free-form living versus social control, local versus central, dreams versus obedience. In this regard, Brand's sentiments precisely matched those of L5's activist core, a group of dedicated would-be colonists led by L5 President Carolyn Hanson, who regularly enlivened the society's newsletters with the inclusion of tub-thumping, eco-sensitive rallying cries. "Declare the Earth a wilderness area: if you love it, leave it," was one. "Decentralize—get off the planet," recommended another. And yet a residue of suspicion lingered in Brand still, leading him to canvas more than a hundred writers and thinkers on the merits of O'Neill's vision. "Is this the longed-for metamorphosis, our brilliant wings at last," he inquired of them, "or the most poisonous of panaceas?"

Most of the luminaries whom Brand consulted had positive things to say about space colonies. But those who opposed them didn't pull their punches. The writer and critic Lewis Mumford, for example, claimed O'Neill's colonies were "only technological disguises for infantile fantasies," and inventor Steve Baer complained that, try as he might, in his mind's eye he just couldn't see Carmel-by-the-Sea: "Instead, I see acres of air-conditioned Greyhound bus interior, glinting, slightly greasy railings, old rivet heads needing paint. I don't hear the surf at Carmel and smell the ocean—I hear piped music and smell chewing gum. I anticipate a continuous vague, low-key 'airplane fear.'" So prolific, meanwhile, was novelist Wendell Berry in his criticisms of O'Neill that Brand felt obliged to lock antlers with him, printing their resulting correspondence at great length.

Berry's fundamental complaint was that O'Neill's vision was in every way conventional—politically, socially, and imaginatively. "If it should be implemented," he said, "it will be the rebirth of the idea of Progress with all its old lust for unrestrained expansion, its totalitarian concentrations of energy and wealth, its obliviousness to the concerns of character and community, its exclusive reliance on technical and economic criteria, its disinterest in consequence, its contempt for human values, its compulsive salesmanship." As if this were not criticism enough, what especially troubled Berry were the easy parallels with America's pioneering past, which he accused O'Neill of invoking naïvely. According to Berry, O'Neill's breathless viewing of our conjectural vistas and insistence on the limitlessness of resources and human possibility made him sound (when he was not speaking like a salesman, that is) like a seventeenth-century European "privileged to see American space and wealth as conveniently distant solutions to local problems," and not like a modern American "faced with the waste and ruin of his inheritance from the frontier."

Similar accusations could justifiably have been leveled against Timothy Leary, another high-profile O'Neillean proselytizer, though so far removed from the environmentalist ambit of Brand and his readers that to speak of them in the same breath would ordinarily seem absurd. Yet the space colony scheme attracted passionate supporters from opposite sides of both the political and ideological divide. In a short polemic called *Neuropolitics*, largely written from Vacaville Prison (where Leary was incarcerated on drugs charges during the 1970s), the self-styled leader of the counterculture and freewheeling champion of mind-bending chemical experimentation stated his libertarian credo in admirably concise form: "Expand! Expend! Explore! Exploit! Exchange!" Leary couldn't have been further from his Whole Earth contemporaries who were holed up (voluntarily) on the opposite side of San Pablo Bay in Sausalito.

Leary came up with a user-friendly acronym for his own vision of mankind's future, S.M.I^2.L.E, which stood for Space Migration, Intelligence Increase and Life Extension. An early convert to the O'Neillean dream, Leary believed that migrating into space offered the species a chance to resuscitate its more enduring visions of challenge and grandeur, a chance to "once again, think noble thoughts about our future." The celestial habitats he called H.O.M.E.s (High Orbital Mini-Earths) were meant to satisfy two counterstrategies for human survival. On the one hand they were to fulfill our "genetic imperatives" to explore and exploit, and on the other, they would enable us to recapture the small-scale dreams of America's frontier past: migrating to H.O.M.E.s, said Leary, would allow us to "re-attain individual freedom of space time and the small group social structures which obviously best suit our nervous systems . . . only in space habitats can humanity return to the village life and pastoral style for which we all long." In short, Leary wanted us to move ever onward, ever upward, and ever backward—and all at once. Such contrariness is characteristic of gurus. But Leary's desire to have things not just both ways but every way points to a fundamental tension in the pro-colonization movement: space colonies, it seemed, could be used to support just about anything.

Why does the desire to leave the planet manifest itself so strongly? Even without resorting to explanations derived from America's frontier history, or even the specific context of the 1970s, the question remains: What do we think we're escaping from? The answer that's hard to avoid when the question is framed that way is, of course, ourselves. After all, O'Neill's vision of the future Earth as a "wilderness" betrays at least a glimmer of self-loathing. The same is true of J. D. Bernal, who imagined his forward-looking colonists making their upward leap at the evolutionary expense of their Earth-bound brethren, left behind to a fate of stagnation. As the one group basked in its aerial splendor, the other would attain undisputed possession of the Earth, but they would "be regarded by the inhabitants of the celestial sphere with a curious reverence." Even more alarming was Bernal's suggestion that his celestial beings convert the world into a "human zoo"—one so intelligently managed its inhabitants wouldn't even know they were in it.

Such melancholic deliberations bring to mind Italo Calvino's description of the city of Baucis in *Invisible Cities*. The city of Baucis is raised so high on stilts that it is lost in the clouds. However, its refined and ethereal inhabitants have arranged things up there in such a way that they have everything they need and they rarely come down. There are three theories about the inhabitants of Baucis, writes Calvino: "that they hate the Earth; that they respect it so much they avoid all contact; that they love it as it was before they existed and with spyglasses and telescopes aimed downward they never tire of examining it, leaf by leaf, stone by stone, ant by ant, contemplating with fascination their own absence."

Ultimately, and in spite of whatever unconscious desires they stirred, O'Neill's colonies failed to get beyond the drawing board stage and into prototype production. There had been seed funding from NASA (to the tune of $40,000 a year for five years), support from Stewart Brand's nonprofit Point Foundation (primarily for O'Neill's annual Princeton conferences), a small fund for research staff, annually replenished by L5 subscription fees, and, for a time at least, favorable political tides that ensured O'Neill safe passage through his Senate hearing and even saw the floating of a High Frontier Feasibility Act, which recommended that the National Science Foundation undertake an objective study of the colonies proposal. But at the end of the day, none of this backing made the slightest bit of difference.

O'Neill's greatest miscalculation was in assuming that the technology of the 1970s was adequate to the task of building Island One. It wasn't, not by a long shot. Visionary though he was, O'Neill was also a product of his time. In a few short years, he had witnessed technological development proceed at a pace unprecedented in history, taking mankind from flinging a small metal ball into low-Earth orbit to rocketing men to the Moon. Who could blame him if he believed that his newfangled electromagnetic lunar mass-driver was just around the corner? Wasn't anything now possible? Moon bases, revolving space stations, celestial power plants, and missions to Mars? The Space Shuttle would eventually destroy such illusions. But in the mid-1970s the Shuttle was very far from being the clunky and overexpensive, semi-reusable, slow boat to China we now know it to be: still half a decade away from its maiden flight, it was a brilliant gleam in the eye of NASA's leadership, the bright hope of engineers and contractors, the darling of the space program.

Effectively billed as a low-cost space taxi and slated for weekly launches, throughout the 1970s the Shuttle was the technical linchpin of every scheme that begged for inclusion in the official space program. O'Neill, in fact, went so far as to base his preliminary timetable on units of Shuttle activity; setting up the lunar mass-driver would, he estimated, require "two years' worth of Shuttle flights," while the next stage of his scheme—beginning the chemical processing of lunar materials—"will take another year's worth of Shuttle flights." In truth, however, the Shuttle was never really meant to undertake missions in lunar orbit. In the words of Apollo astronaut Russell Schweickart, it was designed "to do one job and one job only, and this is to get into low-earth orbit from the surface and back down to the surface, and do it over and over again."

In his introduction to the third edition of *The High Frontier*, published in 2000, Freeman Dyson steps back from the operational nuts and bolts of the matter to paint a broader picture of the problem. Like any large bureaucratic organization, he says, NASA has many parts that are only loosely interconnected. There is the "real NASA" that builds and operates the Shuttle and the International Space Station, and there is the "paper NASA" that studies advanced concepts and promotes long-range ventures. The real NASA is intensely conservative, politically astute, and budget conscious, while the paper NASA, which is adventurous in all these areas, lacks the resources to realize its goals. The paper body will therefore support all sorts of schemes, so long as they are located far in the future and do not call for the development of an alternative infrastructure that would compete with the Shuttle.

When O'Neill published his plans for space colonization, they fit perfectly with the style of the paper NASA. It would give him a public platform and seed funding, and it would talk about Island One as if time were the only factor on which its realization would hang. But the real NASA never took him seriously. Jesco von Puttkamer, who in the 1970s was responsible for advanced planning in NASA's Office of Space Flight (the water-marking department of paper NASA), recalls that "O'Neill's ideas were just what I was looking for." To appreciate precisely what that means, you need to know that, for the most part, von Puttkamer spent his energies on PR. He theorized in popular journals about the search for extraterrestrial life, lectured on "space industrialization," took part in documentary films about technologies of the future, and wrote introductions to *Star Trek* books. Every now and then, he would pack a selection of nice slides and a bagful of proposals and go off to *Star Trek* conferences, where he'd thrill the crowds with promises that trips to Mars and space stations orbiting Jupiter aren't just the stuff of dreams. Later, in 1979, he served as technical advisor to Gene Roddenberry on Paramount's *Star Trek—The Motion Picture*.

Back in the real world, even the grassroots activists in L5 began to turn away from colonies. Under Gerald Driggers, who became president of the society in 1980, they began focusing on more practical, near-term goals, such as a manned space station. Then, in 1987, L5 spontaneously dissolved, merging with the National Space Institute (an industry-led group of NASA cheerleaders) to become the National Space Society. The Space Studies Institute (SSI), a pro-space organization that O'Neill founded in 1977 to seek private sponsorship for what he called "critical path" research, is, meanwhile, still up and running, sponsoring studies into space habitat and lunar-base design and conducting research on mass-drivers and solar power satellites. But the only SSI project to have made it from the design stage to reality is the Lunar Prospector—a veritable Cinderella story for the space advocacy movement. Conceived, developed, workshopped, and expertly designed as a result of SSI initiatives between 1989 and 1992, the Lunar Prospector mission was eventually funded by NASA. In fact, it was selected for inclusion in Dan Goldin's signature robotic extravaganza, the Discovery Program. The year was 1995—the same year, ironically, that O'Neill expected to see the first Island One habitat sail across the skies like a new star in the east. Sadly, O'Neill did not live long enough to see Prospector succeed, let alone to smash a champagne bottle against the flank of the first Island One. He died in 1992 after a seven-year battle with leukemia.

Occasionally, in space policy newsgroups, the subject of colonies rears its head to become a hot discussion topic once again, but the naysayers tend to outnumber the enthusiasts. One of the more thorough rejections of O'Neillean dreaming I've yet come across was posted in one of these newsgroups in 1997 by someone using the handle GroundHog. In a passage reminiscent of Steve Baer's remarks of twenty years earlier, GroundHog opines, "The romance of pioneering in space will wear off real quick once the public realizes there are no holodecks, or green bountiful parks in moon domes, or exciting battles with fierce alien invaders, just 10 cubic meters of cramped quarters, recycling your own urine, living in your own sweat, facing the dangers of decompression daily, seeing the same goddamn faces every day, knowing that down below on Earth people are laughing and loving, breathing fresh air and running in spring sunshine, meeting people and living life."

Moving on to top off the realism of the picture, GroundHog bursts the bubble of patriotism, blown out of all proportion by those who imagine that colonizing space would be a rerun of America's pioneering past. It won't be middle-class Americans who'll be home-steading the off-world habitats, but "Cubans, Haitians, Somalis, Phillipinos [*sic*], Timorese. They are the immigrants of the twenty-first century. They are the ones fleeing persecution and poverty, seeking a better life. They have far more in common with the passengers on the Mayflower than the overfed, overweight, self-satisfied, self-righteous, tax-paying groundhogs sitting behind their computers and filling the Net with wannabe hogwash, boasting about their ancestors' deeds and imagining themselves to be their spiritual heirs."

If GroundHog's rant doesn't represent the final nail in the O'Neil-lean coffin, I don't know what does. As for the frontier agenda, its focus has now largely returned to more conventional objectives, such as Moon bases and Mars.

Although the drive to colonize space continues to animate a handful of fringe activists, such as Marshall Savage and his followers, or Robert Zubrin and his, none of them boasts anything like the popu-lar following that formerly attached to O'Neill—and most of them do little more than rehash arguments in *The High Frontier* anyway. In terms of achieving anything concrete, they have, as a group, had few successes. The notable exception is Biosphere 2, the many-chambered giant greenhouse that sits at the feet of the Santa Catalina Mountains near Oracle, Arizona, like some modern-day realization of one of Tsiolkovsky's Mansion-conservatories. Built with private funds in the late 1980s, and now administered with no apparent sense of irony by the Earth Institute of Columbia University, Biosphere 2 was conceived as a prototype Mars colony, and for a short while—famously—it actually functioned as one.

The moving force behind the Biosphere project was John Allen, an avowed millenarian who held a cultish fascination for those he managed to recruit to his colonizing cause. In 1991, under Allen's direction, the "closed system" of Biosphere 2 became the site of a highly publicized survivalist experiment that saw eight people "sealed" into the biomes, where they endeavored to carve out a self-sufficient eco-nurturing existence, rehearsing for what they imagined would be a similar future in space. The quasi-agricultural, quasi-religious experiment was an instant crowd-puller, and tourists flocked to the Arizona desert to press their faces (and cameras) to the glass, hoping to catch sight of the "colonists." Nothing, to my knowledge, has ever come closer to J. D. Bernal's vision of the Earth as "human zoo"—except here the "colony" was the zoo: the evolutionary cul-de-sac attracting the "curious reverence" of those fortunate enough to reside elsewhere. In any event, the survivalists managed to last only eighteen months in the biomes. Driven out by falling oxygen levels and meager crop harvests, they emerged thin and straggling from their paradise-prison into the hot Sonoran desert, their bright orange Space Agey jumpsuits hanging off their haggard frames, as the media looked on, gloating over their failure.

And yet the extraterrestrial experience has fallen to Earth in ways more unsensational than this. After all, what are "new towns" and gated communities if not attempts at designing environments that aim simultaneously to replicate and improve on their haphazard originals, to divide and nurture, to exclude and to make safe. The Earth abounds in such colonies, though none has taken the principles of planned living further than Celebration, Florida—the town the Disney Company finally built in 1997 as a belated realization of Walt Disney's Space Age vision for EPCOT.

But there is one important difference: while EPCOT was always billed as a "city of tomorrow" (Disney's original plan was for the entire town to be housed within a giant dome and organized like a wheel, with the industrial and commercial heart of things at the wheel's hub and the residential areas moving out in concentric circles), Celebration is a bricks-and-mortar paean to the past. Down to the last detail—the well-placed soda fountains, the rocking chairs on the lawn, the white picket fences—life in Celebration has been designed to re-create the feel of a Norman Rockwell painting, and neighborliness is exalted as next to godliness. Even the sales brochures strike just the right note of nostalgia: "There was once a place where neighbors greeted neighbors in the quiet of summer twilight. Where children chased fireflies . . ." and so on. Thousands of Americans, many of them lamenting a "loss of community" that they attribute to the demands of modern life and yearning to recapture a mythical time of innocence, snapped up houses in Celebration and took a collective leap into a resurrected (and carefully airbrushed) past, hoping to rediscover there an almost spiritual dimension to the everyday. Gleefully, they took possession of their brand-new homes, models of neotraditionalism one and all.

However, in order to build a community that had any chance of functioning according to a set of prescribed principles (and Celebration was based on five: health, education, technology, community, and place), they had to leave behind the real world, where one is free to display political posters in one's living room window as one wishes and to park the car in the driveway for stretches of more than twenty-four hours. These and a host of other restrictions were the price residents had to pay to maintain the illusion that Celebration actually worked. Celebration, in fact, did and didn't work. Over months and then years, a sense of community did evolve among the town's residents, but in a messy, democratic fashion; bonds were forged among parents who opposed the philosophical idealism that animated the town's school (they wanted it to be more competitive) and among those who wished to see some form of representative local government in the town (there was none). And house owners found solidarity in grouping together to protest the poor construction of their housing. This was not the kind of community that the Disney Company could embrace, and it gradually pulled back from its involvement with Celebration. The town worked, in other words, only by deviating from its ideals.

Even more prevalent than socially engineered towns is that most ubiquitous of spacecrafts, the shopping mall. No other semipublic, semi-isolated space achieves quite the same otherworldly feel. Cut off from the sights and sounds of nature and yet filled with fountains and plants, artificial light, downtown piazzas, and all the noise of the fair, the mall is a vision of the future that seems to have become garbled in the process of being translated from concept to concrete.

In a wonderfully acute book called *The Malling of America*, William Severini Kowinski details his excursions through the malls of America, where he finds himself becoming increasingly spaced out by the extraterrestrial nature of his experience. "For here is the mall," he writes, "all this food, clothing, entertainment and information in a sealed structure. The people move swiftly on their appointed tasks wearing various uniforms. They are part of a busy environment that is apparently autonomous. Every facet of its operation, including the air that everyone breathes is controlled. . . . It could be anywhere, or nowhere; it could even be moving about." The only thing missing is a pressurized atmosphere. But, says Kowinski, "Give it a warp drive and a five year mission and you've got this . . . starship."

In the late 1970s and early 1980s, coinciding perfectly with the spread of O'Neillean dreaming, malls proliferated across North America and Europe, and at the same time they grew in size. The West Edmonton Mall in Alberta, Canada, for example, opened in 1981 with more than 800 shops and a hotel, an amusement park, a miniature golf course, a church, a "water park" for sunbathing and surfing, a zoo (who'd have expected such postmodern quotation?), and a 438-foot-long lake. Like that of the space colony, the fantasy of the mall has been explicitly constructed to satisfy our basic sensory

needs, combining kinetic excitement and temperature-controlled sta-
sis within a secure, if somewhat claustrophobic, simulated setting. To
the extent that malls clearly hint at a certain totalitarian oppressive-
ness, it is hardly surprising that they have often stood in for the
dystopian planned perfection of science fiction futures. In fact, the
1976 movie based on William F. Nolan's best-selling novel *Logan's
Run*—in which the social engineering of the Space Age environment
extends to the people, none of whom are permitted to live beyond
the age of thirty—was actually filmed in a mall.

Only cyberspace, it seems, has succeeded in reproducing the
space colony without also conjuring up the interiors of Greyhound
buses and without recourse to greenhouses, piped music, and jumpsuits. Still, that may not be much in the eyes of virtual-reality designers questing after their own holy grail: successfully reproducing the
holodeck, or holographic projection chamber, made popular in the
series *Star Trek: The Next Generation*. In the television show, the
holodeck featured initially as an environment simulator, a place
where crew members could recuperate, wander through green
forests, listen to birds chirping, and rest beside babbling brooks. For
those unfamiliar with *The Next Generation*, being in the holodeck so
far surpasses the experience of residing in a 3D cyberworld like
Alphaworld that you would never know that the forests, birds, or
brooks were anything other than real. You would be thrust, bodily,
right into the simulation, to experience it in its full, multisensory
glory.

What is revealing is that over time the holodeck was developed as
a training facility, where situations and characters were simulated for
purposes of technical and moral instruction. From being a fairground
attraction, it became a learning tool. *Next Generation* viewers were
given to understand that the shift was largely possible because the
computer technology behind the holodeck had improved, becoming
capable of generating animate objects (people included) made up of
a partially stable form of matter. They were not invited to dwell, how-

ever, on the paradox that the new relationship between the holodeck's form and function gave rise to: for as the simulator grew better and better at reproducing reality, the uses to which it was put became more and more abstract. The holodeck's highest purpose, it seemed, was to serve as a thought experiment.

The holodeck's example, invites, I think, an interesting question. For if cyberspace is the outer space of today, then can we say that what the Space Age was seeking all along was not so much an expansion of physical space as an expansion of mind?

CHAPTER 5

ALIENS ON YOUR DESKTOP

Every now and then when I fall to musing in front of my computer screen, daydreaming instead of tapping, my computer makes a sudden bid for independence and takes on a life of its own. Without the least bit of warning, the work on my screen dissolves away to nothing, and something altogether different begins to manifest itself. Instead of toasters with angel wings gently flapping or a twinkling starscape that recedes into an imaginary distance, a series of charts and graphs that looks suspiciously like work and not like time-out begins its tireless procession before my eyes.

One moment I'll be mulling over a page of text and the next I'll find myself facing a colorful frenzy of businesslike activity. Dominating proceedings is a 3D plot of radio frequencies sampled directly from the skies that chugs across my screen in an orderly but animated fashion, looking like (and I'm not hallucinating) a marching army of index cards readying itself for battle behind the closed doors of the office supply cupboard. Elsewhere, a wiggly red line fizzes and jiggles and periodically freezes, holding still the outline of a bar chart resembling the graphic trace of a city skyline, and beneath that, a solid red block slinks slowly across the screen with sluglike single-mindedness. All in all, it's as though a Kandinsky painting jumped off the wall of the Met, poured itself into my PC, and began a silent lock-step samba.

Although this novelty screen-saver gives little away at first blush, on closer inspection it is clear that some kind of intensive computation is under way. Reading the small print running along the axes of the graphs, you learn that the 3D plot represents something called a Fast Fourier Transform—a method of separating out individual radio signals from what is predominantly noise, only using software instead of a radio tuner—and that the wiggly red line searches for regular patterns amid the buzz of radio waves. Another set of inconspicuous labels seems to imply some astronomy-related end, attaching precise figures to Doppler drift rates, Gaussian powers, and the time and date the radio signals were collected at the Arecibo Radio Observatory in Puerto Rico. But the chief design merit of the screen-saver is how well it disguises its real purpose by masquerading as mere eye candy. This is why, despite being thoroughly familiar with what is happening on my computer screen, I have to pinch myself to remember that it is a highly functional software application that has changed the way people think about computers. Because this application not only links one computer to the next, pulling millions of physically disparate machines into conspiratorial collaboration; it also links a community of believers bonded by a desire to explore the stars.

This is the Search for Extra-Terrestrial Intelligence at Home. Better known by the shorthand SETI@home, it is an ingenious free-subscriber program that enables a California-based team of astronomers, physicists, and engineers to borrow computing power from ordinary people eager to participate in a bona fide scientific experiment, and then to put that processing power to use analyzing radio signals from outer space for signs of intelligent life. Anyone can climb on board the enterprise, anywhere in the world, and help search for electromagnetic evidence that we are not alone in the universe. All that is required is a reliable PC with idle processing time to loan out and access to the internet, which is how would-be participants register for the program and obtain the screen-saver. In practical terms, the screen-saver is simply a broker, mediating a functional exchange of computer time for scientific kudos. But in symbolic terms SETI@ home is much more than that. It brings outer space and cyberspace into a new kind of conference, effectively allowing subscribers to tap the cosmic airwaves and "listen" for intergalactic messages that might have originated from distant civilizations.

As the economies of the developed world evolved from mercantilism to industrialism to the no doubt oversold "information economy," so too has the negotiation of space been transformed from exploration—a grand old mercantilist concept—to communication. SETI@home definitively points the way forward. Along with the robotic probes that NASA hurls into space to conduct biochemistry experiments on our behalf and the orbiting Hubble telescope (effectively a prosthetic eye extending our vision into the farthest recesses of the universe), the SETI enterprise to intercept intelligent-looking alien signals epitomizes how the remote handling of information is changing our very perception of space. The traversing of vast distances at light-speed—still the relativistic limit for all movement through space—was once understood to be a question of exponentially increasing velocity. Now it is a simple trick of technology, a function of telepresence, and a by-product of greater connectivity. SETI@home, however, adds a further twist: it democratizes space, opening up access to the citizen-astronauts of the twenty-first century, whom we once gaily imagined traveling back and forth between the planets in customized spacecraft. Only SETI@home brings space to the people instead, parsing it out in bits of code that can comfortably inhabit our desktop computers. The result is that today's citizen-astronauts are web surfers.

· · ·

SETI's online manifestation is a fairly new phenomenon—just three years old, compared to SETI's (the discipline's) forty-plus. The acronym can be confusing, in that it denotes not just a specialist field, but also a method of searching, a dedicated research institution (the SETI Institute in Mountain View, California), and, not least, the scientists who are engaged in searching (hence the term, SETI scientists). Until the advent of SETI@home, which was developed and implemented by a small team of computer scientists at the University of California, Berkeley, the community of SETI scientists extended to no more than a few dozen, most of them in America, who pursued their quixotic quest decade after decade at some of the world's lonelier telescopes, watched with curious interest, and often bemusement, by the larger community of astronomers. Now that the online application has dragged SETI into the fashionable glare of the internet, the enterprise has acquired a raft of enthusiastic supporters—voyeur-participants who have thrown in their lot with the search, with (and this varies from subscriber to subscriber) the belief, advocacy, and clear acknowledgment that looking out there for cosmic companions is worthwhile, whether or not we find them.

In its simplest form SETI@home is a software package that can be downloaded over the internet by anyone using a personal computer. Once installed, it delivers to every such "client" a small chunk of data recorded at Arecibo. Whenever the client machine is not running other programs, or when it is otherwise underemployed, the software kicks into gear and sifts through its small chunk of allotted data for radio signals that are potentially artificial in origin. Then, when the task is complete, it sends the results back to the central server at Berkeley for aggregation with results from other similarly analyzed chunks of data, before grabbing a new piece of digitized space to search. As with any screen-saver, if you move your mouse or tap a key, these activities are immediately suspended—until the next time your concentration lapses. But it is amazing how many processing "cycles" your computer has to spare; even when you are typing as fast as you can with windows open all over the show, your average modern PC is yawning. These are the spare cycles that SETI@home takes advantage of.

At face value, this sounds like any number of other dot-com ideas that appear and then vanish in the internet world like clouds in the afternoon sky. It was even introduced to the web in the appropriate spirit of adventure and with nothing but word of mouth to recommend it. With the nervous backing of the Planetary Society—the space advocacy organization founded by Carl Sagan and Bruce Murray—the program's creators launched SETI@home almost as a lark, hoping to demonstrate on a small scale the potential for distributing data over the internet for analysis. They had expected to get 200,000 to 300,000 users at best, and they worried incessantly about whether those users would tire of the screen-saver, opt out of the program, or surf elsewhere for their thrills. In any event, they surpassed their goal within a couple of weeks, and within a matter of months they'd broken the seven-figure user mark. In an industry where durability is both rare and highly prized, SETI@home has proven its worth. Three years on, it boasts more than 4 million users in 226 countries and territories around the world. It has identified over half a billion signals that merit further investigation and notched up more than 800,000 years of processing time.

As if this were not impressive enough, in the process of outstripping its stated objectives SETI@home has become the largest community computing project that the internet world has ever seen. Far from tiring of the screen-saver, its users have joined forces to set up their own grapevines. They'll meet in chat rooms and newsgroups to swap progress reports, read and write online newsletters, rave about the application in online zines, and club together into teams hellbent on bettering the latest data-crunching record posted on the Berkeley website. As the phenomenon continues to escalate, SETI@home is itself evolving. With roughly 3,000 new users downloading the application every day, it is now far more than a novel solution to the problem of delivering supercomputing power at superlow cost—which is how it began life. It is a veritable underground movement.

What a movement associated with a software application can possibly be, or believe in or stand for, is an interesting question in itself. There are internet subcultures that possess an almost tribal sense of their own identity. I am thinking especially of those cyber-societies modeled after the famous San Francisco–based WELL community, founded in 1985, whose core members came to regard the group as an alternative family, even though they rarely met face-to-face and were physically scattered across the continent. But there are both greater and lesser associative bonds forged online. At the immersive end of the scale, cyber-cities like Alphaworld and the complex fantasy worlds of MUDs invite users to indulge in a shared suspension of disbelief and plunge into baggage-free zones where what you say is the only thing that matters. Who you are, where you live, your sex, race, and religion, all of these real-life anchors of identity are irrelevant. Meanwhile, at the softer end of cyber-culture, newsgroups and chat rooms provide forums where people can congregate around shared interests or pursuits without calling for any banner-waving ideology or tub-thumping cyber-manifestos. They are the cyber-equivalent of hobby clubs, community lectures, and subscription magazines.

SETI@home seems initially to have more in common with the softer cyber-subcultures in that contact between individual users or teams is fairly minimal. Other than in SETI newsgroups—fan clubs, effectively, where people gather to discuss problems with the software, brag about their number-crunching prowess, or excitedly post pictures of unusual-looking signals—communication is formally mediated through the Berkeley website. But if you move up along the spectrum of emotional investment, the most cursory survey of registered users readily reveals that they are all similarly (often passionately) motivated by the desire to find E.T. They believe in the need for searching and in the possibility of finding. What's more, unlike every other internet subculture, which at bottom line consists of talk, talk, and yet more talk, SETI@home users are actually doing something, collectively, to work toward realizing their goal.

This is precisely what online game designer David Gedye had in mind when he came up with the seed of the SETI@home concept back in 1995. At the time, Gedye, a former Berkeley graduate student then gainfully employed in Seattle's booming electronics industry, had been watching a television series commemorating the Apollo program, and he had been struck anew by the way in which the moon shot had given people a sense of common purpose. It was not the usual round of nostalgia that succeeded in moving him, the black-and-white footage of flag-wavings, liftoffs, reentries, and ticker-tape parades, all narrated in the assured tones of American paternalism. It was more the way people united behind the effort to achieve a new scientific milestone. This set Gedye thinking about whether any scientific project in the modern world had the potential to involve people in a similar way, sweeping them up in a tide of hopefulness and, he recalls, "allowing them to set our planet's troubles in perspective." Cloning perhaps? Or genome mapping? Even the hunt for an AIDS vaccine? No one thing seemed to combine all the right ingredients of popular appeal, collective participation, and a clear problem to tackle. Then Gedye thought of involving people in a SETI search. "I knew from online gaming that you could get large numbers of people working together on the internet," he says, "and I knew that people would find it exciting to participate in SETI. The trick was to get it to work." Though the idea might not succeed in unifying the modern world, it could certainly give rise to a community bonded together by a shared goal, if not by a shared set of beliefs.

Gedye managed to persuade computer scientist David Anderson, his former tutor at Berkeley, of the fruitfulness of this line of thinking and then, through the influence of Washington-based astronomer Woody Sullivan, he roped in SETI scientist Dan Werthimer, also at

Berkeley, as well. Gedye was aware that Werthimer had a problem. His SETI project—a broad-ranging, all-sky search that piggybacked the Arecibo receiver and sucked up every radio wave that bounced off the supersensitive dish across 56 million distinct channels—was accumulating radio telescope data at a rate that vastly outpaced the computing ability of his servers. Werthimer needed a way to deal with this mounting store of crude data, and he needed it to be cheap. What Gedye did not yet know was that David Anderson already had the answers. As Anderson himself puts it, "The research I was doing on distributed processing in the late eighties and early nineties was basically a solution in search of a problem. We would run toy programs all the time just to demonstrate that you could use fifty computers at once. It was thrilling, but we didn't have a real application."

Thus, without quite realizing it, Gedye had set the gauntlet down before the perfect listener. A talented but maverick programmer, David Anderson had bounced around the computer science world for years, never quite sure whether his home was on campus or in commerce. While working as an assistant professor at Berkeley and playing around with distributed networks, his extracurricular sorties took him to Sonic Solutions, where he worked as a software architect designing high-end systems for editing digital audio, and then to Tunes.com, one of the largest online music libraries and a forerunner of Napster. SETI@home enticed him back into the academic fold in no small part because in it he foresaw an opportunity to tinker further with the possibilities of distributed networks and perhaps even realize the technology's commercial potential.

Working with Dan Werthimer was a case of opposites attracting. Werthimer, one senses, wouldn't see a commercial prospect if it landed on the hood of his baby-blue Mustang convertible—a vehicle he manages to keep just this side of the wrecker's yard, and which he drives around Berkeley seemingly without a care in the world. Few people are more affable than Werthimer; whenever we've met he's given the distinct impression of being happy with life as he finds it, and he responds to most any statement with a deeply nasal "cooool." As it happens, Anderson, who is dark and brooding to Werthimer's blithe and blond, ended up exploring the commercial viability of distributed processing on his own. Toward the end of 2000, he helped found United Devices, a Texas-based distributed processing outfit that boasts a management team of high-tech rene- gades with impeccable pedigrees; the three principal figures have more than twenty years of programming experience between them, at Intel, IBM, Dell, and Microsoft. Since the tech boom started to go bust practically simultaneously, his timing couldn't have been worse. But United Devices survived the crash, and Anderson still hopes to take on commercial clients requiring massive computational resources for projects such as drug modeling and genome mapping, and then match them up with a volunteer base whose members would be enticed into loaning CPU (central processing unit) cycles by means of inducements ranging from gift certificates and air miles to cash prizes won by sweepstake.

SETI@home, however, has remained a nonprofit enterprise, though not for lack of venture interest. Anderson and Werthimer soon cottoned onto the fact that for this project, at least, subscribers wished to contribute processing time gratis, since the great majority believes that SETI advances the cause of humanity. Now the Berke- ley scientists balk at any attempt to commercialize the project and regularly fight off companies seeking to buy banner space on their website. It is the quest itself that moves them.

"I'd always dreamed of becoming a concert pianist," Anderson told me during a meeting at his impressively chromed but not yet occupied Berkeley office. Tall, rangy, and quick to smile, Anderson, now in his late forties, exudes the easy charm of someone who knows he's clever, and yet feels no need to demonstrate it. When we spoke, he managed to be both informative and confiding. "The only thing I spent more time doing than practicing was messing around with the departmental computer trying to devise ways to represent music with multiple voices and to separate the way tempo changes over time from the notes themselves." Anderson remembers the machine, a PDP11, fondly, "because it was one of the first computers that could sit on a desk as opposed to standing on the floor, and it had all these sexy graphics." But more than that, it represented a personal turning point, because from then on Anderson was hooked on programming instead of performing, and after going on to get a doctorate in computer science—for research that used ideas from linguistics to describe the way computers talk to one another—he was fortunate enough to walk straight into a teaching position at Berkeley. Explaining the arc his career took from there, Anderson gave me a quick course in recent computer history.

Computing is as subject to fads as anything else, and in the eighties the big fad was parallelism. Parallelism is the processing model that gave rise to the supercomputer, which, before distributed processing arrived on the scene, was the only means by which very large, computationally intensive problems could be solved with any degree of proficiency. Those unfamiliar with these machines should think of a supercomputer as a kind of computational mother ship that houses within its mainframe dozens of smaller computers coexisting side by side. Though magnificent in their own way, for these are big, physically commanding machines, the trouble with them is twofold. Stuffed full of microchips and highly specialized to boot, they are a nightmare to program. What's more, these processing titans were, and still are, extremely costly pieces of hardware, and they remain prohibitively expensive to all but a few large corporations and well-heeled institutions.

This is where distributed processing comes in. Distributed processing shifts the burden of parallelism from hardware to software by exploiting the internet in order to connect thousands of physically dispersed PCs into a single network—in essence, a mainframe whose computational components have been scattered over hundreds or thousands of miles and then reconnected via electrons and fiber optics. This network is far more flexible than any supercomputer: you can run one specialized software application one day and another specialized application the next, and all for a fraction of the cost. Not surprisingly, distributed processing has become the fad of the moment, and many of the big players in computing are rushing to stake a claim, if not priority, in inventing it. Sun Microsystems, one of SETI@home's major sponsors, has long had an interest in networking multiple computers, for example. Only the Sun model never broke away from the client-server yoke, which dictated that all the computing resources had to be concentrated in the server while the client machines were dumb receptacles whose main job was to interact with human beings. The company's McLuhanesque mantra, "the network is the computer," was more fully realized elsewhere—notably at the research labs at Berkeley, where David Anderson and others were networking intelligent PCs.

"These days people tend to lump SETI@home together with Napster and call it the peer-to-peer revolution," says Anderson, referring to the upstart online music company that famously drew the wrath of the international recording industry by bypassing it entirely in order to allow listeners to swap music online directly. Anderson is clearly pleased to have been one of the movers behind such an interesting upheaval, even if, as he points out, file swapping and distributed processing are, technically, different species of grassroots activity. In fact, he grows increasingly animated as he describes how peer-to-peer programmers rebelled against the tyranny of the client-server model. "They completely turned things around," he says, turning his long fingers around imaginary cogs. "Once they recognized that ordinary PCs were becoming powerful resources in their own right, they began figuring out how to aggregate these resources out at the edges of the network and in the process they decentralized the network." In this way they succeeded in mimicking the massively parallel architecture of supercomputers, without the headache of having to write programs for multiprocessors and without the crazy costs.

The beauty of the system lies in its economy and invisibility. Because your up-to-the-minute, off-the-shelf PC has so much storage and computing capability, it can participate in a distributed network at the same time that it meets its your other computational needs. Thus you can quite happily search for intelligent life in the galaxy as you pull out a spreadsheet, say, and knuckle down to doing your taxes, while you e-mail your nearest and dearest, or scour the web for a bargain flight to Mexico City. The only time you notice that your computer is working for someone else as well as for you is when you stop long enough for a screen-saver like SETI@home to show itself. Dan Werthimer, who is rightly and unabashedly proud of the application's achievement, is fond of expounding before any audience, even an audience of one, that invisibly, surreptitiously, and almost out of nowhere SETI@home has in short order become the world's most powerful supercomputer. At the slightest encouragement, he'll rattle off how many teraflops worth of calculations it performs compared with other supercomputers—a teraflop is one trillion operations per second—and his eyes will pop with excitement at how many gigabytes it can munch through at mind-boggling speeds. Should he ever find himself in need of a new conversation stopper, he might add that not only is his supercomputer invisible but that in any real sense of the word it doesn't even exist. It is no more, and indeed, no less, than a virtual machine.

Virtual machines and virtual communities. These are tricky things to get your mind around, irrespective of how thoroughly the internet has been domesticated in recent years. Add to this the decidedly trippy notion that a machine running SETI@home is somehow communing with the stars and it is difficult not to get lost along the shadowy border where possibility meets pure fiction. To be more accurate, though, when running SETI@home you are not *actually* listening to the music of the spheres, you're just virtually listening. The application's software is mediating the process, sifting and sorting millions of radio signals as it performs a number of complex, interrelated tasks. These tasks, and the light they shed on the subject of cosmic companionship, are what interest Dan Werthimer.

Dan Werthimer is the original über-geek—an astronomy whiz before he was ten, a SETI junkie by the age of fourteen, and a builder of computer circuit boards by sixteen. Looking back on it all, now aged forty-seven, he'll shake his head and say, "It was a wonderful time to grow up." What he's referring to, primarily, is the fact that the first microchips were becoming available just as he was old enough to begin fiddling with them. Along with the Apple Computer founders Steve Jobs and Steve Wozniak, the teenage Werthimer was a member of the now legendary Homebrew Computer Club, which in the early 1970s met once a month at Stanford University's Fairchild Auditorium. "It was a wild event," says Werthimer. "The first part was a show-and-tell period where people would get up and do a demo, showing off some software they'd written or a computer they'd built. Lee Felsenstein, who moderated the meetings, wouldn't let anyone talk for more than one minute, then he'd start shaking a stick at them. After the demos, people in the audience would shout out questions or throw out problems, and then it was chaos, with everyone running around trying to learn more about what they'd seen and heard."

At first, Werthimer explains, the digital-age Young Turks were simply interested in swapping ideas and know-how, but over time the Homebrew whizzes became more and more business-minded. Apple was founded in 1976, and a dozen more companies would emerge from the club before the decade was out. "A lot of people in that club got filthy rich. But I didn't get filthy rich because I was always thinking about how you might use these chips to search for radio signals," says Werthimer. Thus the pattern of his life was set. Even when Werthimer was a research scientist at Berkeley developing what he calls "gizmos" for the Space Shuttle, which included a small telescope and a spectrometer, SETI was foremost in his mind, and he'd simultaneously be building data-analyzing equipment and writing computer algorithms to get to the bottom of the radio signal conundrum.

Werthimer's offices are situated high in the Berkeley hills, overlooking the tree-lined, white-stone university campus whose trademark campanile can be seen on a clear day from across San Francisco Bay. The building, an appropriately retro-looking minimalist cube of concrete, is called Space Sciences, but you know you've arrived at SETI HQ when you step over the "Welcome All Species" doormat. The large and airy second-floor room that houses operations was just the same as I remembered it when I'd first visited Werthimer there two years earlier—before SETI@home had been unleashed on the public at large, and when a couple of programmers working at a couple of consoles was as busy as the action got. Several computers displaying luscious graphics were humming away quietly as light streamed lazily in through the large windows. All in all, the place remained refreshingly free of clutter and clamor. Somehow I'd expected to find the office transformed into a dynamic nerve center, with people scurrying about frenetically, paper flying, and the phones ringing constantly. How did the skeleton staff of four manage to keep 4 million users happy and still look as if they had all the leisure in the world to search and destroy software demons and fix operational glitches?

"I'll show you how," said Werthimer, motioning me to follow him out of the office and down the corridor to what looked like a cupboard in the wall. Flinging open the wide double doors to reveal a rack of servers working away incessantly as noisy fans cooled their computational ardor, he stood back, placed his hands on his hips, and announced: "This is the Central Brain." It looked more like an art installation. All around the servers, fibers were bunched into thick bright blue and bright orange tubes that ascended the walls and trailed across the ceiling, Pompidou Center–style: these, apparently, attest to the fact that SETI@home is the largest user of the internet in the University of California. There are four servers in all—Asimov, Cyclops, Sagan, and Clarke—and together they manage the whole operation. Data from Arecibo comes in on Asimov, which is the server that also stores the contact details of individual users. Sagan divides it up into work units and then sends the work units out, while Cyclops (named after an early NASA-funded SETI project) and Clarke work at the opposite end of the process, analyzing results coming in from users. This then was the source, the wellspring, the fundamental basis of it all, and I have to admit that the Central Brain possessed a certain shrinelike aura, its semiconcealed nature bringing to mind those Catholic icons you find ensconced in nooks and recesses on street corners in Palermo or Naples.

Having paid homage at the altar of distributed processing, I was ready to settle down to unraveling the mysteries of Doppler drift rates and Gaussian powers and to finding out exactly what my screen-saver was doing whenever it sprang into activity.

The "I" in SETI refers to a specific and necessarily limited definition of intelligence; researchers listen for radio signals on the assumption that alien civilizations are either deliberately or unintentionally broadcasting. We ourselves provide the model, in that we are unintentionally announcing our existence to the cosmos via leaking radio waves that carry everything from *I Love Lucy* to the BBC World Service and *The Simpsons* across the intergalactic seas. Admittedly, these emissions are very weak, nor are they likely to be understood anywhere else but here; but we do not currently have the resources to transmit a deliberate signal at the kind of strength that would qualify as a beacon, at least not for any sustained period of time. Other civilizations, however, might have far greater resources at their disposal than we do and, in addition to leaking radio waves, might be transmitting clear beacon signals, pure and piercing as a sustained operatic note, or precise, regular pulses that, in the first instance, grab attention, and in the second, may contain parcels of digital information. The odds of finding such signals may be small, but the point behind SETI is that it has worked out how to look.

All such signals—beacons, pulses, even leakage—have telltale signs of artifice stamped all over them, making them easy to pick out against the background noise produced by natural astronomical objects. The difference is especially striking once you convert radio waves into sound waves. Natural radiation produced by such things as gas, dust, and clouds of matter in the galaxy sounds like static. It's the same hissing noise you hear when you tune your radio between stations, since, believe it or not, even a receiver as simple as this routinely picks up intergalactic radiation, including radio waves that originated in the big bang. By contrast, artificial signals, including interference from Earth, sound like whistles. These are the narrow band signals that SETI@home seeks out and then scrutinizes, looking for changes in strength and in pitch.

The screen-saver software seeks changes in signal strength by scanning for a whistle sound that gets louder as the telescope moves over it, peaks when it's perfectly aligned, and then gets softer again as the telescope moves away. This kind of sonic fingerprint implies that the source of the sound is a fixed point in the sky; if you plotted the strength of the signal against time you'd get a Gaussian distribution or bell curve. If the signal emanates from a spinning planet or from a satellite orbiting a planet, you can expect an additional aural signature, a change in pitch that corresponds to scaling up or scaling down the frequency of the transmission as the distance to the source of the signal oscillates back and forth. In other words, you would hear a whistle that rises or dips. And that unearthly sound, reminiscent of nothing so much as a theremin—that antique piece of electronica whose faintly nauseating ululations famously feature in the original *Star Trek* theme music—represents Doppler drift. Since no one either inside or outside the SETI community has any idea how fast the frequency might be changing, or "drifting," SETI@home looks at 23,000 different drift rates. Finally, in 2001, a further algorithm was added to the application. This sifts through the data look-ing for three equally spaced pulse signals, where the space could be anything from a thousandth of a second to fourteen seconds.

As if the task of running me through the workings of SETI@home had triggered only latent worries concerning the difficulty of finding anything at all (after all, SETI as a discipline is more than forty years old, and to date it has found nothing), Werthimer sighed and then set off on a downward spiral of speculative patter. "We are much more likely to find an artifact than a deliberate communication, an *I Love Lucy* equivalent or some kind of navigational beacon or radar sys-tem," he said. "I mean, why would anyone want to get in touch with us. We're so primitive." Whittling down the odds even further, he continued: "For the first four billion years of life on Earth, we didn't leak radio at all, then suddenly for a hundred years or so we leak like crazy, and now, if we go digital, we will return to being radio quiet. That leaves a very narrow window for possible detection. It means the chances of locating alien beings who, like us, have just discovered radio, are minimal. What's more we can't detect any intelligent life before that technological watershed or predict what superadvanced technologies older civilizations might use." At this point Werthimer seemed to run out of steam. A natural optimist, he has no appetite for bleak conclusions, so instead he began telling me about laser searches—a new optical SETI enterprise that he has recently obtained funding to pursue—and how SETI@home is expanding to take on data from the Southern Hemisphere recorded by the Parkes telescope in Australia.

I know that it is deeply unfashionable in this age of flash and burn to be seen to try at anything, but SETI@home's rapidly expanding fan club seems to think otherwise. Its members applaud the search qua search. They think SETI is pathbreaking and worthwhile and benefi-cial to the long-term interests of humanity. Besides, they've got com-putational muscle to spare by the teraflop, and they wish to see it put to good use. Perhaps, too, they sense intuitively that SETI is unfalsifiable: no matter how long you keep turning up nothing, you can never state definitively that there are no civilizations out there—you can only keep looking. And so we return to the user base. How can it be characterized? What motives do people have for running the screensaver? And what cultural forces underlie its immense popularity?

Like the internet itself, SETI@home is a truly international phenomenon. Since its launch at the end of 1999, it has spread with an almost viral rapaciousness, infecting people in more than 200 countries with the desire to seek out new life beyond our own small sphere and to find an Otherness that transcends national difference and ethnic diversity. As active and well intentioned as it is wide, this diaspora has turned out to be self-organizing; members actively seek out one another, and numerous volunteers have taken it upon themselves to translate the SETI@home website into dozens of different languages, including Russian, Turkish, and Swedish. I suspect, however, that whoever delivered the Esperanto translation had an agenda of his or her own and, rather than intending to offer practical support, merely wished to remind people that devotees of this prefabricated Europeanese for nerds once nurtured pie-eyed dreams of the kind of community building that SETI@home seems effortlessly to achieve.

Turning to the detailed picture of the breakdown in demographics, we find that the United States leads the pack in SETI@home's league of nations, with nearly 1.75 million users to its name. After America come Germany and the United Kingdom, with over a quarter of a million users apiece, and then the community fans out across the globe from Mongolia to Malawi, Portugal to Paraguay, and Japan to Jordan, stringing together places with as little obvious common ground between them as Guam, Greenland, and Guadeloupe. There are more than 52,000 users in Brazil, 9,000 in New Zealand, 8,000 in Hungary, 32,000 in China, 14,000 in Turkey and India, and 8,000 in Israel, a country that boasts a SETI team calling themselves the "IsraAliens." Most Arab nations can claim membership, dozens of African countries are represented, and there is no island too small or too remote for inclusion. In fact, if you rank all the countries and colonies according to the number of participants per capita, you get an even better sense of the application's extensive reach, since Pitcairn Island emerges at the top of the heap, with 46 people running SETI@home out of a population of 49, closely followed by Antarctica, the Cook Islands, and the Falklands.

For the most part, any spirit of partisanship based on national pride is subsumed within the grander collaborative effort, even if a handful of teams treat SETI@home as a form of social glue, among them gays@stuttgardforS.E.T.I and Poland's Seti@Posnan, where a bit of municipal rallying inspired 206 townspeople to join forces in the hunt for E.T. I stumbled across these two teams while perusing the Berkeley website, which is a dangerously addictive thing to do, since every team that registers is given room to post a one-line descriptor, message of hope, or some other such trifle, and these are extremely diverting. It was here that I found the Baltimore Believers—"just a couple of people at work who think this is a cool thing to do"—and Let's Kick Some Alien Butt, a team of 112 Swedes so taken with their own name that they've taken to selling logo-ed T-shirts. Then there are Project Colossus, whose mantra is "we know we can . . . we know we can . . . we know we can . . . ," and JEDI@home, whose members identify themselves as "servants of the little gold guy"—a cryptic reference to *Star Wars'* Yoda, the dwarfish E.T. with skin like parchment who is possessed of the wisdom of Solomon. Also worth a mention is Motley Fool UK, a team of 45 British SETI fans determined to "poke fun (and pig's bladders on sticks) at the Wise who try and suppress us with their knavish tricks and devilish incantations."

Best of all is a team calling itself The Fred. Gently ribbing The

Borg, the latest alien foe to terrorize the starship *Enterprise*'s hardy crew, this time with the threat of assimilating them into a miserable colony of dronelike man-machines, The Fred claims to be "The Ultimate Collective." Its motto reads, "We are The Fred. You will join us. You will know useless trivia. Resistance is futile."

Computer nerds, science fictions fans, stargazers, and Roswellian mystics (most of whom have banded together in the jumbo-size Art Bell Team, which has 12,000 plus members) make up just the sort of broad alliance that you would expect SETI@home to attract. None of these separate constituencies appears to use the site to work out their differences or air their grievances, however, as the community spirit is much too lighthearted to bear the strain of ideological warfare. At the same time, at the team level, competition is absolutely rife and is fostered by the existence of league tables. In the league of commercial teams, such competitive jostling has seen Sun Microsystems and Silicon Graphics—real-life rivals headquartered across the street from each other in Silicon Valley's Mountain View—vie shamelessly to become SETI@home kingpin. In the race to beat each other, the two companies have been neck and neck near the top of the team rankings ever since SETI@home began. As of this writing, Sun is currently ahead of the game, with over 3,105,000 work units under its belt. But SGI, which has only 392 members to Sun's 460, may yet catch up, since the company has dedicated to the search faster machines that use less CPU time to crunch through more work units.

Bettering your CPU times, finding the best platforms and operating systems for running the screen-saver, accumulating work units, and beating friends and enemies alike are run-of-the-mill obsessions among the SETI membership, and among individuals as well as teams. Everyone wants to be better, faster, smoother, and more productive, thus getting to play out contemporary business culture's do-or-die ethos in microcosm. This number-crunching fury, adapted from gaming culture, is the clearest indication that the vast bulk of SETI@home users are geeks—this, and the fact that the application is most avidly discussed in trade magazines bearing such bracing titles as *Global Telephony, Infoworld, Computer Dealer News,* and *Software Digest.* In addition, browsing the list of company teams is like reading the NASDAQ index unfiltered. Virtually every internet success story of recent years and every microchip-manufacturing mogul has a profile here: Lycos, eBay, Compaq, Intel, Microsoft, Apple, IBM, Dell, Hewlett-Packard, Cisco, and Oracle. Factor in the clutch of telecommunications giants like Ericsson, Nokia, AOL, Sony, Motorola, and British Telecom (whose descriptor reads "BT, ET, whatever . . ."), and the smattering of engineering companies and aerospace contractors like Boeing and Lockheed Martin, and you could be forgiven for concluding that SETI@home had the world's high-tech fraternity more or less at its feet.

Prior to tapping the SETI@home grapevines for information, I believed myself to be a fairly typical user. In return for volunteering the part-time services of my computer, I had the satisfaction of participating in a collaborative scientific experiment combined with a latent, if unrealistic, hope that lurking within one of my very own parcels of data would be the genuine call from beyond. So far, so good, for these motives put me in line with the stated objectives of roughly half the population of users. The point of divergence comes with my laissez-faire approach to the science. I'll admit that I enjoy the scientific thrill of the whole thing—the fact that I can pull up "data info," check up on "data analysis," and keep an eye on the running count of the CPU time that my trusty laptop has so far devoted to searching for life elsewhere. But it is enough for me just to bask in the aura of science. Not so the majority. Most users cannot get enough of the science, and the most frequently visited page on the Berkeley website is the one that allows them to obtain what is essentially an account statement. You just type in your e-mail address and, courtesy of Asimov, out come the stats: the number of work units you've processed, the total CPU time, the CPU time per unit, the date you returned the last unit, how many hours you've been running the screen-saver, and more. You can find out which part of the sky your work units hail from, pore over sky maps and star charts, and set yourself up to race against the clock and trounce your own CPU record.

This navel-gazing preoccupation with computer speeds and productivity ratios is echoed across the newsgroups, where people are forever posting messages that reveal nothing short of performance anxiety. A typical post on alt.sci.seti, for example, might read: "I am using an Athlon 850Mhz with 256MB of memory and I am running SETI client with SETI Driver and SETISpy on Win 2000. It takes me about 11 hrs to complete a WU and SetiSpy ranks my computer as 8.24 CPU cycles/FLOP. This seems slow compared with other people on this newsgroup." It hardly invites sympathy. Or interest.

In fact, given that this kind of souped-up techno-babble fairly represents the day-to-day concerns of the vast bulk of users, it is extremely tempting just to dismiss the phenomenon as a geek convention that a few nongeeks have unwittingly stumbled upon and then misread, trotting off back home to wax lyrical about the way the application has taken the pulse of popular culture or captured the spirit of the times. And yet to a large extent, all the talk of drivers and platforms, of operating systems, megabytes, and RAM, is just a language of goodwill spoken by people who believe that the faster their machines run, the greater are SETI's chances of finding a meaningful signal. It is a roundabout statement of their devotion to the cause. Geeks are idealists at heart, and their everyday preoccupations with what machines can do ought not to be confused with their ultimate motivations for running SETI@home, nor with their utopian-leaning beliefs about what the internet is capable of. Besides, if the last few years have taught us anything at all, it is that what geeks think and feel and believe swiftly finds its way into the mainstream of both business culture and popular culture, affecting the way all of us interact with one another and view society at large.

The question of motivation arises directly in an online poll that has so far attracted responses from over 80,000 users—60 percent of them aged between twenty and thirty-nine and more than 90 percent of them male. Administered by the Berkeley team and updated hourly, the poll invites people to share their reasons for running the application by ticking off a number of second-guessed motives. Nearly 60 percent of those surveyed have ticked the box saying that their principal reason for running the application was to find E.T. for the good of humanity, while more than 16 percent ticked the one saying they ran it primarily to keep their computers productive. Of greater interest however, are the free-form rationales that independent-minded SETI fans are invited to submit, which stand as a collective testimony to user commitment.

Scrolling down the long list of platitudes ("I want to advance science"), wisecracks ("I can't get a date on this planet"), and occasional confessions ("I strongly believe in aliens"), which literally thousands of people have typed in, it soon becomes clear that three interrelated motives predominate.

1. Wanting to participate in an intriguing and worthwhile scientific experiment ("It's a long shot—but it just might work"; "One small step for Man. One giant leap for Mankind"; "Understanding is Happiness"; "To improve the sum of human knowledge"; "It's cool; I'm proud to help with the search"; "To seek out new life . . ."; "To find a race of beings who have it a little more together than we do").

2. Wanting to be connected to something bigger than themselves ("To be a part of the biggest collaborative project ever undertaken by mankind"; "A way for me to personally participate in space exploration"; "To act in a cooperative nature with one million other people to reach a single goal").

3. Wishing to use their computers and the internet productively ("$4000 laptop, this machine's gonna work"; "Because of its value as an experiment in distributed computing"; "As with Linux OS, SETI@home is the internet at its best"; "Because this is what the

internet is all about. We're proving it's not just there for spam, viruses and as a means for porn merchants to make extra cash").

The naked idealism expressed here may well recall the kind of answers that teenagers on the cusp of political awareness pipe up with when quizzed about how they'd like to change the world. But it also points up the unexpected ways in which outer space and cyberspace have met and converged. If the hope for transforming society was implicit in the Space Age—conditional on our successful transformation of space into a resource—it is practically a manifesto for many in the internet generation. That it should rear its head in the quest to find E.T. online is simply par for the course.

Such hopes are very much alive elsewhere in cyberspace. There is the almost religious effort to expand and popularize the computer language known as Linux, the brainchild of Finnish software engineer and sometime hacker Linus Torvalds, who gave away, via the internet, the source code for this operating system—considered by some to be superior to any other available, including Microsoft's Windows, and considered by all to be a direct slap in the face to Microsoft's much reviled monoculture. Or PiHex, a project to calculate the five trillionth and forty trillionth bits of pi; the various schemes organized by Distributed.net to crack encryption codes and find ways to protect online privacy; GIMPS, or the Great Internet Mersenne Prime Search; and Golem@Home, the wonderfully named program to evolve robotic life-forms.

One of the chief reasons that these activities inspire an almost cultish devotion is that they strive to recapture one of the founding principles of many early cybernauts who dreamt that the internet would be the kind of free-ranging, open-to-all-comers place that outer space was once promised to be. A place where people would be valued not for who they were or where they came from, but for the contribution they made to online culture; a place, too, where innovation would be its own reward. This vision has got lost in recent years, trampled on in the e-commerce gold rush and the related attempts by venture prospectors to recast the internet in the image of a shopping mall. For this reason, Torvalds's largesse struck a chord with internet pioneers passionate in their belief that online communities could be genuinely productive at the same time as they scorned a mainline economy enslaved by the interests of profit. Process, Torvalds seemed to be saying, is as important as product, and collaboration is a viable alternative to market competition. The same goes for SETI@home and other distributed efforts. All these projects live up to an ideal that envisions the products of online collaboration as providing direct material, scientific, medical, and social benefits to mankind as a whole, and then stipulates that these benefits be free.

These dreams cherished by cybernauts are New World dreams, generic dreams of hopefulness that drift into view whenever a new frontier comes within our sights—the Americas, then outer space, now cyberspace. They are dreams that belong to new beginnings. And yet cyberspace is a virgin territory much different from those that have gone before. It doesn't exist in any physical form, which is to say that it has no extension in space, no background or foreground, no here and no there; moreover, we can journey into its jungles, shopping arcades, libraries, and singles bars without ever having to leave home. In many ways, it more closely resembles a landscape of the mind. The upshot is that it is not at all clear that we are its colonizers. In fact, it could be argued that with projects like SETI@home and Linux Open Source harnessing people into productive networks, it is cyberspace that is colonizing us. Playing up the eerier aspects of a wired world in which it is becoming increasingly difficult to disentangle our mental circuitry from our electronic circuitry, intellectual historian George Dyson comments (pace Marshall McLuhan in cynical gear), "Everything that humans are doing to make it easier to operate computer networks is at the same time, but for different reasons, making it easier for computer networks to operate human beings."

In his 1997 book *Darwin Among the Machines*, a broad-ranging history of mankind's symbiotic relationship with all things mechanical that begins with Thomas Hobbes's Leviathan and ends with the internet, Dyson makes the wry observation that if today's advanced networks ever developed even a crude kind of consciousness, then they would qualify as the alien intelligence we have been seeking for so long. Now whenever people start talking about thinking machines, most of us automatically default to robotics and the oft repeated promise made by artificial-intelligence aficionados that mechanical beasts with independent spirits will someday be our co-workers and social companions. But Dyson is interested in something far more nebulous, an intelligence that arises organically, as an indirect rather than direct consequence of programming: in kind, a life force not dissimilar to the "vast active living intelligence system" that quietly thrummed to the rhythm of its own thoughts in Philip K. Dick's 1980 novel *Valis*. Dyson is careful to avoid suggesting that, merely by intensifying the combinational complexity of networks, intelligence will somehow arise. And yet he cannot entirely rule out such an occurrence. The increasing erosion of the boundary between life and non-life has already resulted in complex networks developing such organic properties as self-organization, learned behavior, and an ability to evolve. Some species of coded entity, such as bots, viruses, and spiders (or crawlers), even reproduce themselves. Why shouldn't consciousness be next?

Dyson uses the term "digital metabolism" to describe the way biology and technology are currently converging toward a common language based on self-replicating strings of code. For what is DNA but a natural analogue of computer code, but with four bases instead of two? And isn't human thought itself no more than a pattern of electrical signals in a matrix made from carbon rather than silicon?

Of course, there is a valid question mark hanging over how literally we are meant to understand such analogies, since a lot of metaphorical hay gets made at the juncture where bio meets tech—a juncture where a mutual investment in feedback mechanisms, self-regulating systems, embedded programs, neural networks, and so on becomes glaringly apparent. Yet, as the former editor of *Wired* magazine and self-styled cyber-prophet Kevin Kelly points out, more than language is at stake here. Kelly has made a career out of sounding the advent of a neobiological civilization made up of both humans and "living" machines and of predicting that this digital culture will be characterized by "the swarm"—with many minds directing a superorganism. An avid beekeeper, he has found the perfect zoological template for the diffuse, distributed computer networks of today, and he firmly believes that just as the beehive has developed features of intelligence that supersede what any individual bee is capable of, so the aggregate properties of diffuse networks will exceed the sum total of the network's programmable properties. Perhaps such neobiological aspirations are what SETI@home users have in mind when they talk about wanting to "participate in the greater human collectiveness" or "expand our collective intellect."

Kelly's views are popular with the cyber-fraternity, where there's a marked tendency to think of our global electronic networks in animist terms, irrespective of the metaphysical difficulties that that involves. Admittedly, you'll find such thinking arrayed along a spectrum that stretches from cyber-critic Howard Rheingold's straightforward celebration of the internet's collectivism—what he calls "grass roots, group minds"—to the out and out mysticism of writers such as Louis Rossetto, one of the co-founders of *Wired* magazine. In an online interview about internet culture, Rossetto has enthused, "What seems to be evolving is a global consciousness formed out of the discussions and negotiations and feelings being shared by individuals connected to networks through brain appliances like computers. The more minds that connect the more powerful this consciousness will be."

Like many of today's cyber-gurus Rossetto is a fan of the religious philosophy of Pierre Teilhard de Chardin, the French Jesuit priest and paleontologist who prophesied that mankind would achieve a "planetary consciousness" as a result of co-evolving with technology. Writing in the first half of the twentieth century, Teilhard de Chardin found inspiration for his animist philosophy in everything from rocks and animals through to the nervous system; all these things, he believed, possessed a spark of the divine or, to use the neologism he coined, "tangential energy." Drawing on his observations of the nervous system, where increasing complexity produced sharp jumps in intelligence, Teilhard de Chardin argued that this tangential energy was continually striving to break out of organic life into new forms. It was as if—and this is where he finds his current support base—communication had the transcendent goal of consciousness.

Because George Dyson is an analyst of digital culture and not a cheerleader, he is less cavalier with his terminology than either Kelly or Rossetto and, by the same token, more concerned with the metaphysics behind hive consciousness and Gaian minds. Yet he, too, believes in the "emergent properties" of complex, self-organizing systems. Life and intelligence have, after all, emerged once before from less alive and less intelligent components. What makes Dyson's argument so compelling, however, is not his reliance on precedent so much as his insistence that emergent properties defy explanation. Those who profess to understand them do so only by sleight of hand, he says, and yet none of this implies that emergence is not real. Emergence, rather, is what is left after everything else has been explained. By thus styling emergent properties as something that exists in between the spaces of what we know and understand, Dyson introduces an ineffable quality into the functioning of diffuse, distributed networks. It's an approach that rings true because it draws attention to the gaps in our understanding of how life itself evolved, to the fact that there is still a mysterious set of steps to unravel between the known existence of an organic, amino-acid-rich soup and the appearance of the first single-celled bacteria. We know that life emerged, but we don't know how.

To some degree Dyson is guilty of his own sleight of hand, in that without actually saying as much, he implies that the emergence of life and intelligence might as well be a miracle. Still, his is a miracle of physical causality—a miracle that rationalists can believe in. It explains why one quite commonly finds people who understand that computer intelligence (such as it is) is a matter of connecting up hundreds of miniature transistors on miniature circuit boards, believing that these machines are nonetheless capable of magic.

The SETI@home constituency embraces a fair number of such cyber-mystics, including many who labor under the illusion that they themselves, directly, are participating in a new type of space exploration. Indeed, David Anderson regularly receives e-mails from users convinced that as a result of downloading SETI@home their PCs have acquired the sensory ability to scan distant stars for signs of alien existence. To my knowledge, however, only one user has been inspired to mystical heights reminiscent of Teilhard de Chardin: going by the name of Zurd, he says, "SETI is not just about searching for other life forms," it's about working toward a time when "the consciousness of the Earth itself might be awakened, when all humans on Earth become collectively networked."

I suspect that a similar mystification of the internet underlies University of Toronto professor Allen Tough's "Invitation to ETI," a bizarre website that cordially requests E.T. to come online and "establish a dialogue with humankind." Of course, the good professor may just have watched too many Steven Spielberg movies (remember the scene at the end of *Close Encounters of the Third Kind* where humankind and spacekind literally end up making heavenly music together?). And yet, absurd as it might seem, Tough's invite indirectly speaks to the concerns of so many SETI@home users who yearn to be part of something collective and utopian—and who believe, moreover, that the boundaries of cyberspace should be not only permeable but ever expanding, as if mirroring our own ballooning universe. In this alternative cosmos, why shouldn't E.T. be invited to the ball?

Then again, as George Dyson suggests, perhaps a propensity to believe in life elsewhere is causally linked to a propensity to believe in life online—or, if you prefer the language of emergent properties, the belief that life evolved by networking. Either way, E.T. has yet to pick up on the electronic hum of collective human thought and log on.

CHAPTER 6

GROUND CONTROL TO MAJOR TOM

On a midsummer's day in the northern hemisphere of Mars, a beach-ball-like object the size of a Volkswagen Beetle dropped out of the sky. It bounced across the airless landscape, finally coming to rest on the arid floodplains of Ares Vallis. Minutes later, the object deflated, its component air bags falling lifelessly to the ground like a set of collapsed lungs, and a second skin consisting of glinting solar panels fell away to expose the precious cargo within: a small six-wheeled buggy called Sojourner. The date was July 4, 1997. The Martian sky above was hazy and salmon colored, and as the twenty-two-pound rover cranked into life, gingerly raising an antenna to take the ambient surface temperature before driving off to investigate a bunch of rocks, teams of scientists on Earth popped open the champagne and celebrated their success. Pathfinder had landed.

A week later, summer crowds began pouring into movie theaters to see *Contact*, the new feature film based on Carl Sagan's best-selling novel about SETI. Still buzzing about Pathfinder's success, people were now being invited to dream of cosmic encounter. Already, in March, NASA's Lunar and Planetary Science Conference had devoted itself to the debate concerning whether or not Martian meteorite ALH84001 presented clear evidence of fossilized life, making headlines around the world. Now a real-life mission and major feature film were taking up where the conference left off, teasing our recumbent Space Age hopes with new possibilities. At the same time, the scientists whose esoteric work *Contact* so effectively publicized were getting ready to restart Project Phoenix, a sophisticated radio search for intelligent signals virtually identical to that in the movie. In the remote Appalachian Mountains, they would spend night after night huddled around computer screens in the cramped control room that nestled at the base of the Green Bank Observatory's radio dish, attempting to pick meaningful signals from the noise. And, in New Mexico, thousands of believers gathered in Roswell to celebrate the fiftieth anniversary of the crashed UFO. It is hard to resist speculating that something more than simple coincidence lay behind the convergence of science, entertainment, and what can only be described as faith.

If you look at Pathfinder and Project Phoenix, that "something more" seems to be a set of ideas whose time had come. Although superficially very different, both projects hint at new directions in space exploration that might finally afford us the sense of connectedness (to one another and to the cosmos) we once looked for in the Space Age. Recognizing that long-distance human travel in space is not going to happen, at least not for centuries, both projects have managed to close the gap between here and there—Earth and elsewhere—by exploiting the culture of entertainment and the mechanics of communication. Both are remote operations, reliant on electronic sensors and imaging devices, and on the ideas of telepresence and information transfer. In this sense, Pathfinder and Phoenix are of a piece: post–Space Age expressions of our continuing yearning to know what, or perhaps who, is out there. More than anything else, this open-ended longing accounts for the way in which both projects gripped the public imagination.

Pathfinder proved that when NASA got things right, it could still muster something of its old sparkle, overcoming the constraints of spirit-sapping budgets and overcautious management to produce scientific thrills sufficient to dazzle a jaded public. The mission was a wake-up call to thousands of people who hadn't shown the slightest interest in space for decades. Many people found themselves suddenly riveted to their television screens by splashy animatronic trailers that showed exactly how Pathfinder would parachute into the Martian atmosphere, inflate its air bags for landing, and then bounce its way to a halt, rolling across the rock-strewn plains like a piece of high-tech tumbleweed. Not only did media coverage of Pathfinder end up trouncing the prime-time competition; it thoroughly eclipsed coverage of the Roswell celebrations.

Pathfinder gave Earth a first taste of what virtual space exploration might be like. Sojourner was our prosthetic eye: we saw what it saw as it panned across the rouged rubble of the Martian terrain. When it encountered a rock ("Barnacle Bill," "Yogi," or "Scooby-Doo," in the user-friendly parlance of the mission), so did we. To the extent that the mobile rover was remotely controlled by an Earth-based operator, Pathfinder spoke to a whole generation of trigger-happy video gamers weaned on joysticks: Mission Control had never felt more hands-on. What's more, the whole experience was delivered to our screens in real time—allowing for the ten-minute delay in transmitting sounds and pictures from a distance of 35 million miles. Compared with the 1976 Viking landers, which plopped onto the Martian landscape like lead weights and then relayed home photographic stills in fits and starts, Pathfinder was positively interactive.

Although Pathfinder's principal goal on the public relations front was to demonstrate that NASA's "faster, better, cheaper" imperative (the credo of former administrator Dan Goldin) delivered results, its chief impact on the public was in getting them to reconceptualize space exploration. Robotic probes had never been smarter. Distant planets had never been made to feel more proximate. It didn't take much of an imaginative leap (and the media held our hands as we jumped) to picture a coming Space Age in which exploration would be the domain of cute and cuddly superrobots and experienced via long-distance electronic communication. Rovers were just the beginning: in time, all our extraterrestrial yearnings could be satisfied remotely.

If Pathfinder spoke to our dream of space travel and met its needs vicariously, SETI spoke instead to our desire for contact and communion. Rather than drawing its virtual-worlds lexicon from robotics and video gaming as Pathfinder had done, SETI taps into our familiarity with the internet, and to the fact that we already have at our fingertips instantaneous long-distance messaging—chatty avatars that let us bare our souls to the inhabitants of simulated worlds—and remote access to rafts of encyclopedic knowledge just hanging in the ether. From this starting point, it seems feasible (if not inevitable) that we might one day intercept electronically coded messages beamed our way from afar (SETI scientist Jill Tarter calls it the "dial tone") and talk back to the stars in strings of ones and zeros.

Perhaps the way forward lies in playing these two hands, the robotic and the communicative, in tandem, since each complements the other. For example, while robotic space exploration may soon be capable of conjuring up a seamless sense of being there, no amount of mechanical finessing can make us feel emotionally invested in the universe. Only SETI, with its all too earthly (and achingly mortal) yearning for cosmic encounter, can address this essentially metaphysical need. Interestingly enough, NASA has already attempted such a two-hander. In one of its first toe-dipping forays into the science of remote probes, the agency rolled together robotics and metaphysics within a single SETI-inspired package. The result was Pioneer 10.

In 1972, when Pioneer 10 was launched, nothing of its kind had been seen before. It was the fastest man-made vehicle ever built, with a postlaunch speed of 32,174 miles per hour, and a "cruising" speed three times that—more than fifty times the muzzle velocity of a high-speed rifle bullet. It would be the first spacecraft to survey

Jupiter and its moons and, using a gravitational slingshot from Jupiter, the first spacecraft to exit the solar system. Once it had cast itself into deepest space, abandoning the solar system for the call of the unknown, Pioneer 10 would begin the second and more uncertain part of its journey: to carry to the stars our hopes that we might one day find cosmic companions. For soldered to the chassis of the spacecraft was a 6-by-9-inch gold-anodized plaque that in crude pictorial form announced our existence to the universe.

The plaque was the work of Carl Sagan, America's unofficial Astronomer Royal, and SETI's founding father and Sagan's Cornell colleague Frank Drake. They were both brilliant and mad to discover extraterrestrial life. Sagan had pushed NASA to include the plaque on the mission, as a symbolic gesture, he said, and after getting an eleventh-hour go-ahead, he and his then wife, Linda Salzman, sat down with Drake and began brainstorming ideas, determined to compress as much information as possible into the tiny space allotted to them. Within a few hours they settled on an engraving of a naked man and woman standing beside a pulsar map—a new form of cosmic cartography devised by Drake for the express purpose of disclosing our cosmic coordinates to anyone (or anything) who cared to puzzle it out. Like all of Sagan's pet projects, the Pioneer plaque stirred a flurry of media interest and was then left to its own devices, alone if not quite forgotten.

Curious to discover what had become of Pioneer 10, I logged on to the internet, where NASA maintains an extremely lively up-to-the-minute presence. There I learned that despite covering more than 300 million miles a year, this speedy vessel still has a very long way to travel before it comes anywhere near another star system. To be precise, it will be 30,000 years before it sails relatively close to a faint red dwarf in the constellation of Taurus known as Ross 248—"relatively" meaning three light-years distant (a light-year being the distance that light traverses over the course of a year, traveling at a speed of 186,000 miles per second). This is the nearest pass it will make before shooting farther into deep space. Even now, more than thirty years after leaving the Earth, Pioneer 10 remains within the heliosphere, where it continues to be subject to the sun's magnetic influence. Cosmically speaking, it is still in our own backyard.

The same goes for its twin, Pioneer 11 (equipped with an identical plaque), and also for the two Voyager craft that set out after the Pioneers a few years later. Like their predecessors, the Voyagers were pre-programmed to make a reconnaissance of the outer planets before plunging into the void to meet their unknown fate. And again, Sagan managed to place his imprimatur on the missions. Instead of engraved plaques, however, the Voyagers carry Earth's Greatest Hits—copper phonographs, each containing a pictographic brochure of our planet's varied attractions (skyscrapers, waterfalls, trees) as well as an inventory of earthly sounds (everything from an urbane greeting from then U.N. Secretary General Kurt Waldheim to the mating call of a humpback whale).

I suspect that the real obstacle to Pioneer and Voyager's fulfilling the metaphysical dimension of their missions is not so much the vastness of intergalactic distances per se as the fact that we'll never know whether or not another civilization happens to chance upon them. Even if such an encounter were to take place thousands of years in the future (and the odds are minute in the extreme), another gap of thousands of years would have to pass before our descendants (should they happen to live that long) came to learn of it (if they were both able and lucky).

That said, it's hard not to feel sentimental about these robotic emissaries, which for the time being have almost nothing to impart to us beyond the heartbeats they transmit back, letting us know they're still there. Pioneer 10, in particular, has become something of a space-faring mascot now that it has outlasted mission expectations. Going by the book, it ought to have made the transition from super-probe to space junk in 1997, its instruments arthritically seizing up once and for all and its ever more feeble transmissions fading to nothing, like a flatlining EKG. But despite being almost out of juice, Pioneer 10 has gone on transmitting beyond its sell-by date, and now its every surprising transmission, no matter how weak, is to be cheered and welcomed.

NASA's Pioneer 10 web page gets more than 1,000 hits a day and more than 20,000 a day when the probe is in the news. Ever since I joined the ranks of concerned bystanders, I've been regularly checking up on its well-being. The last time I checked, shortly after the probe's thirtieth birthday in March 2002, it had just passed the 7.4 billion mile mark, its Geiger Tube Telescope instrument was still functional, and as it headed into deeper oblivion, it was still valiantly beaming signals home with what little power it could muster—now roughly equivalent to that needed to illuminate a Christmas tree bulb.

As if to acknowledge an old family friend, SETI scientists display a keen interest in the health of Pioneer 10. In fact, they try to track the probe each day during observational runs as a means of checking that their computer systems are working properly. Ironically, for practical purposes, the Pioneer signal might as well be an intelligent E.T., which is, of course, what SETI scientists are scouring the heavens to find. It is regular, narrowband, and faint, while exhibiting Doppler drift—just what you would expect from a broadcasting alien—and if SETI astronomers can pick it up as a distinct beacon against the background noise of the universe then, in theory, they should be able to detect the real thing.

Over the years, the task of locating Pioneer 10 has acquired ritualistic importance for SETI astronomers—much like the bottle of champagne they always have chilling in the observatory refrigerator just in case the longed-for call from beyond arrives. During observing sessions, all the astronomers who are around and awake huddle in front of the computer screen and wait for Pioneer 10 to make its scheduled appearance, or to be more accurate, for the Earth's rotation to carry them round to a position that points in the probe's direction. Then, after a bit of muted cheering and shy back-patting, they'll let out a collective sigh and return to whatever they happened to be doing, content that all is right with the universe.

A couple of years back I witnessed the scene for myself when I spent a few days watching SETI astronomers at work at the Arecibo Radio Observatory in Puerto Rico. I had always understood that dramatic equatorial settings were par for the course when it came to the practice of world-class astronomy, the better to "view" as many stars as possible, north and south. But the radio telescope in Arecibo is in a class of its own. One thousand feet across and cradled within a natural limestone sinkhole in the middle of the jungle, it really is a sight to behold; a modern-day wonder of the world whose physical remove from towns, shops, and the benefit of decent roads makes it all the more arresting.

Getting there from the old Spanish capital of San Juan took most of a morning, with speedy freeways giving way to bumpy one-lane roads that in turn gave way to a twisting, potholed lane lined with banana trees and clapboard houses and along which motor vehicles wound their deliberate way, dodging dogs, chickens, and playful children. I'll never forget the way the telescope revealed itself bit by bit, like a coy fan dancer doing her seductive best, as the observatory's driver ascended the hillside, rounding one bend after another. First I glimpsed a single support tower, rising stark and white out of the obscuring foliage. Then it disappeared. The next time it showed itself, there were two. In this manner the telescope's support towers became visible one by one until something like the bended legs of an overgrown metal crab whose sunken body was below my line of vision seemed to sit like a mirage on my horizon. And yet this was nothing compared to the dish itself, large as an ogre's soup bowl and shimmering under the sun—beneath it you could fit twenty-six football fields.

SETI astronomer Jill Tarter, who looks forward all year to the two three-week observational runs that her scientific team is able to secure at Arecibo annually, has evolved her own way of paying homage to this beast. Tarter is a force of nature in her own right, a woman who combines breathtaking scientific brilliance with great eloquence, an easy charm, and a smattering of personal quirks—among them, a fondness for wearing her hair in pigtails and for salsa dancing whenever the opportunity presents itself. At Arecibo she has acquired a new quirk. Following her nightlong observing shifts, she runs headlong into the cool misty dawn to jog once around the telescope dish before retiring to bed for the day, exhilarated and exhausted.

While at Arecibo I more or less took up residence inside the observing room, which occupied part of a five-story concrete building that rose solidly out of the jungle not far from the edge of the dish. I had decided to keep vigil there with everyone else as one nearby, bright, or otherwise promising star after another was scanned for intelligent-looking radio emissions across 56 million individual channels, much as one would scan across a car radio looking for a station amid the static. This was Project Phoenix, the ongoing SETI program that began in Australia in 1995, moved to West Virginia in 1997, and then wound its way to Puerto Rico. Oblivious of the rotating geography, the astronomers simply picked up where they'd left off after each change of locale and continued to work methodically through Phoenix's list of 1,000 Sun-like stars that lie within 200 light-years from Earth.

The observing process was painstaking and laborious—"like watching paint dry," said SETI astronomer Seth Shostak, his eyes hypnotically glued to his computer screen. Like Tarter, Shostak is affiliated with the SETI Institute in California. In his mid-fifties, he has a round, expressive face and short gray-black hair, and he is a veritable font of SETI knowledge, which he delivers for the most part backhandedly, like a stand-up comic grousing about his favorite pet hate. Every now and then, when an interesting-looking signal would

briefly stir a bit of excitement, he would say, "Now here's a new crit-
ter," and for a few tense moments, as hearts raced in anticipation, the
astronomers ran through their backup routine at breakneck speed.
First they moved the telescope on and off the source of the signal to
make sure they could rule out ground-based interference, and then
they checked to see if the "remote follow-up" at Jodrell Bank,
halfway round the world in Cheshire, England, had also picked up
the signal. It seldom took more than a couple of minutes to unmask
a false positive (that is, a signal heard at one listening post but not
the other), at which point people's moods instantly deflated. Still,
with each new star plucked from the Phoenix shortlist, hope flick-
ered into life once more. And so the observational shifts proceeded,
through a succession of emotional ups and downs, with hope succeeding disappointment, succeeding hope.

The evening I saw Pioneer 10, I looked on as Shostak tapped
away on various keyboards to guide the telescope to its target before
retreating to a back room, where he stationed himself in front of a
couple of computer consoles. Outside in the fading light, the supersensitive receiver, suspended on a 900-ton platform hundreds of feet
above the giant dish, responded to his bidding and slowly slewed into
place, clanking and whirring as it did so. The effect of this distinctive
sound was remarkable; like a call to the faithful, it instantly drew all
and sundry to Shostak's side at the consoles. A few moments passed
as electromagnetic radiation from the stars was translated into electrical information in the control room and, before long, what looked
like a blizzard of snowflakes manifested itself on-screen.

It was odd to think that all that mechanical power possessed by the
awesome arrangement of machinery in the jungle beyond the window
ended up being converted into such gentle graphics, with each
"snowflake" representing a point source of electromagnetic radiation.
But the best was yet to come, for when Pioneer 10 showed up on-
screen, making parallel tracks in the snow, joined at regular intervals
by horizontal struts, it put me in mind of nothing so much as Jacob's

ladder—the Biblical bridge linking Heaven and Earth that so well served the purposes of two-way communication. Had Pioneer 10 taken the form of any other archetypal symbol—a circle, say, or a swastika—it would have tugged equally well at emotions buried deep in the unconscious mind. But that it should take the form of the very thing it aspired to model itself on functionally was almost too much. Gazing at the screen in front of me, as Shostak chattered merrily on, I understood why the astronomers found its appearance so moving.

SETI is often compared to a religion—usually, it must be said, by its critics. But, in fairness, the resemblance holds, largely because of the seeking and searching that underpins the enterprise, technically and metaphorically. Unlike other scientific experiments, SETI searches do not yield conclusions (at least they haven't so far). They just elaborate on methodology. At best, they suggest that a particular star or a particular part of the sky may be discounted as a rich hunting ground for alien intelligence—and then, only discounted using this very specific and narrow method for divining its existence.

It takes a certain kind of scientist to work for such minimal rewards, staking professional gratification on the very long odds of stumbling across a genuine beacon beamed our way from afar. But according to Shostak, most people make the mistake of focusing on the product (the signal) at the expense of the process (the searching, and all the theorizing and computer customizing that that involves). Over the course of my stay in Puerto Rico, Shostak kept comparing Arecibo to a monastery, suggesting that it was a place where SETI astronomers enacted their devotions, sharpened their minds, and reaffirmed their conviction that, somewhere down the line, the signal would one day come. Sure, they'd be disappointed every time what looked like a promising candidate signal turned out to be interference, whether from a radar, satellite, cell phone, aircraft, or even another observatory. But at the end of the day, it was the searching itself, daily repeated like the round of prayers running from matins through vespers, that sustained them.

Nowhere is the fundamental religiosity of SETI more evident than in Sagan's *Contact*—a novel, first published in 1985, that argues, against its own avowed scientism, that reason pursued to its extreme will eventually come full circle to meet faith. The irony of this unlikely epistemological shakeout will not be lost on readers who've noted how deliberately Sagan set about styling the novel's heroine, Ellie Arroway (a convincing blend of himself and Jill Tarter, who was Sagan's close friend), as a passionate skeptic: the effort palpably strains the book's pages.

SETI astronomers pride themselves on their skepticism. At Arecibo, Tarter had lectured me on its importance to the integrity of the SETI process. "By being skeptical, we make sure that the requirements for an acceptable signal are very stringent," she said—her command of matters gentle but absolute. "We expect to find noise, and in the face of that expectation the signal has to prove itself to us." The point is, however, and Sagan knew it, that once a signal succeeds in proving itself, this wall of skepticism comes crashing down, disintegrating into foamy insubstantiality like a wave melting to nothing on the seashore. In its place there is only a longing for communion.

In *Contact*, Ellie Arroway detects just such a signal, which distinguishes itself from the background noise of the cosmos by booming out a repeating sequence of prime numbers. Beneath this beacon lies a deep-level message, which, once decoded, proves to contain instructions for building some kind of marvelous traveling machine. The device transports Ellie and several of her colleagues through an elaborate network of interstellar passageways or "wormholes," depositing them right at the galactic center where Ellie, who finds herself on a miragelike beach, encounters a representative of an alien supercivilization. This gentle creature, who comes to her in the visible form of her beloved but long-dead father, explains that his race has been busy restructuring the universe in order to slow down its rate of expansion. But despite performing such God-like feats, he claims that he and his kind are no more than Caretakers: their business is to stabilize the universe and to maintain the intergalactic way stations and highways that an even more advanced race of Tunnel Builders constructed long ago.

On her return to Earth, Ellie is infused with an extraordinary sense of interconnectedness; she feels at one with the species and the cosmos, much as if she had experienced a revelation. Unfortunately, all the scientific evidence of her trip has unaccountably disappeared, which rather turns the tables on things. Now she is the believer and the rest of the world a gallery of skeptics against whose arguments she is able to brandish nothing more than her faith. "Here I am, the bearer of a profound religious experience I can't prove," she says, pointing out the frustration of her situation to her preacher friend Palmer Joss.

Now if the novel had ended here, on this interesting and equivocal note, it would have raised valid questions about the nature and limitations of scientific knowledge. And indeed, this is where the movie version starring Jodie Foster ends, leaving audiences with plenty to chew over. But Sagan did not end his novel here. Unable to resist asserting his own faith, he delivers Ellie from the torment of Humean ambiguity by having her discover a universal message numerically encoded within the number pi (the constant ratio relating the circumference of a circle to its diameter) thereby proving that a master intelligence had designed the universe. Ellie's discovery of an artist's signature "built into the fabric of the universe" constitutes the kind of fundamental truth that religions are built on—and of course Ellie's religion is also Sagan's religion. While *Contact* doesn't contain the full credo, it does set forth one of its central tenets: "Part of my message," says Ellie, "is that we're not central to the purpose of the cosmos. What happened to me makes us all seem very small."

I sometimes wonder whether Sagan, who repeatedly invoked a

wide-eyed reverence for the cosmic depths in order to disabuse us of a misplaced sense of self-importance, ever read Gaston Bachelard, the French scientist turned *philosophe* who famously attempted to scale our relationship to the universe. Intent on pinning down the psychic tic that leads us to look toward the vast heavens for personal meaning, Bachelard suggested that there exists a correspondence between external immensity and inner intensity. When someone meditates on the infinite universe, he argued, something of its grandeur is conferred on him or her, and he or she experiences an expansion of being. In this quasi-religious state, the mind, freed from its own kind of gravity, is able to experience a new purity. Probing deep space thus becomes akin to searching for one's soul.

This kernel of Bachelard's thinking is echoed over and over by Sagan, not just in *Contact*, but in his numerous books on astronomy and cosmology as well as in *Cosmos*, the landmark television series that made him a household name. Sagan positively delighted in reminding people of the stark post-Copernican extent of our cosmic insignificance. He was fond of referring to the Earth with flat disparagement, calling it a clod or hunk of metal and rock and, in his later years, a pale blue dot, and he would use his legendary oratorical eloquence to expound on how irrelevant in the grand scheme of things was virtually everything that happened here. None of this is meant to imply, however, that Sagan thought life was cheap. Far from it: for in spite of his Darwinian conviction that mankind was neither the first, nor the last, nor the brightest, nor the best in the universe, mankind was what we were and what we should therefore learn to love. All that cosmic melodrama he loved to evoke, like an ancient God taunting his wayward children with thunderclaps and floods, was really Sagan's way of saying how precious mankind was.

Sagan was an exemplary model of the kind of agnostic seeker that Bachelard had in mind when he developed his peculiarly spiritual thesis. His intellectual obsession with cosmic infinity was fundamentally inward-looking. Everything out there, he believed, rebounded back on us. If we just let the universe fill us with awe, we would be both aggrandized by it and, at the same time, calmly reconciled to our limitations. In fact, Sagan had originally wanted to call his television series *Man and the Cosmos* in recognition of this two-way correspondence, but after his wife, Ann Druyan, convinced him the title was sexist, he dropped the idea. Had Sagan lived long enough to see Pathfinder and experience Mars interactively, as the rest of us did, I'm convinced he would have extended his insights to eulogize the extraordinary sense of bi-location we felt as we simultaneously experienced being there and being here. Sadly, he died just months earlier, but not before he managed to get *Contact* made into a film, and not before he got Voyager to pay one last homage to Earth.

Having built a towering career out of helping us learn to feel at home in an indifferent cosmos, near the end of his life Sagan turned his attention back toward the Earth. In fairly rapid succession he published three books that fixed mankind at the center of his concerns, as an evanescent, frequently misguided, but nonetheless potent life force. At the same time, he began urging NASA to turn Voyager around so that its camera could snap one last shot of the Earth. More than fifteen years had passed since Sagan had stood on Florida's beaches and watched the space probe tear into the skies on its one-way journey to the stars. Now, as it neared the outer limit of the solar system, he longed for it to glance back toward home, just once—before it grew too late to capture the Earth's "pale blue dot." NASA eventually complied with Sagan's wishes, but only after fussing over whether Voyager's sensitive instruments could survive pointing straight into the Sun: the result was a blurry picture in which the Earth appears as a pinprick crescent only 0.12 pixels in size.

It was absolutely typical of Sagan to want to leave posterity not with a glorious frame-filling image of our lush green-blue world—of the kind Apollo bequeathed us, with its conflicting connotations of mankind's Promethean prowess and ultimate fragility—but rather with the boggling thought that the grandeur (and folly) of all human existence could be contained by an insignificant speck at the edge of the galactic swirl. Transcending this, he seemed to imply, was an existential matter, and not the province of a technological fix.

In the wake of the film *Contact*, Jill Tarter found herself famous. The phone lines at the SETI Institute were jammed for weeks, and Arecibo became what travel agents call a "destination." The media lapped up everything to do with SETI: to journalists and broadcasters the very idea of searching for aliens rationally seemed unconventional, wayward, sexy. SETI scientists weren't used to this. Accustomed to seeing themselves as a beleaguered group, an easy target for congressional cuts and for cheap quips about hunting for Little Green Men, they tended to come across in interviews as cautious, even defensive. They were certainly not nearly as enamored of the media as it was of them.

It was also clear that many of them still hadn't recovered from the shock of being blindsided by NASA. For decades, NASA's funding of SETI had been patchy and nervous, but after Nevada Senator Richard Bryan, a longtime SETI foe, led a successful campaign to ax SETI funding for the fiscal year of 1993, NASA never again went to bat for SETI in Congress, and government funding for Project Phoenix and other searches has never been restored. The space agency claims to bear SETI no animus, yet to this day it scrupulously omits any mention of radio searches whenever it promotes its own Origins Program, a high-profile, interdepartmental effort dedicated to searching for evidence of life elsewhere in the solar system via the exclusive employment of smart probes. Considering that two of the three Mars probes launched since Pathfinder have been unmitigated failures, disappearing unaccountably before landing, the agency may come to regret shortchanging SETI, now the most prominent torchbearer for a virtual Space Age.

Although SETI was subsequently rescued through the private support of a handful of Silicon Valley moguls, including Intel's Gordon Moore and Microsoft co-founder Paul Allen, SETI scientists still chafe at their official exclusion from the space establishment. Being part of NASA gave them a certain respectability that they are unwilling to relinquish, even though the tech community leaders who gallantly stepped in to fill the funding void are offering a far more ambitious vision for SETI. From their point of view, tuning in to an alien signal would be the apotheosis of the communications revolution they themselves ushered in, the ultimate in long-distance dialing. Already, a handful of commercial enterprises like Starlite offer to hook up the internet to the stars. But the siliconaires know that in this area, SETI has no equal, since it is not the messages we transmit that will bring about an epistemological revolution. It's the reply.

At the SETI Institute in Mountain View, California, the atmosphere is distinctly familial. Talk to one scientist there and he or she suddenly grows concerned that you should be talking to someone else, as if each of them were interchangeable or, at the least, just one more cog in the wheels that keep SETI interests turning. Conducting interviews there, I quickly sensed that the cause was more important than its individual champions, who appeared by and large to give themselves up to it, like nuns or monks taking holy orders. It is certainly true that once admitted to the ranks of the community scientists seldom leave without first dying.

But while the SETI community is very much an insider's realm, made up of friends and colleagues whose associations go back years, it understands the value of repaying loyal hangers-on. Plenty of part-timers and volunteers have won a place within the fold through sheer persistence, and they continue their cheerleading on an almost daily basis. It's the turncoats who are not easily accommodated. Every important book on the subject of SETI, for example, has expressed puzzlement, sadness, or dismay at the defection of Soviet

SETI scientist Iosif Shklovsky, who co-wrote the influential pro-SETI tome *Intelligent Life in the Universe* with Carl Sagan, but who later took a dim view of our chances of ever establishing contact with extraterrestrial civilizations.

At the center of it all, presiding over his clan like a watchful paterfamilias, sits Frank Drake, the founder of the discipline. In 1960, Drake, then a young research scientist at the National Radio Astronomy Observatory in Green Bank, West Virginia, decided to act on an experimental whim he'd been wanting to test out for some time. He trained the antenna of the observatory's 85-foot telescope onto two nearby stars, hooked up the amplifier to a pen and chart recorder, donned headphones, and began to listen. He was hoping to find radio emissions that bore the mark of intelligence; signals, in other words, that had been manufactured. Sweeping his single-channel receiver up and down the microwave band at 1420 MHz, the frequency of neutral hydrogen, where interference is minimal, Drake spent several weeks listening for extraterrestrial signals, stopping only when he was satisfied he'd reached the limits of what he could do with such basic technology. Thus was SETI born.

The timing of the Green Bank search is important; for while space exploration was officially being given over to the money-guzzling theatrics of state-sponsored corporate science, here was a venturesome astronomer gamely conducting space science on the wing, using whatever equipment came to hand. That, at least, is how the SETI mythmakers would have it.

Since then, the quietly spoken Drake, now seventy-one, silver haired and bearing a more than passing resemblance to Ernest Borgnine, has applied what energy he could to SETI research while holding such prestigious positions as lecturer in astronomy at Cornell University and director of the Arecibo Observatory. When he was offered the position of chairman of the board of the SETI Institute in 1984, Drake was finally able to assume the full responsibilities, emotional as well as practical, of heading up this strange *cosmo nostro*. It is a role he clearly enjoys, even if he is rather too open to the flattery of die-hard SETI fans. If the mood takes him, for example, you may catch him referring to himself, albeit with the winking swashbuckle of Indiana Jones, as the "Protector of the Truth." Yet, beneath the playfulness, this romantic title is a testament to the seriousness with which Drake intends, even now, to continue fighting in SETI's corner, defending it against pseudo-science, misplaced mysticism, and the occasional sniggering from the ranks of academia.

"I cannot accept that we're alone in the universe," Drake told me when I spoke to him in the institute's dimly lit boardroom, "and no one will ever prove that we are." He chuckled throatily, pleased with his own conundrum. Drake, of course, is equally unable to prove the opposite at present, but he does a pretty good job of trying. He was extremely convincing, for example, in a public debate held in Silicon Valley in the spring of 2001, where he banged heads with University of Washington geologist Peter Ward, co-author of *Rare Earth*—a book that garnered a huge amount of publicity when it was published the previous year because it makes the currently unfashionable argument that life is extremely rare, if not entirely unique to this planet.

During the debate, Drake shared the podium with a single potted Madagascar orchid of a type known as *Angraecum sesquipedale*. This orchid is characterized by having a long tube dangling from its flower that is roughly a foot in length and inside of which is hidden a stash of nectar. At one time the plant had fascinated Charles Darwin, who was baffled that its nectar was so inaccessible when this class of orchid was known to be insect-pollinated. Darwin determined that there must exist a species of moth with a proboscis long enough to reach the nectar. That was in 1862. Forty-one years later, his prediction was confirmed when an unusual-looking moth was found in Madagascar: the color of a dead leaf, it had a wingspan of five inches and a proboscis ten inches long.

Drake told his audience that he wished to celebrate this instance of parallel evolution, where one life-form needed the other and could not exist without it. Life, he announced, is extremely audacious; wherever it can, it finds extraordinary ways to adapt. Making a quick calculation, I realized that the forty-one-year gap between prediction and confirmation was precisely the amount of time that had elapsed between the Green Bank search and the debate I was hearing. Was I getting carried away with magic numbers, or had Drake chosen to tell this story because he believed in its talismanic quality? I never got the chance to ask him and in any case it didn't matter much, because the story did the job of captivating the crowd, whose members were invited to extrapolate from the exoticism of parallel evolution to the mind-bending possibilities of exobiology (or extraterrestrial biology).

In recent years, Drake has thrilled from the sidelines as extrasolar planets have begun popping up with surprising regularity on astronomers' radars. He has always believed that the galaxy contains "many planets like the Earth that have given rise to a diversity of life-forms we cannot imagine." And yet the evidence offered by extra-solar planets is purely circumstantial; it ups the probability that life exists elsewhere without constituting the least bit of proof. The same goes for analogical arguments based on evolutionary history. Even if biologists were able to prove that evolution has selected for intelligence on Earth (and as yet, they cannot), they would still never know if the example of Earth's fossil record is typical, because it remains the sole example we've got. Only a signal would tell us for sure that intelligence thrives elsewhere in the cosmos. The problem is—at least it is a problem for a culture that wants results—SETI hasn't been able to find one.

Drake isn't worrying about it. "I don't fight it," he says. "I always tell people that the chances of success on any given day are very small—it may take decades, it may take centuries. At the same time, I'd hate to think we'd miss the signal because we weren't looking in the right place or in the right manner." Thus, in the twilight of his professional years, Drake has begun agitating for a broadening of the

SETI sieve to take in infrared and laser searches. It was not so long ago that SETI scientists stood aloof from a whatever-it-takes approach, feeling that they'd only begun to explore the possibilities of using radio. Now they're thinking again. I suspect, though, that in Drake's case the change of heart betrays a deeper yearning, since for all his rationalizing and scientific circumspection, his bet hedging and avowals of skepticism, his historical perspective and his track record in more conventional areas of astronomy, what he would like more than anything else is to see a bona fide signal arrive in his lifetime.

Given the ardor of most SETI astronomers, it is remarkable that they've collectively demonstrated so much restraint over forty-one years of seeking a signal and not finding it. These are people who walk, talk, eat, think, and sleep signal, and yet in all this time only a couple of overzealous astronomers have fallen foul of the illusion that they've actually found one.

And that's not counting the drama of the night of August 15, 1977, when an interesting-looking signal made its presence felt as the constellation of Sagittarius was passing over Ohio State University's "Big Ear" radio telescope. The signal, which produced a huge spike in intensity right beside the hydrogen line (a protected radio bandwidth that is out of bounds for terrestrial communication needs) and which turned itself on and off like a beacon, lasted just as long as it would take for a star to pass through the telescope's view. It was exactly the sort of signal that SETI scientists predict an alien civilization would send. Noticing what was happening, the stunned duty astronomer wrote "Wow!" on the margin of the computer printout. But the signal never repeated itself, despite weeks and months of subsequent searching. To this day, no one knows what lay behind the "Wow!" signal, and although it appeared just once, flaring brightly for but an instant, SETI scientists still consider it to be one of the all-time best candidate signals.

An altogether more dramatic cry positive took place in 1964, when Soviet radio astronomer Nikolai Kardashev called an international press conference to announce that he had found a supercivilization broadcasting from the far-off constellation of Pegasus. Now if anyone at the time was going to find a signal, you could have put money on its being the Soviets. They invested in SETI far more heavily than the Americans throughout the sixties and seventies, even if they employed more basic telescopes, consisting not of dishes that fed a concentrated beam into a strategically placed feed, but of wire antennae mounted on posts. Spurred on by the edgy competitiveness of the Cold War, the Soviets may well have viewed the decisive capture of an alien signal as an opportunity to run ahead of Western scientists in a second and very different space race. But the simpler explanation is that while Drake and his colleagues were battling for credibility, the Soviet scientific community had little trouble grasping the idea that a search for alien intelligence might be a rational thing to support and, as a result, they embraced SETI energetically.

Kardashev was Iosif Shklovsky's star pupil at the Sternberg Astronomical Institute in Moscow. A direct beneficiary of the state-sponsored push to get SETI up, running, and triumphing in the USSR, he spearheaded the first Soviet search in 1963, and a year later he organized a conference in Armenia for Soviet scientists interested in ETI. Formal, portentous, and boasting plenty of high-profile participants, the conference was typical of the grandiosity with which the Soviets intended to practice SETI. With an official verve of which the Americans could only dream, the authorities put themselves at Kardashev's disposal, and immediately he set about building a coordinated network of telescopes across the USSR, stretching east to west from Vladivostok on the Sea of Japan to Murmansk, near the Finnish border.

Kardashev was clearly someone who made things happen—searches, conferences, telescope networks—someone who knew how to play the system. But his real passion was theory, and to this end he made bold predictions about the kind of extraterrestrial life-forms that might exist throughout the universe, devising a taxonomy of alien civilizations that ranked them according to their skill in obtaining energy.

At the bottom of the heap languished Type I civilizations, essentially our technological peers. Like us, these simpletons are able to utilize only what energy radiates their way from the Sun, whether in the form of sun-enriched hydrocarbon molecules like petroleum or natural gas, the heat gradient that causes winds or tides, or direct photovoltaic energy—and then, if they really are like us, much of that energy would still escape them. Type II civilizations, which may be millions or even billions of years in advance of us, are able to exploit all of the energy that their sun radiates. In characterizing such civilizations, Kardashev probably had in mind an idea popularized by the physicist Freeman Dyson in 1959. Dyson proposed that advanced, energy-hungry civilizations might be able to redistribute planetary material in such a way as to construct giant spheres around their parent stars, in order to trap and draw all their available light and heat. Finally, at the top of the developmental tree are Type III civilizations, veritable masters of the universe who think nothing of turning a cluster of stars in their galaxy into a kind of cosmic power plant.

In 1964 Kardashev thought he'd stumbled upon a Type II civilization.

It was while he was examining cosmic radio sources at the Crimea Deep Space Station with his colleague Evgeny Sholomitsky that Kardeshev's quarry first revealed itself to him. A clearly extraterrestrial source of radio waves of a type never seen before was pulsing in the vicinity of CTA-102 (or radio source number 102 listed in Caltech Catalog A). At first blush it wasn't the sort of signal you'd expect from an alien civilization; broadband rather than narrow, it didn't much resemble a beacon. And yet its principal emission frequency of 900 megahertz was one that Kardashev considered optimal for interstellar communication, in that it represents a tiny oasis of quiet bounded on one side by cosmic noise and on the other by quantum noise. If anything was emitting here, Kardashev concluded, it deserved closer attention.

The evidence that really swayed him, however, was Sholomitsky's study of the signal's variations in intensity, which showed that the emissions from CTA-102 fluctuated in a regular 100-day cycle. Plot this on a graph and you get a perfect sine curve; the object, in other words, pulsed steadily. For months the two astronomers tracked the signal and it rewarded them with an unvarying pattern. It was a regular cosmic clock, and its source was so powerful that Kardashev could not help but imagine a Type II civilization thriving around CTA-102.

The fact that CTA-102 was optically invisible only heightened his suspicions, because the beauty of a Type II civilization is that it emits no light (who knew what feats a Type III civilization might be capable of?). Having harnessed all the energy of its home star, perhaps even enclosing it within a Dyson sphere, it would appear to the ordinary observer to be shrouded in darkness. Dyson had predicted that such a civilization would betray itself only by the trail of waste heat that its technological activities produced and that the place to detect this "exhaust" energy would be the infrared region of the spectrum. Sure enough, when CTA-102 was put to the test, it revealed itself at the violet end of the infrared band.

Against the wait-and-see advice of the more senior Shklovsky, Kardashev and Sholomitsky rushed to announce their find, using the high-profile SETI conference in Armenia as a springboard. They were hoping to make a splash and they did. The news attracted worldwide press coverage and worldwide astronomical scrutiny. Though not unwelcome, the process of peer review proved to be the Soviets' undoing, overturning their claims within a matter of months.

In April 1965, six months after it announced Kardashev's gold strike, the *New York Times* ran a second article reporting that CTA-102 had been identified as a new class of astronomical object known as a quasar, or quasi-stellar object. Quasars appear at first to be stars, but in fact they are turbulent galaxies at the outer edge of the universe that are receding from us at great speeds. Each one of them has an energy output equivalent to hundreds of billions of stars. It is now thought that quasars have black holes at their cores that swallow up the matter in the galaxy, causing intense radio emissions of the kind the Soviets picked up. However, the interesting history of CTA-102 doesn't quite end here, because the *New York Times* coverage of the mysterious radio source was unwittingly responsible for entwining an altogether different set of claims into the story.

Enter Betty and Barney Hill, an educated, mixed-race couple from New Hampshire, who claimed to have been abducted by aliens in 1961 while driving home from a vacation in Canada. After spotting a bright star that appeared to be following them, they stopped the car to get a better look. Then Barney got out, taking his binoculars. Focusing his instrument on the light, he resolved the star into a spaceship whose occupants could be seen staring at him from behind a large window. Terrified, he ran back to the car and sped himself and his wife away, but not before they heard a "beeping" sound and felt a strange "drowsiness" come over them. They arrived home toward dawn, some two hours later than they had been expecting to get back.

The Hill case has long intrigued ufologists because it is the first documented instance of "missing time." But what supposedly happened during those two lost hours did not come to light until 1963, when Boston hypnotherapist Benjamin Simon treated the couple. Betty had been having terrible nightmares ever since the UFO sighting, and Barney had been suffering anxiety attacks bad enough to give him ulcers. Neither had responded to conventional medical treatment, and through a series of referrals they were led to Simon.

Under hypnosis, Betty and Barney, who were seen separately, related how they'd been captured by the aliens—stocky gray creatures with long noses—and subjected to a range of crypto-medical examinations aboard the UFO. Betty complained that she'd been prodded, probed, and stripped, that the aliens had attempted to extract her teeth, and that they'd stuck a needle into her navel, causing her intense pain. At the end of this ordeal, she'd asked the alien "leader" where it came from, and it obliged her by showing her a "sky map," which she drew for Simon, complete with various lines representing "trade routes" connecting the different stars. By now, Simon had drawn his own conclusions. While he did not doubt the Hills' integrity, nor the genuine trauma they'd experienced, he believed the case to be a folie à deux—a shared delusion in which each person leads the other further down the path of self-deception.

Following her treatment, Betty became active in UFO study groups. She bought books about astronomy, and together with Barney, she made cathartic visits to the site of their abduction. Then she read the *New York Times* article about Kardashev's supercivilization and instantly recognized her own UFO star map in the drawing of the constellation Pegasus that was published to show the position of CTA-102. She quickly concluded that the Soviet's pulsing radio source was a beacon to guide the aliens back to their home star of Zeta Pegasi. Establishing this link in time for it to be included in John Fuller's *The Interrupted Journey* (the 1966 best-selling account of the Hills' abduction experience), Betty unleashed a flurry of public interest in her star map, even though the first round of excitement about CTA-102 had by then died down.

Two amateur astronomers, Marjorie Fish and Charles Atterberg, independently set about trying to discover precisely which piece of the cosmic jigsaw Betty was in privileged possession of. Fish pored over star atlases, concentrating on sunlike stars; she visited Betty, from whom she learnt that the map was three dimensional and holographic, and she built elaborate mobiles, using weights suspended on strings. Eventually Fish concluded that the aliens' home star was in fact a double star called Zeta Reticuli. Atterberg, meanwhile, came up with a very different map. His took in the three stars that Carl Sagan had identified in the book he wrote with Shklovsky as being the "nearest stars of potential biological interest."

Then Robert Sheaffer entered the fray. A computer-systems programmer working at NASA's Goddard Space Flight Center and a noted debunker of UFOs, Sheaffer plotted the positions of the planets in the northern sky for the night Betty and Barney Hill were supposedly abducted and concluded that the bright moving light that struck terror in their souls had all along been the planet Jupiter.

With its endless twists and frequent comic turns, the story of CTA-102 is something of an embarrassment to today's SETI scientists, concerned, as ever, with respectability. Even without the Hills' involvement, the CTA-102 fiasco is bad science. Kardashev so much wanted to believe that he had located a Type II civilization that he conducted his research in reverse, selecting only what empirical evidence fitted his theory and ignoring the rest. It's a pitfall that is easy enough to fall into for astronomers moved as much by faith as by curiosity.

Indeed, Sagan himself was at one time convinced that he had found E.T.

It was in the late eighties, and Sagan had just helped secure funding for Harvard SETI scientist Paul Horowitz, his friend and colleague, to undertake a high-powered multichannel radio search of the skies at the Oak Ridge telescope near Boston. He had even inspired Steven Spielberg to donate $100,000 to the cause. Among the candidate signals that Horowitz's data-crunching processors offered up in the very first weeks of the search, there were several that refused to be explained away by any other means: a series of signals clustered along the galactic plane. Sagan was sure these were intelligent in origin (for no other reason than the galactic plane was where he had always believed that life lurked undetected), and were it not for Horowitz's insistence on caution, he would most likely have blustered into print. As it was, he kept his counsel. The cause of the signals, however, was never resolved.

Because we cannot travel to the stars to verify our experimental hunches, we require them to speak to us, to offer up their secrets in hints and allusions, by means of bottled messages and energy traces. Obviously the margin for error is enormous. But while SETI scientists tend to differ in their thinking about how the signal will arrive, where it will come from, what it will look like, and whether or not we stand a chance in hell of ever decoding it, one thing they agree on is that for practical purposes (probes notwithstanding), nothing more than information may be transferred between the stars. For this reason, they cannot abide being tainted, as they see it, by association with believers in UFOs, contactees, abductees, and other sad, deluded, or mystically misguided souls. They don't even talk about aliens—only extraterrestrials—since aliens belong to pop culture and not to science.

And yet, as Betty Hill's entanglement in the Kardashev story suggests, the line is more often than not blurred. After all, who is to say whether Hill's exuberant projections about aliens, star maps, and trade routes are any more or any less valid than Kardashev's wish-fulfilling fantasies about supercivilizations? Both loop directly into Space Age expectations of a universe populated by star-farers and colonizers, tunnel builders and energy hoggers—expectations so ingrained that they color our very perception of the universe. The Hill-Kardashev conjunction also suggests that regardless of what clothes it wears (science, religion, mythology), the slow-to-evolve human psyche still has trouble adjusting to the post-Copernican reality of our loneliness, inconsequentiality, and ultimate smallness. Not everyone, after all, is big enough, as was Sagan, to see the grandeur in that. Besides, SETI is not above peddling its own brand of cosmic mysticism.

In 1971, after more than a decade of stop-start searching and shoe-string funding, disheartened SETI scientists in America were finally given leave to let their spirits soar and allow their religious imaginations to roam free among the stars. The source of inspiration came from an unlikely quarter: a scientific report called *Project Cyclops*. Written by Bernard Oliver (a singularly eminent computer engineer who directed Hewlett-Packard's R&D lab and led the team that developed the pocket calculator), with some help from NASA SETI scientist John Billingham, the report had the ostensible goal of persuading NASA to invest $20 billion—real Space Age money—in constructing a giant array of radio telescopes powerful enough to scan far-off galaxies. This was SETI throwing down the gauntlet to Big Science; it was make or break, join us or forsake us, do or die. And, of course, it failed. But the report did furnish SETI with a mystical endgame scenario that many scientists within the community cherish to this day: the Encyclopedia Galactica. Oliver and his NASA-funded research team envisaged the Encyclopedia Galactica as an immaterial and protean pool of universal knowledge, which, in so far as it exists at all, exists as a series of ghostly vibrations amid the cosmic airwaves. Tune into it, they claimed, and you can eavesdrop on the chatter of ancient civilizations that have been in contact with one another for eons.

Oliver believed that mankind stood to gain a great deal from partaking in this "extensive heavenly discourse" because he took it for granted that civilizations that managed to develop beyond that phase of "technological infancy" when societies are inclined to flirt with self-destruction would not only be long-lived, but would possess all those fairy-tale qualities that we tend to attach to longevity: wisdom, patience, benevolence, selflessness, and so on. Perhaps, he ventured, they had even discovered the secret of immortality. What seemed beyond dispute was that through their (virtual) mutual contact they would have compiled a free-floating library containing nothing less than "the totality of the natural and social histories of countless planets and the species that evolved: a sort of cosmic archeological record of our Galaxy ... that would make plain the origin and fate of the universe." This was godly knowledge indeed, and as Oliver saw it, it was there for the taking, at least for races clever enough to find ways to tap it. As if further incentive were needed, he enthused, "Access to this 'galactic heritage' may well prove to be the salvation of any race whose technological prowess qualifies it."

Leaving aside for a moment this teasing post–Space Age prospect of salvation without ascension, what is truly remarkable is the extent to which Oliver's vision of a fluid congregation of pure minds reads like a manifesto for the internet twenty years before the fact. Not long before Cyclops was proposed, the U.S. Department of Defense's Advanced Research Projects Agency (ARPA) had begun funding a small group of unorthodox computer programmers and engineers who believed there was a future in what they called "interactive computing," and who swiftly developed an interlinked communications network that allowed government research agencies to interact directly with their military (and later aerospace) contractors. ARPAnet was of course the forerunner of the internet, but it took a full two decades before interactive personal computers became available to citizen-users. As Howard Rheingold, who has studied the rise and influence of virtual communities, points out, the computer-using population first had to expand from "a priesthood in the 1950s, to an elite in the 1960s, to a subculture in the 1970s." In fact, long before the public learnt to surf the web, university professors and research scientists alike reveled in the internet as an exclusive club where like-minded people could congregate and exchange ideas—if not an Encyclopedia Galactica, then perhaps an Encyclopedia Scholastica.

Once crawler software like Mosaic (the technology behind Netscape's search engines) enabled the explosive development of the world wide web, the idea of disparate minds achieving near spiritual communion went public, thereby sustaining an ideal that the Space Age never could, because the Space Age never allowed for participation. Admittedly, the new mind-space has what you might call an ontological problem (of a similar order to that of the Encyclopedia Galactica)—namely, its existence is purely ethereal. Even William

Gibson, who coined the term "cyberspace" in his 1984 novel *Neuro-mancer*, had to concede that the new frontier his "console cowboys" spent their energies pioneering was nothing more than a "consensual hallucination." And yet it is because rather than in spite of its funda-mental immateriality that cyberspace has proved to be as engrossing an elsewhere as outer space, and it is both capacious enough and suf-ficiently "real" for it to accommodate an almost wholesale trans-planting of our extraterrestrial ambitions.

Of these, perhaps the most tenacious is the belief that we might start over somewhere new and realize the utopias we've always dreamt of but never quite managed to build here on Earth. Since its inception, cyberspace has been a breeding ground for neotribalism, with every minority group you can think of rushing to stake its claim in the ether and attempting—through Usenet groups, bulletin boards, chat rooms, and conferencing—the kind of mind-meld that is just not possible in a world handicapped by terrestrial geography. Commenting on the success of such colonizing efforts, techno-utopians tend to reach for hyperbole: cyberspace, they will tell you, is a New Eden where all may eat from the Tree of Knowledge with-out fear of punishment or persecution (for which, read censorship). Or it's a Heavenly City, where our virtual selves can rise like souls immortal to new heights of fulfillment, commune with kindred spir-its, and, as in Alphaworld, create and destroy worlds at will. Such are their hopes for the new deep space.

The archetype for many of these budding cyber-utopias, however, began life more modestly in 1985, when Stewart Brand (who'd been so vocal a proponent of O'Neillean space colonies in the seventies) took possession of a VAX minicomputer the size of a fridge and the PicoSpan software needed to run it and invited readers of his *Whole Earth Catalog* to log on. Both the hardware and software were dona-tions from Larry Brilliant, a Michigan-based vendor of computer conferencing equipment who approached Brand in the first place, correctly surmising that the Sausalito-based intellectual magpie and avowed technophile would give him access to a ready-made user base. The result of this collaboration was the Whole Earth 'Lectronic Link, or the WELL for short.

Brilliant's conferencing equipment would prove to be the key to a groundbreaking exercise in community building whose success has since become legendary among cybernauts. At the outset, however, it was not at all clear what would transpire when people dialed up their modems and began to participate in electronic discussions that ranged over topics as diverse as parenting and politics, or hacking and earthquakes. Only with time did it become apparent that people would bring to online conferencing the same passion they brought to real-life interactions, that they'd hang out for hours in the WELL's virtual pub, that personalities would emerge and that (eventually) the bonds people forged between one another via their modems would be cemented offline.

As a business, the WELL never managed to progress beyond meeting its operational costs, but as an experiment in living it excelled itself. In the eyes of user Roman Sender Barayon, who thought of the community as "a disembodied tribe," the WELL's break with convention was equivalent in boldness to the Open Land communes of the sixties. The WELL was also a statistical success, with membership growing from a few hundred in 1985 to 2,000 in 1987 and more than 3,000 by the end of the decade. Many users habitually spent five to six hours a day on the WELL, giving and receiving advice, swapping medical opinions, and helping one another with work or research. Then, as the community developed more of a sense of itself, users began to tap it in order to raise money for the treatment of sick "WELLbeings," mobilize support for direct action campaigns such as freeway cleanups, or to address issues pertaining to the WELL's internal affairs. "The WELL took over my life," Howard Rheingold confessed recently to WELL biographer Katie Hafner. The point is, for WELLbeings like Rheingold, immersed in life online, the WELL didn't mirror reality; it *was* reality.

The WELL set the standard for the all-or-nothing immersiveness and participation that subsequent cyber-communities would come to demand from their users. Rheingold himself went on to found just such a community, Brainstorms, where conversations followed the same threaded, linear model established by the WELL. Because for a brief time I was a member of Brainstorms, I can personally vouch for the fact that the conferences were stimulating and the communards welcoming. But enjoyable as I found the experience of having instant access to an incessant stream of juicy real-time banter, I couldn't commit myself to this virtual life in a convincing enough manner (I simply didn't post frequently enough—didn't grab or add enough ideas from or to the ether), and my account was quietly terminated. It was a virtual death of sorts, even if I was not much inclined to mourn it. Although I could understand the buzz that cyber-critic Erik Davis calls our "ecstasy of communication," I didn't feel it.

I think Davis is right when he suggests that part of what drives so many netheads in their quest for information rapture is an unconscious expectation that our increasingly incorporeal information systems are expanding consciousness itself. For many programmers and cyber-theorists, not to mention many SETI@home users, the ecstasy Davis describes is just more confirmation that the compact between mind and machine extends beyond sharing mechanisms of information-processing to embrace a mystical spiritualism: networking, in other words, is the new mind-expansion, and it is every bit as trippy as the old-fashioned, chemical kind. It was exactly this kind of mysticism that Umberto Eco wrote about in his novel *Foucault's Pendulum*, in which the lead character gives his laptop the name of a renowned medieval Kabbalist before diving into the data stream to trace the tangled web of connections among Freemasons, Rosicrucians, Illuminati, and Knights Templar, and to experience an information ecstasy that corresponds to the glorious all-as-oneness of divine knowledge. Had Eco known about Bernard Oliver's galactic brotherhood, he would have probably thrown that, too, into his techno-

spiritual stew. As it was, he seemed to be saying that computer technology had opened the door once more onto mysticism. And no
sooner had it opened, than in jumped the whole techno-utopian
crew, raving about "group minds," Gaian forces, and the planetary
consciousness of Teilhard de Chardin.

It is almost impossible to approach this nexus of ideas, where
quasi-religious mysticism meets high-tech culture meets the Space
Age desire for a communion of minds, without touching on the
bizarre group suicide of thirty-nine members of the Heaven's Gate
cult—web page designers who dispatched themselves with a deadly
cocktail of vodka and phenobarbital in order to rendezvous with
their mother ship. The San Diego suicide made headlines across the
globe in the spring of 1997, when the bodies were found in a
markedly theatrical mise-en-scène; draped in purple ceremonial
robes, they were neatly laid out on mattresses and bunks, while suit-
cases containing personal belongings stood sentinel beside each
one—the better to prepare them for life aboard the UFO they
believed had come to take them home. The deliberate staging of the
event, steeped in ritual and melodrama, was shocking. It was made
worse by the media playing and replaying a series of videotaped
recordings that cult members left behind explaining their actions, for
as we watched one buzz-cut believer after another step up to the
camera to elucidate his or her science fiction faith, profound sense of
alienation from the world, and belief that human bodies were merely
dispensable "containers" for our immortal cosmic souls, it became
increasingly difficult to avoid concluding that Heaven's Gate had
died, at least in part, for the cause of infotainment.

From the extraterrestrial perspective, however, the cult's desperation looked somewhat different. It looked, in fact, like just another
case of cosmic homesickness, where the ailing soul, troubled by its
own estrangement from itself and in search of spiritual uplift—and,
ultimately, transcendence—longs to break entirely with Earth's surly
bonds and soar heavenward (recall that Wally Schirra felt that by

giving gravity the slip he'd been born again). Heavens Gate's solution to the problem was of course exceptional. And yet the specific (some would say Gnostic) disdain in which cult members held their physical bodies is shared by a whole raft of techno-extremists convinced that the human body is no more than a faulty and corruptible receptacle for the self and that the next evolutionary step is to discard it. It is now almost an article of faith among fringe technophiles and mainstream artificial-intelligence pioneers alike that the body is merely a husk we need to slough off en route to greater self-realization. MIT's Marvin Minsky calls it a "meat machine." In common with cultish groups like the Extropians (whose techno-fetishistic disciples view all cybernetic aids as evolutionary enhancements), Minsky dreams of a time when we will be able to "upload" ourselves entire, as if we'd just walked off the pages of a William Gibson novel. In true Extropian fashion, he believes that we must move beyond incarnation, grow out of our carbon adolescence into silicon maturity, and meet our posthuman fate as cyborgs. This is a sentiment echoed up and down the virtual corridors of cyberspace by those who wish to escape matter entirely, plunging heart and soul into the new cyber-religiosity. As virtual-reality animator turned cyber-guru Nicole Stenger confided to sociologist Sherry Turkle, "On the other side of our data gloves . . . we will all become angels." The ideal of a fleshless paradise enlivens a great deal of cyber-utopian thinking.

The term "cyborg," incidentally, was actually coined at a NASA conference in the sixties by scientists Nathan Kline and Manfred Clynes, who proposed enhancing astronauts technologically so that they could feel more at home in outer space. But the fleshless paradise of cyberspace, with its "metaphysical economy" (the term comes from cyber-guru Stephan Hoeller) and its promise to separate immortal mind from fallen matter, arrived before space science could make any serious progress with the cyborg dream.

One of the most important documents to argue for cyberspace as a New Eden of the mind was penned in a rage of indignation in 1996 as a direct response to the federal government's attempt to introduce legislation that would impose regulations on the internet. Its author was Wyoming cattle rancher John Perry Barlow. Many cybernauts would sell their grandmothers to Bill Gates for Barlow's credentials. Besides being a genuine cowboy, Barlow is the son of a Republican senator, a former songwriter for the Grateful Dead, and a passionate defender of cyber-rights. In 1990, with Lotus founder (and big-time SETI funder) Mitch Kapor and Sun Microsystems whiz John Gilmore, Barlow founded the Electronic Frontier Foundation (EFF), an advocacy organization dedicated to anti-censorship, cyber-rights, and privacy issues. After cutting its teeth defending hackers against FBI raids, the EFF went to war in 1996 over the congressionally mandated Communications Decency Act, which, if implemented, would license all manner of censorship. Barlow's anti-government outpouring, an impassioned piece of rhetoric on the internet, provocatively entitled "A Declaration of the Independence of Cyberspace," circulated rapidly through cyberspace and drew 50,000 named plaintiffs who fought and won their case in the Supreme Court the next year. The Communications Decency Act was officially struck down as a muzzle on free speech, and Barlow became a cyber-hero.

Barlow's declaration wastes no time setting out its goals. It begins:

> *Governments of the Industrial World, you weary giants of flesh and steel, I come from Cyberspace, the new home of Mind. On behalf of the future, I ask you of the past to leave us alone. You are not welcome among us. You have no sovereignty where we gather. We have no elected government, nor are we likely to have one, so I address you with no greater authority than that with which liberty itself always speaks.*

Having established cyberspace's independence, Barlow goes on to underscore its difference.

Cyberspace consists of transactions, relationships, and thought itself, arrayed like a standing wave in the web of our communications. Ours is a world that is both everywhere and nowhere, but it is not where bodies live. . . . Your legal concepts of property, expression, identity, movement, and context do not apply to us. They are based on matter. There is no matter here.

By making a fetish both of liberty and of disembodied fulfillment, Barlow pours into the familiar mold of Jeffersonian thinking a vision that effectively amounts to a rerun of the extraterrestrial dream: a vision of cyberspace as a golden place that is nowhere on Earth. In the process, he casts the government in the role of Old World tyrants bent on thwarting the noble attempts of New World citizens (read, cybernauts) to build a liberty-loving "civilization of Mind" outside its realm of jurisdiction. It's a clever rhetorical move because it frees him to expound on the virtues of cyberspace, all the while implying that government oppression is preventing them from being realized. It also accounts for the high-minded tone that Barlow adopts when he claims that anyone may enter the borderless paradise of cyberspace "without privilege or prejudice" and express their beliefs without fear of being "coerced into silence or conformity." Indeed, he goes so far as to suggest that cyberspace might yet remind politicians of what good governance can and should be when based on "ethics, enlightened self-interest, and the commonweal."

For me, the most striking aspect of Barlow's declaration is the way it seeks to shape cyberspace into a newfangled America of the mind, just as Gerard O'Neill (that other great extraterrestrial dreamer) wished to build an "America of the skies," as Carl Sagan so accurately diagnosed it. The implication, in both cases, is that the America of "flesh and steel"—the America that is weighed down by gravity—has betrayed its founding principles and ossified into the kind of imperial power that the original colonists sought to leave behind in Europe.

Like O'Neill again, Barlow looks to the myth of the frontier as the cure for this betrayal. In the popular tradition that follows Frederick Jackson Turner in romanticizing the wide open spaces of the Wild West, and the virtuous traits Americans developed in response to the challenges of colonizing it (self-sufficiency, fearlessness, a rugged individualism), the frontier is the wellspring of spiritual, moral, and national renewal. Though Barlow is not the first cyberguru to apply frontier mythology to the code cowboys, outlaw hackers, WELL-style homesteaders, and other early pioneers of cyberspace, none other has put the mythology through its paces to quite the same degree. The irony is that Barlow, writing in 1996, did not know how apt the comparison would prove to be. At the time cyberspace had not yet fallen victim to venture-capitalist greed, and it had still to capture the full attention of the telecommunications and entertainment industry giants who would soon swoop in and carve it up between them as greedily as the large nineteenth-century railroad companies swallowed up the West. Within only a few short years, cyberspace's wide open spaces would give way to the crowded, jarring, neon-lit shopping malls of today's world wide web, making it hard to believe that lawlessness or adventuring ever reigned there.

That cyberspace eventually succumbed to the demands of commerce is consistent with a traditional pattern whereby groundbreaking exploration is invariably followed by large-scale colonization, as long as there is money to be made. Virgin land is good only if it can be deflowered; hence the certain starvation of any exploratory venture that follows the disappointment of its commercial backers. Had would-be lunar prospectors, for example, seen sufficient opportunity for profiteering, whether from mining, chemical processing, or even tourism (ironically, the one space business making news today), the Space Age might have played out rather differently—especially since it was readily apparent that there was no military gain to be had from the Moon. But commercial sponsors never built trading posts in the wake of NASA's explorer-pioneers who risked their lives just to plant the national flag on virgin *luna firma*. Even for all the money spent on getting there, capitalists did their calculations early on and concluded that working the Moon was a no-pay prospect.

Thus has it ever been. We like to think of exploration as somehow pure, driven by intellectual curiosity and by the noble desire to test the human spirit against the world, but if capital does not flow back along the new channels opened up by explorers, those channels will dry up. To the extent that commerce has always been necessary to sustain exploratory zeal, one might well ask how long the court of Castile, for example, would have gone on funding the conquistadors if their only function had been the claiming of empty lands, or even the conversion of heathens to the new faith. Or indeed, whether the Portuguese and Spanish crowns would have bothered going head to head to discover a sea route to India had they not been driven by the avaricious desire to source the lucrative spice trade.

While NASA officials have long understood the need to show that they weren't ignorant of space's potential appeal to commerce (so they could run it up the flagpole whenever someone in Congress brought it up), the agency has never in fact needed to rely on commerce—nor will it have to anytime soon. This has led to a paradoxical situation in which the agency is forever talking up the possibility of manufacturing pharmaceuticals or developing new alloys in space, and of needing to make space attractive to a whole new range of paying customers, and yet has shown itself to be singularly inept at handling the occasional commercial propositions that actually come its way. One small example will do: Princeton University physicist Bob Dicke approached NASA in the 1970s about placing reflectors on the Moon that would help scientists study its motion. Costing up the work needed to customize off-the-shelf reflectors, he estimated that he could supply the equipment needed for his experiment at a cost of $5000 per unit. NASA accepted the proposal but insisted on making the project an in-house affair and contracting out the fabrication of the reflectors to one of its longtime aerospace partners. As a result, NASA ended up paying $3 million per unit.

I can't help wondering if NASA officials have not always known in their heart of hearts that there was more at stake in paying lip service to commerce than the expedient goal of appeasing Congress. Because—if one takes one's historical metaphors seriously—without successfully accommodating the interests of business, space could never measure up to the "new frontier" legacy, much less become the "final frontier" that Gene Roddenberry, fueled on Turnerism, hoped it would be. It would only be another Everest or another South Pole—which is to say, it would merely be a place whose emptiness and isolation piqued our vanity. The irony is that the frontier comparison actually holds true for cyberspace precisely because business was able to thrive there. First came the cowboys, outlaw hackers, and homesteaders, and then came the Gold Rush: by the time anyone thought to question all the madness for colonizing, the electronic New World had been thoroughly settled. Cyberspace, it seems, is an America of the mind less because of its wide open spaces than because a rerun of the how the West was won could be staged there.

As I neared the end of writing this book, I was seized with the idea that I needed to see a Shuttle launch. I thought that experiencing the sheer violence of the launch—all that power and steam and steel and thunder—would somehow rescue the Space Age for me from the death to which I'd helped condemn it. The idea held the further appeal of symmetry; I would end my journey as I had begun it, at Cape Canaveral—only this time I would take away the kind of visceral thrill I remembered experiencing as a child in the 1960s. But the more I pondered whether or not to go, the more ludicrous my impulse seemed. After all, I had made reluctant peace with the Space Age's passing, so why reopen an old wound? More to the point, I no longer needed to witness such a dramatic spectacle of separation to appreciate the conflict that plainly continues to vex us: the struggle between the desire to tear ourselves free from the known world, and our fundamental inability to escape not just our formative history but also memory itself. The whole project of writing this book, I now know, was a way of scratching that troubling itch.

In spite of having occasional pangs for an era now passed, I can see that the future of space lies not with transport but with information and, even more, with imagination. Like the holodeck that virtual-reality engineers are striving to create, space's most rewarding function may be to serve as a thought experiment. To this end, a little-known and undersold project simmering on one of NASA's back burners might just point the way forward, and it has the added advantage of managing to speak of hope and renewal without recourse to the myth of the frontier. Its name is Triana, and the man responsible for getting it off the ground is none other than former Vice President Al Gore.

In 1998, Gore announced plans to put a satellite in space that for twenty-four hours a day, every day, would broadcast live images of the planet over the internet and on cable television. Called Triana, after Rodrigo de Triana, the lookout who first saw the New World from the *Santa María*, this satellite would be placed into orbit at L1 (the stable Lagrangian point between the Earth and the sun). From the distance of about 1 million miles from Earth, always facing the planet's sunlit side, it would study both celestial bodies and provide scientists with a constant source of invaluable environmental and meteorological information. Triana was a favorite project of Gore, who enjoyed a reputation as a computer buff and environmentalist, but the vice president remained closely associated with it only long enough to persuade NASA officials that it was worthwhile. That, however, was too long for the project to shake off its party political taint—its detractors, for example, insisted on calling Triana "Gore-Sat"—and in a partisan vote the House Science Committee cut from NASA's 2000 budget a total of $32 million that had been set aside for Triana. Since then, Triana's fate has hung in the balance. First the project won a brief respite after an independent panel from the National Academy of Sciences gave it a favorable report, but then President Bush's recent pruning of NASA's 2002 budget put it back on ice, even though Triana was already built and ready to go. The latest word is that NASA is now discussing the possibility of launching Triana on a European Ariane rocket and is also talking with a private company keen to find a high-profile mission for the Ukranian-built Tsyklon rockets that it is trying to market.

Should Gore's satellite yet see the light of day, it's hard to say whether it would fulfill its Gaian charter. Would it make us feel all warm inside as we turned on our computers to come face-to-face with fulsome real-time images of the bright spinning Earth before we checked our morning e-mail? Perhaps we'd simply feel queasy as we struggled to assimilate the fact that the internet we already think of as our window on the world had become literally that. There is, after all, a delirious dimension to having so much at our fingertips—the Encyclopedia Terra, no less—without having to exert ourselves in the least to obtain it. It's sublime and power crazed in equal parts. Then again, at a Lagrangian point, stabilized between the Earth's gravity and that of another planetary body, with the forces of exploration and gravity, of community-creation and community-dwelling held in balance, Triana's symbolism is that of reassuring equilibrium. Either way, Triana is a marvel for managing to embody so many of contemporary culture's post–Space Age obsessions simultaneously—the thrill of bi-location that we experienced with Pathfinder, the push for godly knowledge symbolized by the all-at-once rush of information, even latent ideas about cyberspace as the new home of planetary consciousness. All of which suggests that Vice President Gore either had a prophetic sixth sense or else a particularly canny group of advisers.

For my own part, as a Space Age dreamer who is left having to accommodate myself to our own world, much like the Apollo astronauts themselves, I'd like to see Triana launched. For one thing, it neatly subverts the traditional apparatus of surveillance in order to create a public resource, shoving aside Big Brotherish overtones with an almost playful nonchalance to make room for something that approaches humanity's Third Eye. Too far away to spy on us and invade our privacy, Triana would nonetheless be close enough to produce images to tug at our heartstrings and perhaps even boost our flagging belief in humanity's collective potential. Moreover, it seems to me that Triana's holistic perspective fruitfully splits the difference between Sagan's humbling, fraction-of-a-pixel abode, as captured by Voyager, and Apollo's overwhelming, bigger-than-us, frame-filling living planet. As a result, it may succeed, in genuine Bachelardian fashion, in reconnecting us with the larger picture without sacrificing the intimate scale we cherish and in which we best function. Best of all, and without shouting about it, Triana affirms that there are meaningful signals to be picked out of the noise. Yet in refusing to channel them for us, it leaves us free to make what we will of our earthly confinement. Who knows, but from there all our extraterrestrial hopes may reignite.

$$\textit{works consulted}$$

CHAPTER 1: The Sky's the Limit

William D. Atwill probed the minds of developers in central Florida in *Fire and Power: The American Space Program as Postmodern Narrative* (Athens, Ga.: University of Georgia Press, 1994).

Jesse Lee Kercheval's autobiography is *Space: A Memoir* (Chapel Hill, N.C., and New York: Algonquin Books, 1998).

Population, road, and employment statistics are in Eden Ross Lipson's "Newsletter" on Brevard County, prepared for the Institute of Current World Affairs as part of a study called *New Towns and City Planning 1966–1970* (March 1970). Lent by the author.

Oriana Fallaci wrote about the launch towers in *If the Sun Dies* (New York: Atheneum, 1965), translated by Pamela Swinglehurst.

Norman Mailer wrote about prelaunch excitement in *Of a Fire on the Moon* (Boston: Little, Brown, 1970).

Krafft Ehricke was the pundit who proposed thinking of the space vehicle as a natural successor to the wheel and boat in "The Extraterrestrial Imperative," *Bulletin of the Atomic Scientists*, November 1971, pp. 18–26.

For the eponymous expression, see Joseph Corn, *The Winged Gospel: America's Romance with Aviation, 1900–1950* (New York and London: Oxford University Press, 1983).

Alfred Lawson's predictions were published in his editorial "Natural Prophecies" for *Aircraft*, October 1916.

The Wally Schirra quotation can be found in Fallaci's *If the Sun Dies*.

Among Gerard O'Neill's visionary books is *2018: A Hopeful View of the Human Future* (New York: Simon & Schuster, 1981).

For the mystical origins of the Soviet space program, see David F. Noble, *The Religion of Technology: The Divinity of Man and the Spirit of Invention* (New York: Knopf, 1997).

The film *Powers of Ten,* which Morrison made in collaboration with furniture designers Charles and Ray Eames, first appeared in 1968, and was then expanded in 1977. It also spawned a book: Philip Morrison and Phyllis Morrison, *Powers of Ten: A Book About the Relative Size of Things in the Universe and the Effect of Adding Another Zero* (Reading, Conn.: Scientific American Library, 1982).

Robert Jastrow's book is *The Enchanted Loom: Mind in the Universe* (New York: Simon & Schuster, 1981).

Keay Davidson's excellent biography is *Carl Sagan: A Life* (New York: Crown, 1999).

For updates on Team Encounter, log on to www.teamencounter.com/index_static.html.

Timothy Leary pondered his various "life after death" options in *Design for Dying* (New York: HarperEdge, 1997).

CHAPTER 2: One Small Step

Tom Wolfe's *The Right Stuff* (London: Jonathan Cape, 1980) described the history and mythology of the original Mercury and Gemini astronauts—the "first seven."

For background on the early space program, see Walter McDougall, *The Heavens and the Earth: A Political History of the Space Age* (New York: Basic Books, 1985).

I owe the idea of astronauts as screens to Dale Carter, *The Final Frontier: The Rise and Fall of the American Rocket State* (London and New York: Verso, 1988).

Gallup polls are cited in Howard E. McCurdy, *Space and the American Imagination* (Washington, D.C.: Smithsonian Institution Press, 1997).

William Burrows, *This New Ocean: The Story of the First Space Age* (New York: Random House, 1998), is particularly good at describing how Soviet advances spurred American ones and vice versa.

Arthur C. Clarke, *The Exploration of Space* (New York: Harper & Brothers, 1951).

More detail on the movers and shakers behind the Space Age can be found in Tom Crouch, *Aiming for the Stars: The Dreamers and Doers of the Space Age* (Washington, D.C.: Smithsonian Institution Press, 1999).

Michael Collins's hair-raising personal account of the Apollo 11 mission can be found in *Lift Off: The Story of America's Adventure in Space* (New York: Grove Press, 1988).

Norman Mailer's unequaled analysis of our Space Age ambitions is *Of a Fire on the Moon* (Boston: Little, Brown, 1970).

Arthur C. Clarke continued his interest in the space program with *The Promise of Space* (New York: Harper & Row, 1968).

Many of the Apollo quotes can be found in Peter Bond, *Heroes in Space, from Gagarin to Challenger* (Oxford: Basil Blackwell, 1987), and Andrew Chaikin, *A Man on the Moon: The Voyages of the Apollo Astronauts* (New York: Viking, 1994).

David F. Noble makes a number of interesting observations on the essentially Christian character of the space establishment in *The Religion of Technology: The Divinity of Man and the Spirit of Invention* (New York: Knopf, 1997).

The seminal work on Gaia is James Lovelock, *Gaia: A New Look at Life on Earth* (London and New York: Oxford University Press, 1979). See also Lovelock's *The Ages of Gaia: A Biography of Our Living Earth* (New York: Norton, 1995).

The Lovelock interview is at www.salonmag.com/people/feature/2000/08/17/lovelock.

Richard Macey quoted Story Musgrave in "The Xentric Files: Here's a Real Story from Space," www.smh.com.au/news/0002/08/national/national5.

Edgar Mitchell has written up his credo as *Psychic Exploration: A Challenge for Science* (New York: Putnam, 1974). His lecture can be accessed at www.noetics.org.

Arthur C. Clarke's 1953 classic, *Childhood's End,* is available in reprint editions (e.g., New York: Ballantine, 1987).

Clarke's essay "Space Flight and the Spirit of Man" is reprinted in *Voices from the Sky: Previews of the Coming Space Age* (New York: Harper & Row, 1965).

Oriana Fallaci included her letter to her father in *If the Sun Dies* (New York: Atheneum, 1965), translated by Pamela Swinglehurst.

Timothy Leary's comment is from *Neuropolitics: The Sociobiology of Human Metamorphosis* (Los Angeles: Starseed Press, 1977). See also Wynn Wachhorst, *The Dream of Spaceflight: Essays on the Near Edge of Infinity* (New York: Basic Books, 2000). More than Leary, Wachhorst plays up the sexual overtones of this rite of passage, referring to the Apollo 11–Saturn V edifice as "man's collective erection" and "the hotrod of an adolescent species bent on tearing itself from mother Earth."

J. D. Bernal speculated on the rise of Spacekind in *The World, the Flesh and the Devil: An Inquiry into the Future of the Three Enemies of the Rational Soul* (1929; reprint, London: Jonathan Cape, 1970).

Arthur C. Clarke's comparison of space exploration to prehistoric evolutionary leaps can be found in "Space Flight and the Spirit of Man."

For "spore bearers," see Loren Eiseley, *The Invisible Pyramid: A Naturalist's Analysis of the Rocket Century* (New York: Scribner, 1970).

Buckminster Fuller's essay "The Universe Is Technology" is reprinted in *Worlds Beyond,* edited by Larry Geis and Fabrice Florin (Berkeley: University of California Press, 1978).

Peter Russell's convoluted arguments are in *The Global Brain: Speculations on the Evolutionary Leap to Planetary Consciousness* (Los Angeles: J. P. Tarcher, 1983). See also Frank White, *The Overview Effect: Space Exploration and Human Evolution* (Boston: Houghton Mifflin, 1987).

James E. Webb's business book is *Space Age Management: The Large-Scale Approach* (New York: McGraw-Hill, 1969).

Alex Rowland's "Barnstorming in Space: The Rise and Fall of the Romantic Era of Spaceflight, 1957–1986," in *Space Policy Reconsidered,* edited by Radford Byerly Jr. (Boulder, Col.: Westview, 1989) is good on how NASA fell from its pinnacle.

C. S. Lewis's 1943 novel *Perelandra* is available in reprint editions (e.g., New York: Scribner, 1996).

John Witte's "Home" can be found in *The Norton Anthology of Literature,* edited by J. Paul Hunter et al. (New York: Norton, 1986).

J. G. Ballard's book of short stories is *Memories of the Space Age* (Sauk City, Wis.: Arkham House, 1988).

For more detail on space adaptation syndrome, see Frances Ashcroft, *Life at the Extremes: The Science of Survival* (London: Flamingo, 2001) and Albert Harrison, *Spacefaring: The Human Dimension* (Berkeley: University of California Press, 2001).

Robert Zubrin's colonial manifesto is in *The Case for Mars: The Plan to Settle the Red Planet and Why We Must* (New York: Simon & Schuster, 1996).

For space talk and other highly original takes on the Space Age, see David Lavery, *Late for the Sky: The Mentality of the Space Age* (Carbondale and Edwardsville: Southern Illinois University Press, 1992).

CHAPTER 3: Forever Roswell

Among the many books written about Roswell and aliens, I found some that were particularly helpful: Benson Saler, Charles A, Ziegler, and Charles B. Moore, *UFO Crash at Roswell: The Genesis of a Modern Myth* (Washington, D.C.: Smithsonian Institution Press, 1997); Stanton T. Friedman and Don Berliner, *Crash at Corona: The U.S. Military Retrieval and Cover-up of a UFO* (New York: Paragon House, 1992); Kevin D. Randle and Donald R. Schmitt, *The Truth About the UFO Crash at Roswell* (New York: M. Evans, 1994); Philip J. Klass, *The Real Roswell Crashed-Saucer Cover-up,* (Amherst, N.Y.: Prometheus Books, 1997); and C. D. B. Bryan, *Close Encounters of the Fourth Kind: Alien Abduction, UFOs, and the Conference at MIT* (New York: Knopf, 1995).

Whitley Strieber's *Communion: A True Story* (New York: William Morrow, 1987) marked the start of the Gray's ascendancy.

For a sympathetic history of alien sightings see Jerome Clark, *The UFO Encyclopedia: The Phenomenon from the Beginning,* 2 vols. (Detroit: Omnigraphics, 1998). And for a skeptical history, see Robert E. Bartholomew and George S. Howard, *UFOs and Alien Contact* (Amherst, N.Y.: Prometheus Books, 1998).

Stephen Jay Gould's "A Biological Homage to Mickey Mouse" can be found in *The Panda's Thumb: More Reflections in Natural History* (New York: Norton, 1980)

Star Trek actors and ribbon-cutting ceremonies have a long association. Even NASA employs actors from the cult series to energize space fans. See Constance Penley, *NASA/Trek: Popular Science and Sex in America* (London and New York: Verso, 1997).

Orson Welles's radio version of *War of the Worlds* is the subject of Howard Koch's *The Panic Broadcast: Portrait of an Event* (Boston: Little, Brown, 1970).

You can find the original 1947 article that appeared in the *Roswell Daily Record* at dspace.dial.pipex.com/ritson/scispi/roswell/recorder.htm.

Toby Smith, *Little Green Men: Roswell and the Rise of a Popular Culture* (Albuquerque: University of New Mexico Press, 2000), provides good background on military cover-ups in the area, including Project Mogul.

A book that treads a careful path between the New Physics and physics as we know it is Lawrence Krauss, *The Physics of Star Trek* (New York: Basic Books, 1995).

The standard biography of Robert Goddard is Milton Lehman's *This High Man: The Life of Robert H. Goddard,* (New York: Farrar, Straus, 1963).

An essay that intelligently addresses the spiritual needs of ufologists and contactees is J. Gordon Melton, "The Contactees: A Survey," in James R. Lewis, ed., *The Gods Have Landed: New Religions from Other Worlds* (Albany: State University of New York Press, 1995).

On *The Lord of the Rings,* see Patrick Curry, *Defending Middle Earth: Tolkien, Myth and Modernity* (New York: St. Martin's, 1997). See also David Sander, "Joy Beyond the Walls of the World: The Secondary World-Making of J. R. R. Tolkien and C. S. Lewis," in George Clark and Daniel Timmons, eds., *J. R. R. Tolkien and His Literary Resonances* (Westport, Conn.: Greenwood Press, 2000). For Tolkien sales in America, see Julian Dibbell, "Lord of the Geeks" in *The Village Voice,* June 6, 2001 (www.villagevoice.com/issues/0123/dibbell.php).

James Blish's "Surface Tension" is reprinted in Robert Silverberg, ed., *The Science Fiction Hall of Fame: The Greatest Science Fiction Stories of All Time* (New York: Avon, 1970).

For missile silos, see Samuel H. Day, ed., *Nuclear Heartland: A Guide to the 1,000 Missile Silos of the United States* (Madison, Wis.: Progressive Foundation, 1988). See also "A Room with an Apocalyptic View," in Wired News, www.wired.com/news/culture/0,1284,47577,00.html.

CHAPTER 4: Space for Rent

Delve into Alphaworld at *www.activeworlds.com/worlds/alphaworld/Alphaworld*. One user, Zeigan, has written a guide for new users, available on *www.emf.net/~estephen/alpha.html*. Explore the Alphaworld map at *mapper.activeworlds.com/aw*.

Agent Rookie's Report is at *www.geocities.com/CapitolHill/2333/rookie. html*.

For the idealism of cyber-communities, see Stacy Horn, *Cyberville: Clicks, Culture, and the Creation of an Online Town* (New York: Warner Books,), and Sherry Turkle, *Life on the Screen: Identity in the Age of the Internet* (New York: Simon & Schuster, 1995).

"Mock's Mudding Guide" gives you a sense of the wide range of existing MUDs and MUD users. It's at www.moock.org/muds/placestogo.html.

Mr. Bungle's misdeeds were first brought to public attention by Julian Dibbell in "A Rape in Cyberspace," *The Village Voice*, December 21, 1993. The essay later became the first chapter of Dibbell's book *My Tiny Life: Crime and Passion in a Virtual World* (New York: Owl/Henry Holt, 1999).

The best of the online debate on the LambdaMOO rape includes Rebecca Spinhower's "Virtually Inevitable: Real Problems in Virtual Communities" (1994) at *http://world.std.com/~rs/inevitable.html* and Elizabeth Reid's "Identity and the Cyborg Body" (1994) at *www.rochester.edu/College/FS/ Publications/ReidIdentity.html*.

Moria's manifesto, "Colony Alpha, the Construction of an Active World: A Dream in Virtual Space," is at www.stanford.edu/class/history34q/readings/ ActiveWorld/ActiveWorld.html.

Richard Crews's journal is available at *www.luf.org* (from the home page, click on Space Environments Ecovillage, then click on SeeProgress).

For space colonization, see Marshall Savage, *The Millennial Project: How to Colonize the Galaxy in Eight Easy Steps* (Denver: Empyrean, 1992; reissued, New York: Little, Brown, 1994).

Gerard O'Neill's essay on migration to the stars is "The Colonization of Space," *Physics Today* 27 no: 9 (1974). See also his *High Frontier: Human Colonies in Space* (New York: William Morrow, 1977).

Konstantin Tsiolkovsky's *Beyond Planet Earth* was originally published in Russia in 1896. I consulted an English-language version translated by Kenneth Syers (New York: Pergamon Press, 1960).

J. D. Bernal's hollow globes are described in *The World, the Flesh and the Devil: An Inquiry into the Future of the Three Enemies of the Rational Soul* (1929; reprint, London: Jonathan Cape, 1970).

Krafft Ehricke's vision of space cities can be found in "The Extraterrestrial Imperative," *Bulletin of the Atomic Scientists,* November 1971, pp. 18–26.

Freeman Dyson is quoted in Kenneth Brower, *The Starship and the Canoe* (New York: Holt, Rinehart and Winston, 1978).

For background on L5, see Michael Michaud, *Reaching for the High Frontier: The American Pro-Space Movement, 1972–1984* (New York: Praeger, 1986).

The Gerald O'Neill quotes are all from *The High Frontier*. See also Tom Heppenheimer, *Colonies in Space* (Mechanicsburg, Pa.: Stackpole Books, 1977).

Carl Sagan's praise is quoted in Stewart Brand, *Space Colonies* (Sausalito, Calif.: Whole Earth Catalog, 1977).

The Club of Rome's pessimistic study was published as *The Limits to Growth: A Report for the Club of Rome's Project on the Predicament of Mankind* (New York: Universe Books, 1974).

Gerard O'Neill addressed the limits argument in "Space Colonies and Energy Supply to the Earth," *Science* 10, December 5, 1975.

The NASA response can be found in John Billingham and William Gilbreath, eds., *Space Resources and Space Settlements: Technical Papers Derived from the 1977 Summer Study at NASA Ames Research Center, Moffett Field, California* (Washington, D.C.: NASA, 1979).

Timothy Leary's polemic is *Neuropolitics: The Sociobiology of Human Metamorphosis* (Los Angeles: Starseed Press, 1977).

Italo Calvino's 1974 *Invisible Cities* is available in reprint editions (e.g., London: Vintage, 1997).

Russell Schweickart is quoted in Stewart Brand, *Space Colonies*.

Background on the Lunar Prospector mission can be found at the Space Studies Institute's website at www.ssi.org.

GroundHog's rant was posted in the newsgroup sci.space.policy on February 13, 1997. See http://members.aol.com/oscarcombs.wannab.htm.

For Biosphere 2, see John Allen and Mark Nelson, *Space Biospheres* (Oracle, Ariz.: Synergetic Press, 1986). See also Abigail Alling and Mark Nelson, *Life Under Glass: The Inside Story of Biosphere 2* (Oracle, Ariz.: Biosphere Press, 1993).

For the rise of the American New Town, see Nicolas Dagen Bloom, *Suburban Alchemy: 1960s New Towns and the Transformation of the American Dream* (Columbus: Ohio State University Press, 2001).

On Celebration, see Andrew Ross, *The Celebration Chronicles: Life, Lib-*

erty and the Pursuit of Property Values in Disney's New Town (New York: Ballantine, 1999). See also Kathleen Hogan's M.A. thesis on Celebration at http://xroads.Virginia.edu/~MA98/Hogan/celebration/intro.html.

For shopping malls, see William Severini Kowinski, *The Malling of America: An Inside Look at the Great Consumer Paradise* (New York: William Morrow, 1985).

CHAPTER 5: Aliens on Your Desktop

Howard Rheingold, *The Virtual Community: Homesteading on the Electronic Frontier* (New York: William Patrick Books/Addison-Wesley, 1993) is an excellent introduction to cyber-communities. See also Sherry Turkle, *Life on the Screen: Identity in the Age of the Internet* (New York: Simon & Schuster, 1995).

Two of the best articles on peer-to-peer culture and distributed processing are Elinor Abreu's "Pass It On: Peer-to-Peer Technology Is Moving out of the Dorm Room and onto a Corporate Network Near You," at www.thestandard. com (see Past Issues Archive for February 5, 2001) and Howard Rheingold's "You Got the Power," *Wired*, August 2000.

A thorough account of developments in computing can be found in Paul Ceruzzi, *A History of Modern Computing* (Cambridge, Mass.: MIT Press, 2000).

Janelle Brown takes a stab at uncovering the links between a fondness for gadgets and an obsession with aliens in "The Geeks and the Aliens: Why Are the Tech Industry's Brightest So Determined to Spearhead the Hunt for Extraterrestrials?" at salon.com (see archives) and in *Final Frontier*, October 1998.

Visit the Berkeley website at www.setiathome.ssl.berkeley.edu. To get a sense of the larger SETI context, browse the SETI Institute website at www.seti-inst.edu.

For more about Linux OS, see Glyn Moody "The Greatest OS That (N)ever Was," *Wired*, August 1997.

What kind of space is cyberspace? There's plenty of food for thought in Margaret Wertheim, *The Pearly Gates of Cyberspace: A History of Space from Dante to the Internet* (New York: Norton, 1999), and William J Mitchel, *Space, Place and the Infobahn* (Cambridge, Mass.: MIT Press, 1995).

For the relationship between computer networks and human beings, see

George Dyson, *Darwin Among the Machines: The Evolution of Global Intelligence* (New York: Helix/Addison-Wesley, 1997). The classic artificial-intelligence bible, which prophesied that thinking machines would not only become our companions, but would soon surpass us, is Han Moravec's *Mind Children: The Future of Robot and Human Intelligence* (Cambridge, Mass.: Harvard University Press, 1988).

Kevin Kelly joined the debate in *Out of Control: The Rise of Neo-Biological Civilization* (New York: William Patrick Books/Addison-Wesley, 1994).

Louis Rossetto is quoted in Erik Davis, *Techgnosis: Myth, Magic and Mysticism in the Age of Information* (New York: Three Rivers Press, 1998).

Jennifer Cobb Kreisberg characterizes Teilhard de Chardin's techno constituency in "A Globe Clothing Itself with a Brain," *Wired,* June 1995.

For holodecks and other marvels of the data glove, see Michael Heim, *The Metaphysics of Virtual Reality* (Oxford: Oxford University Press, 1993).

CHAPTER 6: Ground Control to Major Tom

Detail on the Pathfinder mission can be found at mars.jpl.nasa.gov/default.html and at nssdc.gsfc.nasa.gov/planetary/mesur.html.

Carl Sagan's *Contact* (New York: Pocket, 1997) was originally published in 1985.

William J. Broad, "Astronomers Revive Scan of the Heavens for Signs of Life," *New York Times,* September 28, 1998.

A good introduction to the issues and methods behind SETI can be found in Seth Shostak, *Sharing the Universe: Perspectives on Extraterrestrial Life* (Berkeley, Calif.: Berkeley Hill Books, 1998).

Track Pioneer 10 at spaceprojects.arc.nasa.gov/Space_Projects/pioneer/Pnhome.html.

For background on Project Phoenix see, Dennis Overbye, "On the Trail of SETI—The Truth That NASA Dares Not Speak!" *Wired,* January 1997, and Jill Tarter, "SETI and the Religions of Extraterrestrials," *Free Enquiry* 20, No. 3, Summer 2000.

Compare Gaston Bachelard's *The Poetics of Space,* trans. Maria Jolas (Boston: Beacon, 1969) with Carl Sagan's *The Cosmic Connection: An Extraterrestrial Perspective* (New York: Anchor/Doubleday, 1973).

For the discontinuation of congressional funding of SETI, see Steven Garber, "Searching for Good Science: The Cancellation of NASA's SETI Program," *Journal of the British Interplanetary Society* 52 (1999).

Janelle Brown's "The Geeks and the Aliens: Why Are the Tech Industry's Brightest So Determined to Spearhead the Hunt for Extraterrestrials?" at salon.com (see archives) and in *Final Frontier,* October 1998, explains why the likes of Paul Allen and Nathan Myhrvold want to find ET.

Drake has written a scientific autobiography, which traces SETI's early history: Frank Drake and Dava Sobel, *Is Anyone Out There? The Scientific Search For Extraterrestrial Intelligence* (New York: Delta Books, 1992). See also Alfred Roulet, *The Search for Intelligent Life in Outer Space* (New York: Berkley Medallion, 1977).

In the early sixties, Drake devised a famous formula for calculating the probability of finding intelligent—i.e. broadcasting—life:

$$R_* \times F_e \times n_e \times f_l \times f_i \times f_e \times L = N$$

R_* is the average rate of star formation over the lifetime of the galaxy; F_e the fraction of stars with planetary systems; n_e the number of planets per star with ecologically suitable environments; f_l the fraction of planets (n_e) on which life arises; f_i the fraction of planets (f_l) on which intelligence develops; f_e the fraction of planets (f_l) on which technological civilizations arise; and L the lifetime of the high-tech civilization. N thus emerges as the number of extant technological civilizations in the galaxy. Given that the galaxy contains more than 100 billion stars, you don't need very high percentages for the remaining variables to find a significantly large number of technologically advanced civilizations. But more than forty years after its formulation, only the first two variables—the total number of stars and the fraction of stars with planetary systems—are anything but a wild guess. Drake talks of his eponymous equation as though it were a mere trifle—he originally jotted it down on the back of a napkin to give scientists attending an international meeting he had convened something to talk about. Still, he is clearly pleased by the healthy afterlife it has gone on to enjoy, even if he remains surprised by its ubiquity.

The Kardashev story is well-covered in David E. Fisher and Marshall John Fisher, *Strangers in the Night: A Brief History of Life on Other Worlds* (Washington, D.C.: Counterpoint, 1998).

Walter Sullivan wrote both articles on CTA-102 that appeared in the *New*

York Times: "Space Signals Said to Hint Life Afar" (October 26, 1964) and "Radio Emissions from Space Spur Disagreement Between American and Soviet Astronomers" (April 18, 1965).

The Hills' story was told in John Fuller, *The Interrupted Journey: Two Lost Hours "Aboard a Flying Saucer"* (New York: Dial, 1966).

More on the Hills can be found in Carl Sagan, *Demon-Haunted World* (New York: Random House, New York, 1995); Curtis Peebles, *Watch the Sky: A Chronicle of the Flying Saucer Myth* (Washington, D.C.: Smithsonian Institution Press, 1994); and Ian Ridpath, *Messages from the Stars: Communication and Contact with Extraterrestrial Life* (New York: Harper & Row, 1978).

Bernard Oliver led the team who wrote *Project Cyclops: A Design Study of a System for Detecting Extraterrestrial Life* (NASA Ames Research Center, 1971).

Howard Rheingold outlined the expansion of the computer literate in *The Virtual Community: Homesteading on the Electronic Frontier* (New York: William Patrick Books/Addison-Wesley, 1993).

Katie Hafner's eponymous history is *The Well: A Story of Love, Death and Real Life in the Seminal Online Community* (New York: Carroll & Graf, 2001).

For the "ecstasy of communication" and the spiritualization of cyberspace, see Erik Davis, *Techgnosis: Myth, Magic and Mysticism in the Age of Information* (New York: Three Rivers Press, 1998).

For Heaven's Gate and other techno-millennial cults, see Marina Benjamin, *Living at the End of the World* (London: Picador, 1998).

Visit the Extropy Institute at *www.extropy.org*. See also Ed Regis, "Meet the Extropians," *Wired*, October 1994.

Nicole Stenger is quoted in Sherry Turkle, *Life on the Screen: Identity in the Age of the Internet* (New York: Simon & Schuster, 1995).

Joshua Quittner profiles the activists behind the EFF in "The Merry Pranksters Go to Washington," *Wired*, June 1994.

John Perry Barlow's "A Declaration of the Independence of Cyberspace" is available at www.eff.org. More on the politics of net culture can be found in Tim Jordan and Aden Lent, eds., *Storming the Millennium: The New Politics of Change*, co-edited with Adam Lent (London: Lawrence and Wishart, 1999).

For Frederick Jackson Turner, see George Rogers Taylor, ed., *The Turner Thesis: Concerning the Role of the Frontier in American History* (Lexington, Mass.: D.C. Heath, 1972).

The Bob Dicke example comes from Francis. J. Hoban, *Where Do You Go After You've Been to the Moon?* (Malabar, Fla.: Krieger Publishing Company, 1997).

For Triana, see Brian Berger, "NASA Considers Two Foreign Options for Launching Triana," *Space News,* February 7, 2002, and Toni Feder, "Satellite Seeks Space Ride," *Physics Today,* August 2001. See also triana.gsfc.nasa.gov.

about the author

MARINA BENJAMIN has worked as a museum curator, a television writer, a professional blackjack player, and a journalist, writing for the *Manchester Guardian,* the *Financial Times,* and the *Independent.* She also served as arts editor of the *New Statesman* and then as deputy arts editor of the *Evening Standard.* She is the author of one previous book, *Living at the End of the World,* and now divides her time between London and San Francisco.